# The Francophone Bande Dessinée

# FAUX TITRE

## 265

Etudes de langue et littérature françaises
publiées sous la direction de

Keith Busby, M.J. Freeman,
Sjef Houppermans et Paul Pelckmans

# The Francophone Bande Dessinée

Edited by

Charles Forsdick, Laurence Grove
and Libbie McQuillan

AMSTERDAM - NEW YORK, NY 2005

Cover design: Pier Post

The paper on which this book is printed meets the requirements of
'ISO 9706: 1994, Information and documentation - Paper for documents -
Requirements for permanence'.

Le papier sur lequel le présent ouvrage est imprimé remplit les prescriptions
de 'ISO 9706: 1994, Information et documentation - Papier pour documents
- Prescriptions pour la permanence'.

ISBN: 90-420-1776-7
Editions Rodopi B.V., Amsterdam - New York, NY 2005
Printed in The Netherlands

**Contents**

LIBBIE MCQUILLAN
The Francophone Bande Dessinée: An Introduction............................7

YVES COTINAT [TANITOC]
Style, havanes & vanités.......................................................15

CHARLES FORSDICK
Exoticising the *Domestique*:
Bécassine, Brittany and the Beauty of the Dead..............................23

LAURENCE GROVE
BD Theory Before the Term 'BD' Existed......................................39

JUDI LOACH
*De nouvelles formes naissent*:
Le Corbusier and the bande dessinée.........................................51

LAURENT MARIE
*Le Grêlé 7/13*:
A (Communist) Children's Guide to the Resistance............................73

WENDY MICHALLAT
*Pilote*: Pedagogy, Puberty and Parents.....................................83

MATTHEW SCREECH
Jean Giraud / Moebius:
*Nouveau Réalisme* and Science Fiction......................................97

TERESA BRIDGEMAN
Figuration and configuration:
mapping imaginary worlds in BD.............................................115

ANN MILLER
Narratives of Adolescence, Ethnicity and
Masculinity in the Work of Baru............................................137

DOMINIQUE LE DUC
Femmes en Images et Images de Femmes:
L'Héroïne de *La Femme Piège* d'Enki Bilal..................................149

LIBBIE MCQUILLAN
Les Bidochon assujettis académiques........................................159

ROGER SABIN
Some Observations on BD in the US........................................175

MURRAY PRATT
'The Dance of the Visible and the Invisible':
AIDS and the Bande Dessinée................................................189

JAMES STEEL
*Let's party!* Astérix and the World Cup (France 1998)................201

List of Illustrations..............................................................219

# The Francophone Bande Dessinée: An Introduction

## Libbie McQuillan
## University of Glasgow

In the UK, the study of the Francophone *bande dessinée*, BD, is as yet something of a minority interest within the field of Francophone cultural studies. Nevertheless, it is increasingly becoming a fashionable research area. A protean medium such as the BD inevitably opens itself to differing areas of scholarly inquiry: the inherent flexibility of the hybrid medium has precipitated several different critical responses in recent years. But there is more to this growing awareness of the BD within the British and Irish academy than a mere recognition of the varied possibilities of the comics form. Perhaps what first drew the attention of British and Irish scholars was the peculiarity of the BD's cultural recognition and more general widespread popularity in France and Belgium. In comparison with Anglo-Saxon traditions of the comics form the cultural esteem in which BD is held could not help but seem strange. In both countries the announcement in the 1980s of future State-funded projects made way for the opening of national institutes of conservation and research in *Centre belge de la bande dessinée* (CBBD) in Brussels in 1989, and the *Centre national de la bande dessinée et de l'image* (CNBDI) in Angoulême in 1990.

BD study is relatively new in Britain and Ireland. Indeed this book is the first collection of essays exclusively dedicated to the study of Francophone BD published in an English-language academic context. As such, it would at first appear that the editors of this book are attempting to innovate and initiate a new area of research. However, the BD has been under critical scrutiny in France and Belgium for almost forty years. The intellectualisation of the BD has a history, and this history is, in part, entangled with the history of its institutionalisation. It was precisely the process of critical inquiry, initiated in the early 1960s by a handful of dedicated enthusiasts, the *Club des amis de la bande dessinée*, that acted as the initial catalyst for the process of the Francophone BD's critical canonisation.

In France BD may very well now enjoy an international reputation for quality, artistry and adulthood, and profit from generous State subsidies. However, this has not always been the case. Post-war censorship legislation—the law of July 1949 censuring the moral content of children's *illustrés*—relegated the BD to a juvenile pastime. BD's ambivalent past during de Gaulle's Fifth Republic did not, however, stop the medium becoming quickly and commonly accepted as an adult activity in the 1970s, when the new adult BD first arrived in France. In historical terms, very little time elapsed between the explosion in the mid-1960s of the widely mediatised *Astérix* phenomenon and the decision in 1982 to build a State-funded home for BD in Angoulême. In France, during a brief twenty-year interlude, BD graduated from being a legally protected medium for children to become a showpiece promoting French culture in embassies around the world. The reasons for this shift in status are many and varied. However, one of the main reasons for this turn-around in post-war BD's fortune was the process of BD's intellectualisation, which culturally promoted, historically chronicled and critically celebrated the artistic revolution within the private world of BD creation during the late 1960s and 1970s.

The first steps towards this process of intellectualisation were taken, in 1961 in a somewhat obscure science fiction review, *Fiction*. The journal, which for the main consisted of Anglophone short stories in translation, published an article that longed nostalgically for 'L'Age d'or de la bande dessinée', the golden age of 1930s American superhero comic strips (see Strinati 1961). This article gave birth to a short series of articles in the same vein and a subsequent survey to quantify the extent of the BD's popularity amongst the journal's readership. Finally, this led to the official establishment, in 1962, of the CBD (*Le Club des Amis de la Bande Dessinée*), and its corollary journal *Giff-Wiff*, edited by Francis Lacassin.

The CBD was soon to promote itself as a learned society. These original *bédéphiles* were historically responsible for the first prolonged media interest of the comics form in France. Eventually the efforts of the club led to the introduction of one of the first courses on the history and aesthetics of the BD in France, run by Lacassin at the Sorbonne. The 1960s saw the introduction of the first fairs and conventions promoting BD. For the first time entire books, rather than short articles were devoted to the subject. In 1965, the first international congress on the BD, at which several members of the CBD and several French cartoonists attended, was held in Bordighera in Italy. It was only a matter of time before the French organised a similar event of their own.

In 1967, the exhibition, 'Bande dessinée et figuration narrative', was held at the Musée des Arts décoratifs in Paris. The exhibition organised by SOCERLID (a splinter group of the CBD), was a success and shortly afterwards similar events were organised in the provinces. In 1966, the previously hostile *Ligue de l'enseignement* organised a conference in favour of the BD. The tide for post-war BD was finally turning.

Contemporaneous with the success of René Goscinny and Albert Uderzo's *Astérix* series, such fairs and exhibitions held nation-wide put BD in the French cultural spotlight. The *bédéphiles* not only helped promote the BD, but also profoundly influenced BD critical discourse. The group was responsible for popularising both the term *bande dessinée* and its abbreviation BD. Comparing the medium to cinema and encouraging an archival research of BD's history, *Giff-Wiff* was responsible for the introduction of certain discourses surrounding BD. It is to be noted that both the meta-language of the pseudo-cinematic discourse and the scholarly investigations into BD's past were adopted in order to promote BD not as an aspect of mass culture but as a respectable adult art form—the 9$^{th}$ art.

Towards the end of the decade, the *Astérix* phenomenon—albums were selling millions of albums with each edition—brought BD to the attention of the general public. A BD vogue swept French pseudo-intellectuals. The initial journalistic response was, characteristically, more interested in the possibilities of intellectualising BD than in the media itself. BD was not, as yet, a widely respected form and even though there was a general interest in *Astérix* there was, as yet, no critical thinking on BD to which the commentator could refer. Indeed, given the novelty of the attention surrounding BD, it is not surprising that BD as a form was so misunderstood or that initial critical reactions were based upon the reception of other comparable media. The fact that a common word even to describe the medium itself was not officially decided upon until the late 1960s perhaps best highlights this problematic.

Whilst *Astérix* mania was sweeping the French press at the end of the 1960s, in 1968, Pierre Fresnault-Deruelle was completing his undergraduate dissertation, *Tintin, bande dessinée: une approche sémiotique*, which he later developed into a thesis. Fresnault-Deruelle was one of many young scholars who in the 1970s turned their critical attention towards BD. Fresnault-Deruelle is perhaps the most famous, since most published, academic writer on the BD of the period. In the 1970s in French and Belgian universities many theses and even more undergraduate dissertations were to be devoted to various aspects of the BD. Most of the work of the period that went beyond the undergraduate level looked to semiotics for its inspiration and self-justification. Such works were, however, more often semiotic in inspiration than in application.

The first ever university course on BD was a practical course introduced in 1970 at Vincennes University. Although one imagines that such adventures must have proved popular with students and with young researchers, BD was ultimately not so popular with university institutions or its hierarchies. Despite some high profile events such as a 1976 issue of *Communications* dedicated to BD, or the French Academician René Clair's 1974 address on BD to the Institut de France, the enthusiasm of a handful of partisans in French academic circles did not establish anything more than a brief vogue for BD study (see Covin, Fresnault-Deruelle and Toussaint). Significantly, the majority of academic treatises and papers appearing at this time dealt with the adventures of the Brussels school, thereby, for the first time, turning the critical focus on Franco-Belgian creation. However, the intellectual legitimacy of all these studies promised by the support of semiotics and later psychoanalysis was but short-lived.

In the 1970s the creative BD world itself was in turmoil. This crisis ultimately proved positive and acted as a catalyst for the revival of French BD. Inspired by the changing international social climate and heavily influenced by the American comix model, young artists detached themselves from traditionally structured publishing houses in a bid to publish independently their own creations. Such personal ventures lead to the establishment of *L'Echo des Savanes* (1972), *Métal Hurlant* (1974) and *Fluide glacial* (1975). In the 1970s, the creation and explosion of this fresh talent was celebrated at the by then annual fairs and conventions.

In particular, in Angoulême an unusually large crowd turned out for a BD exhibition in December 1972. The next year Angoulême was chosen as the site of the first national festival of the BD. Presumably the choice of Angoulême as the location of the fixture was based on the singular success of the salon the previous year. By the 1980s, Angoulême had become a nationally recognised event and it therefore seemed natural that the CNBDI should be based there when the announcement of its creation came in 1982. The national festival of Angoulême brought the power to consecrate the form officially with prize givings and exhibition space. Thanks to such conventions, during the 1970s, there was an ever-growing awareness of the extent of French talent past and present.

Towards the end of the decade Etienne Robial's BD publishing house founded in 1970, Futuropolis, started the task of republishing the 'classics' of French BD such as Alain Saint-Ogan's *Zig et Puce* (1925). The name of Robial's new publishing company was itself a reference to the first French BD science-fiction character, Futuropolis (1937). Bringing attention to long forgotten works, Futuropolis started the process of re-appraising the history of French BD production. Jacques Glénat's BD publishing house, Glénat, also emerged in the mid-1970s. Glénat's seminal fanzine, *Schtroumpf: Les Cahiers de la bande dessinée* (1969), interviewed the emerging artists of the 1970s. Providing impressively complete bibliographies of the artists' works, and enquiring into their creative motivations by understanding BD through a close dialogue with artists, this magazine helped install the cult of the BD author.

Regardless of such a rapid succession of internal developments within the BD critical and creative world, it was not until government intervention of the 1980s that the cultural canonisation of BD took an organised, definitive shape. In France the Socialist government, elected in 1981, announced the Angoulême project in 1982 as part of a much wider series of grand cultural projects. The realisation of the CNBDI, with its huge waves of glass, marked the CNBDI unmistakably in the architectural style of François Mitterand's *grands travaux*. As with other architectural adventures of the 1980s, such as the Louvre's new pyramid, the Bastille opera house or the Villette science-park in Paris, the period's hallmark wide expanses of glass openly declared France's aspirations for the future to the rest of the world.

The CBBD's opening in 1989 anticipated that of the CNBDI. In contrast to the provincial location of Angoulême, the CBBD was centrally located in the heart of historic Brussels. At the cost of a hundred and thirty million Belgian Francs, the Belgians chose to restore the Victor Horta art nouveau building, la maison Waucquez. Costing a projected thirty million Belgian francs to run a year, money came both from the State intervention and private sponsorship.

Despite the accomplishments of the BD critics, no amount of scholarly or enthusiasts' ink would have ever been able to legitimise BD culturally to the extent achieved by the 1980s State patronage. On the other hand, both governments were in a sense acting retrospectively. Official consecration only came when it had become abundantly clear that BD had acquired its adulthood and there was therefore no longer any risk of national embarrassment with this new enterprise. Both the artistic revolution within the BD world and its accompanying intellectualisation had helped give BD its new *titres de noblesse*. But without this culminating State intervention, BD would not exist such as it does today, nor enjoy the general esteem in which it is now held.

Within the critical field during the 1980s changes were afoot. Encouraged by the new officialised status of BD and an economically booming industry, a new breed of critics emerged from Glénat's *Cahiers de la bande dessinée*. Under the direction of Thierry Groensteen, who was to become later the director of the CNBDI's BD museum, the *Cahiers* became the main forum for BD inquiry. The magazine was originally a specialist guide for BD consumption, but with an intellectual edge. The *Cahiers*, however, widened its scope of interest under Groensteen's direction and increasingly concerned itself with critically thematising the BD.

The *Cahiers*' focus on the specifics of the comics form was to initiate the emergence of a series of theoretically insightful works in the 1990s. Various French and Belgian theoretical works in the 1990s, which were to help flesh out the specifics of the BD, were orientated around reading. How to approach the visuality of the BD, how to 'read' a BD was explained via demonstrating how a BD was 'made up' with panels and page layouts. This was the ostensible approach of works such as *Lire la bande dessinée* (Masson 1985), *Case, planche, récit* (Peeters 1991), *Pour une lecture moderne de la bande dessinée* (Baetens and Lefèvre 1993) and *Système de la bande dessinée* (Groensteen 1999), works which have become, in a short space of time, indispensable theoretical guides to BD study.

British and Irish academics have therefore come late rather than early to the study of BD. The essays contained in this book adopt a variety of critical perspectives. It is taken as read that BD is a rich and diverse medium, open to meaningful academic commentary. No apology is made for the academic study of the comics form. Such an assumption, however, relies heavily on the current status of the modern Francophone BD itself, and the battles already won by French-speaking artists and critics. The BD industry is currently in a healthy state, with sales expanding at a rate considerably higher than the national average for any other book genre. And thanks to the emergence of small-scale independent press groups such as Amok, Fréon and Ego Comme X in the 1990s, whose authors for the main have emerged from the new BD art-school culture of the 1980s, the avant-garde reputation of BD is still very much alive. Given the current sophistication of its output in France and Belgium and the medium's official State patronage, the BD does not have to battle against preconceived notions of limitations on its form and content as it has to in Anglophone countries. Both the history of BD and its current continued success allow the medium to be a theoretically stimulating medium whilst at the same time allowing a unique insight into contemporary Francophone culture.

Just as this work borrows from the general Francophone perception that BD is both capable of being adult and artistic, so too this work borrows from current Francophone criticism. Much of the theoretical appreciation of the BD in this collection builds on and complements current theoretical understanding as laid out in the 1990s by French and Belgian scholars. What is perhaps entirely different is a new cultural distance when approaching this material. This is perhaps most readily felt in certain socio-historical takes on the subject.

Although this collection is not intended to offer a history of the BD, this book contains essays focusing on material spanning a significant period of BD history. Material covering most of the century, from Bécassine to Baru, from, as Laurence Grove has put it, 'BD before the term BD existed' to a consideration of contemporary material. Linking these two chronological BD extremes, are discrete studies of some of the century's most important material, i.e. magazines such as *Vaillant/Le Jeune Patriot* (1944), *Pilote* (1959), and *Fluide glacial* (1975) as well as emblematic artists such as Moebius, Tardi, Bilal. Material that signalled crucial turning points in BD history is accordingly revisited and re-examined. Although most of this material has been previously discussed in a Francophone context, the cultural distance of the authors has led to insightful readings and reappraisals. The eclectic approach of the authors reflects the current diversity of research interest in the British Isles. Approaches range from the socio-historic, via theories of comedy, to narratologically based analysis.

Although not all the authors are British, research has been carried out within the Anglophone academy and therefore belongs to this new strand of scholarship.[1] In the last five years BD has emerged as an object of study within French departments in the British Isles. This is not simply because to some the BD option may appear slightly more cutting-edge or innovative than a course on French film, but rather because both the medium and its history give the researcher much to contemplate. BD study may still be embryonic, even pioneering, in an English-language context, but it is a medium that has been uniquely intellectualised and institutionalised in France and Belgium for over forty years. It was perhaps high time that we took notice.

## Bibliography

Covin, Michel, Pierre Fresnault-Deruelle, and Bernard Toussaint (eds) 1976. *BD et son discours*, special issue of *Communications*, 24.
Strinati, Pierre 1961. 'Bande dessinée et science fiction: l'âge d'or en France 1934-1940', *Fiction*, July, 92, 121-25.

---

[1] That is with the exception of the French artist Yves Cotinat [TANITOC], a member of the Ego Comme X group, whose paper in this volume explains the stylistic decisions inherent in the author's creative process.

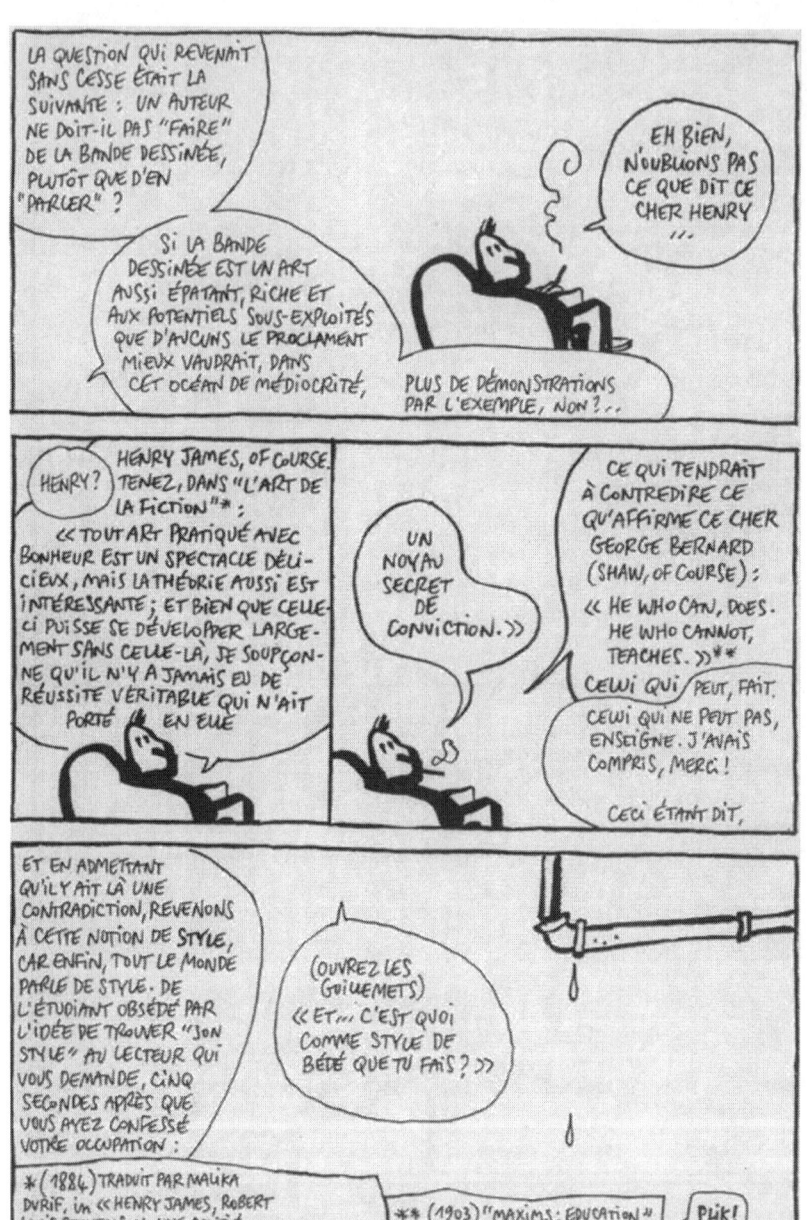

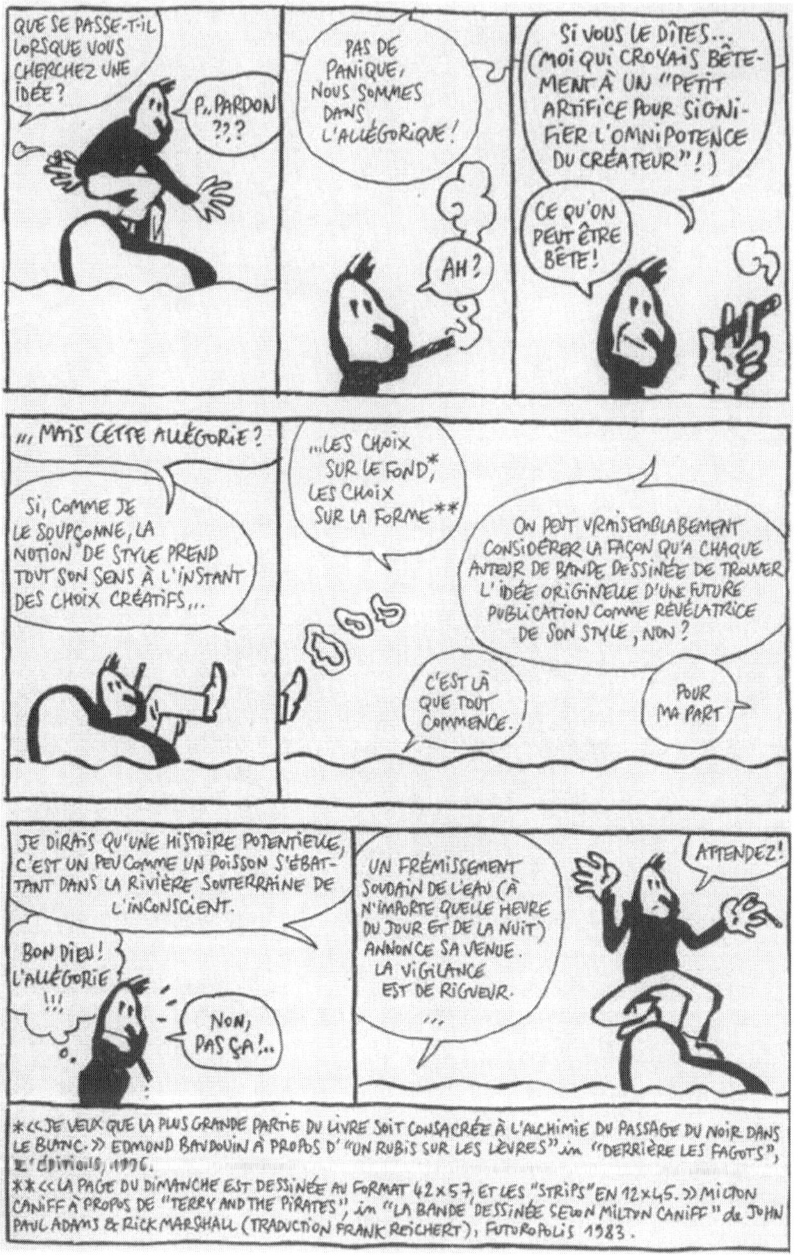

# Exoticising the *Domestique*:
## Bécassine, Brittany and the Beauty of the Dead

### Charles Forsdick
### University of Liverpool

Locked away like an embarrassing elderly relative, Bécassine was long subject to unofficial censorship that has only gradually been lifted. The increasingly archaic *mise en page* of her character—with its clear division of text and image—seemed progressively to conceal a way of life and a series of attitudes rapidly outmoded after the end of the First World War and buried entirely after the Second. The recent republication of the whole series of Bécassine albums suggests, however, the beginnings of a radical reassessment. A popular conception of Bécassine—seasoned traveller, adventurer seeming to thrive on regular crises—is that she is Tintin in drag, with a *coiffe* instead of quiff. Such reductively nostalgic readings are clearly belied by the many polemics that the character has provoked. This article will look in some detail at what is perhaps the most hostile reaction to *Les Aventures de Bécassine*, the Breton response itself, which has ranged from total rejection to more recent instances of subversion (such as the recurrent nationalist image of Bécassine as Che).[1] It will suggest that both previous and contemporary reactions to this particular BD character are highly problematic, not least because they depend on received ideas freighted via a variety of media which do not necessarily include the BD itself.

A particular characteristic of bande dessinée culture is the tendency for characters to spill beyond the limits of the *planche*—to 'dépasser le cadre de la bande dessinée' (Le Bourdonnec 1996, 42)—and to enter the popular imaginary as autonomous figures who may only have a passing resemblance to the original on which they are based. This

---

[1] Such subversion is similar to that carried out by Acadian activists on Longfellow's Evangéline. See Viau 1998, 145-55.

process is particularly true of the Breton character Astérix, product of a specific ideological niche in post-war French culture, who nevertheless has acquired a much more general, representative status. This transformation was made clear at the opening of the Parc Astérix when—in both official advertising material and press accounts—a common rhetorical strategy was used to praise this home-grown theme park as reality whilst condemning Disneyland Paris as pure fantasy (Loselle 1997, 1-3). The distinction between the attractions depends on an abstraction or exemplification of two cartoon characters: according to the common French perception of the USA as a country without history and hence without authentic origin, Mickey Mouse can never be more than a fictional creation; Astérix, on the other hand, originating in ancient Gaul, represents accordingly the ancestral origins of the French. History is presumed to have such a stable content that it cannot be corrupted by any amount of simulation, illusion or comic exaggeration.

This evocation of the *exception française* and of Franco-American culture wars is a reminder of a specific strand of bande dessinée history, to which another Breton character contributes—especially in terms of form. There is no Parc Bécassine—and, if the violent 1939 response to filming of Pierre Caron's *Bécassine* is to be used as an indication, such a project would be foolhardy.[2] However, the character Bécassine, first incorporated in *La Semaine de Suzette* in 1905 and appearing sporadically until the closure of that publication in 1960, reveals a stubborn rejection of American format (especially the use of *bulles*) and an adherence to a traditional combination of descriptive texts juxtaposed with 'vignettes à l'Epinal'. This rooting of the BD in a French tradition of popular iconography offered indigenous origins to an art form seeking cultural specificity. Yet the failure of *La Semaine de Suzette* to survive the 1960s suggests the obsolescence of this attempt to force differentiation or to forge authenticity. Bécassine also is a character who spills beyond the page, but her exemplification is radically different from that of Astérix. It starts at the very beginning of the character's existence and is fuelled by an early instance of merchandising: the loyalty of readers of *Suzette* was encouraged by the weekly provision of dress patterns for the doll Bleuette. Amongst these dresses were costumes for Bécassine, supplemented by a number of other items inspired by the character, such as the mechanical toy *Bécassine casseuse d'assiettes* (1914), or a patriotic lampshade (1917).

There are two sure indicators for a cartoon character's achievement of autonomous status beyond the page: parody in a

---

[2] *Bécassine*, film de long métrage, 1939. Réalisation: Pierre Caron; Scénario: René Pujol; 91 minutes.

pornographic pastiche; and use as an inspiration for neology. Tintin, of course, fulfils both criteria: Jan Bucquoy's *La Vie sexuelle de Tintin* was the first book in Belgian censorship history whose seizure was demanded by booksellers themselves; and the eponymous hero's name has been the source of a variety of neologisms: e.g. 'tintiniser' (Bourdil 1991, 31). Bécassine too has been the subject of at least two pornographic pastiches (Amouricq, 1992; Jando and Pablo, 1974)—as well as the source of the fascist vampire Pencassine featured in the programme *Cocorico*; what is more striking, however, is the range of new words derived from her name: the adjective 'bécassinien' (Le Bourdonnec 1996, 39), the nouns 'bécassins' (Lebesque 1970, 113), 'bécassinades' (Lebesque 1970, 212)—even 'bécassinoclastes'.

The majority of these derived words refer directly to the sociology of Brittany and the sense of inferiority that characterises much Breton self-representation. As a comment by Le Bourdonnec on the 'syndrome "bécassinien"' suggests, Bécassine has come to represent a denigrated vision of the Bretons—and, moreover, has been seen as an agent in such processes of devaluation:

> Le refoulement identitaire génère une sorte de dépression qu'ont mis en évidence quelques spécialistes en psychiatrie. La négation de la langue, expression de sa personnalité et de ses origines, débouche nécessairement sur un refus, une honte de soi. La Bretagne portera, jusqu'au renouveau des années 70, ces stigmates du syndrome 'bécassinien'! (Le Bourdonnec 1996, 39).

The reception history of this *bonne bretonne* is, accordingly, radically divergent from that of her near contemporaries, the 'Pieds nickelés' (Pennacchioni 1982, 103). Whereas the tear-away heroes of *L'Epatant* are celebrated for an anarchic subversion of established authority, the heroine of *La Semaine de Suzette* is found guilty as an accessory to processes of indoctrination, of perpetuation of gender stereotypes. Bécassine was a constant in this weekly paper, whose influential status is suggested by its wide circulation. She was first introduced in a series of 111 free-standing *planches*, recounting various domestic crises, and dependent on a formulaic structure: Bécassine receives an order, the terms of the order are taken literally; confusion ensues—e.g. sent to purchase 'petits suisses', she returns with a number of Savoyards (1914). The popularity of these early anecdotes led to their development into full-length series, in which the main character was given a pre-history and provided narratives with sequence. The attraction of Bécassine for her initial petit-bourgeois readership is complex: on the one hand, she represents the exotic, slightly anachronistic world of the aristocratic household and, consequently, instead of serving a pedagogic role, allows access to dreams of a former social code in which the servant was available daily; on the other, the character's excessive respect of such a code allows readers to distance themselves from it and assert their own modernity.

Such excessive respect, often manifesting itself in specific acts of stupidity, is central to the criticism that Bécassine has undergone. Her stupidity would seem to be innate, encoded in her name and nickname— Annaïck Lebornez contains the epithet 'bornée'; Bécassine, as readers are reminded throughout the albums, refers not only to a bird (the snipe), but also contains the pejorative semantic overtones of 'jeune fille niaise'. But the reference to the bird itself with its prominent beak is ironic and reflects the diminutive size of Bécassine's nose, for the suggestion of stupidity in onamastic detail is supplemented by aspects of physionomy: at birth, her tiny eyes are supplemented by a 'bouche minuscule' and a 'nez si petit qu'on le voyait à peine' (Caumery and Pinchon 1913, 1). The shrunken nature of these organs of sense suggests a restricted interaction with the outside world, and the tininess of the character's mouth (which disappears altogether in a number of albums) reflects a clear difficulty of self-expression. A phrenological examination in *Bécassine pendant la Grande Guerre* corroborates this early evidence:

> Alors M. Proey-Minans promena lentement ses doigts sur la boule qui sert de tête à Bécassine. « Parfait ! murmurait-il: voici la bonté, le dévouement, la simplicité d'esprit... Quel document pour l'ouvrage que je prépare ! » (Caumery and Pinchon 1916, 14)

and a recurrent source of humour in the albums is the headache from which she suffers whenever she is obliged to think. In response to Bécassine's attempt to give Bertrand a suit of armour to protect him at the Front in *Bécassine dans la Grande Guerre* (Caumery and Pinchon 1916, 3), Mme de Grand-Air exclaims: 'Cette Bécassine!... pas de cervelle, mais tant de coeur!', and this comment reveals that Bécassine's stupidity is more complex than some critics have suggested, for it is incorporated in a process which privileges *servitude* (rooted in particular in an acceptance of social hierarchy) as opposed to *servilité* (Pennacchioni 1982, 112).[3] It is therefore possible to incorporate Bécassine in a sequence of fictional servants, and her unquestioning

---

[3] This devotion is taken to absurd limits, especially when it is yoked to the patriotic fervour of the early albums in which Bécassine's self-sacrifice takes on grotesque proportions: in *Bécassine mobilisée*, the heroine takes on a job as a tram conductor so that she can pay her mistress's board and lodging, only to lose the job when she diverts her tram—full of passengers—to protect Mme. de Grand-Air from a rain storm (Caumery and Pinchon 1918).

devotion would seem to ally her to, for example, the Félicité of Flaubert's 'Un coeur simple'. But whereas Félicité's service is literal, rooted in unquestioning acceptance of social and religious codes (and hence derisory), the literal nature of Bécassine's service depends on her stupidity alone and accordingly escapes derision *per se* (Martin-Fugier 1979, 156). The aristocratic social order (rooted in the late nineteenth century) which she represents—and to a certain extent even protects—seems then to escape criticism and emerges unscathed.

A common strand of the recent criticism which attempts recuperation of Bécassine has focussed precisely on the value of the albums as socio-historical document. Such rehabilitation counters the hostile treatment which the character has received since the anti-Bécassine movement in Brittany in the 1930s. Claire Bretécher summarises the principal elements of this hostility:

> [L]'intolérance autour de Bécassine m'agace sous prétexte qu'elle est Bretonne (hurlements des Bretons), domestique (hurlements des gens de gauche) et gourde (hurlements des féministes). Moi, je la trouve moins nulle que Superman... Mais je ne suis pas sûre que les enfants d'aujourd'hui puissent s'y intéresser sauf si elle se déguise en tortue ninja. (Cited in Le Guen 1994).

Critical responses to Bécassine accordingly remain mixed, polarised even, ranging from uneasy rejection or violent polemic to eulogy of the albums as a document of social realism—according to Francis Lacassin, 'une sorte de réplique légère et souriante' to Proust (Lacassin 1969, 39). The transformation of *Les Aventures de Bécassine* into *A la recherche* with pictures is in fact a commonplace of a certain strand of criticism characterised by self-assured, unproblematised nostalgia which grants the BD the status of pre-ideological or even non-ideological document.

Certainly, the Bécassine albums published between 1913 and 1939 reflect three particularly animated decades of French history and present in their *planches* a series of the major political events, social shifts and technological advances which these years encompass. Bécassine herself represents 'la fin des terroirs', the industrialisation of rural France, the shift from subsistence polyculture to specialist farming—and the resultant rural exodus (aided by the expanding railways) which transformed Paris into what Loussouarn calls 'la première ville bretonne du monde' (Loussouarn 1969, 23). Lacassin describes the series of albums as 'le roman de la société française de l'entre deux guerres' (Lacassin 1969, 39), but what such observations ignore is that it is the ideological discourses articulated in the text rather than documentary subject matter which makes these such valuable sources for an understanding of the context from which they emerge.

Pinchon and Caumery represent a world emerging from the nineteenth century, but fractured irreparably by the effects of the First World War. They remain obsessed, nevertheless, by social station, and reveal a profoundly reactionary attitude towards trade unionists, the *nouveaux riches*, and any other group which would seem to threaten the stability of the increasingly obsolescent social structure represented by Bécassine and Mme de Grand-Air. What is striking is that it is actually Bécassine herself who remains static whilst those around her evolve. Frozen in time, a point of reference for a lost social order, by the time of the publication of the last of the first series of albums in 1939 Bécassine is a patent anachronism, left behind by modernity but paradoxically remaining a source of certainty for those uneasy about the implications of that modernity. It is this temporal otherness of Bécassine which, I will argue, marks her character from the start—from the first album, *L'Enfance de Bécassine*—, and which is particularly instructive in considerations of the representation of Brittany.

Numerous critics, rejecting the violence of certain Breton reactions to Bécassine, claim that the choice of Brittany was a matter of chance, the cultural origins of the character potentially interchangeable with any other region of France:

> Monsieur Languereau aurait pu imaginer une Bécassine savoyarde, normande ou auvergnate; elle n'aurait été ni plus sotte ni plus intelligente. S'il a choisi finalement une Bretonne, c'est parce qu'il avait entendu parler des bévues d'une petite bonne originaire de cette province, et écrit deux pages à ce sujet, en 1905, dans le premier numéro de la *Semaine de Suzette*. (Vitruve 1991, 122).

The choice of Brittany is not, however, quite so arbitrary: on the one hand, Bécassine represents a specific Parisian ethnotype, the *bonne bretonne*, who emerged from a particular matrix of late nineteenth-century circumstances; on the other, the perceived denigration of Brittany found in the Bécassine albums is part of a specific tendency in French culture to use representations of Brittany in order to accentuate characteristics which supposedly belonged to the French provinces in their entirety (Bertho 1980). Consciousness of this process is crucial to an understanding of the Breton response to Bécassine, which is triggered not only by the potentially metonymic substitution of character for a whole country or region (a representativity which is, after all, suggested in *L'Enfance de Bécassine*: 'cette petite qu'est la Bretagne à elle toute seule' [Caumery and Pinchon 1913, 9]), but also by the (especially

Parisian) success of the BDs in which she appears.[4] Bécassine—the servant of Parisian nobility, identified as stupid as a result of her name and actions, semi-literate, static as France changes around her—is slowly transformed as a result into a focal point of Breton grievances about their mistreatment and misrepresentation at the hands of the French: 'Just as Little Black Sambo symbolised for Americans the happy, simple black, the cartoon figure of the servant girl Bécassine symbolised for generations of Frenchmen the happy, stupid Breton. The Bretons were the servants, the prostitutes, the cannon fodder of France, and escape from Brittany into French civilisation was held out by schools to Breton children as the only route to dignity and self-respect' (Berger 1977, 166).

The hostile reactions to such ridicule reached their height in the late 1930s in the attack by three Breizh Atao members on the wax-work of Bécassine in the Musée Grévin. This attack in June 1939 was an intervention in the particularly bitter controversy surrounding the filming of a film version of the Bécassine stories starring Paulette Dubost.[5] The film is a peculiar distortion of the BD character in which not only is Bécassine's stupidity accentuated—she is shown in the first scene, accompanied by a pig on a lead (which she thinks is a jaguar), pretending to read a Russian newspaper, and claiming Chicago is in Japan—, but also the social and cultural hierarchy implicit in the plot is emphasised by the chasm between Mme de Grand-Air in her château and the more modest abodes of the local population. Such accentuation of aspects of the earlier albums is ironic since the final Pinchon and Caumery album published in the same year—*Bécassine en roulotte*— shows Bécassine's employer losing her airs and holidaying by the sea with the post-*Front Populaire* masses.

The sense of demolishing a stereotype which underlies the actions of the *Bécassinoclastes* was pushed further in a slightly earlier response to 'ceux qui ont tenté de ridiculiser les Bretonnes en les représentant sous les traits d'une marionnette frisant la bêtise, l'ignorance, et affublée d'un accoutrement ridicule, tournant en dérision le costume breton féminin' (Calvez and Caouissin 1937, 5). The play *Bécassine vue par les Bretons* is an attempt to undermine the comic

---

[4]     On this success, see Gaumer and Moliterni 1994, 54: 'On a beaucoup écrit sur *Bécassine*; on y a vu une chronique d'une époque révolue, une description d'une classe sociale en mouvement et même une "véritable fresque proustienne". Dans l'esprit de Caumery et Pinchon, *Bécassine* se voulait essentiellement une oeuvre divertissante, sans prétention; il s'agissait avant tout de procurer un peu de bonheur aux nombreuses lectrices de *la Semaine de Suzette*... Le moins que l'on puisse dire, c'est que ses créateurs ont réussi leur pari au-delà de leurs expériences.'

[5]     For an account of the filming, see Dubost 1992, 70-72.

version of the *bonne bretonne* by presenting the stoic resignation of the fifteen-year-old Mona, the protagonist who is forced to leave Brittany to go into service in Paris to support her two brothers and three sisters. This reclaiming of an ethnotype and the allied attempt to restore its dignity is a reponse to the trivialisation of rural exodus in the manufacture of Bécassine dolls designed for Parisian consumption. Focussing again on commodification and exemplification rather than representations in the actual BD, the play creates a paradoxical tension in claiming that the fictional Bécassine is an unpatriotic figure, ridiculing the Breton sacrifice in World War I. The heroine Mona is a strong, eloquent character, and it is young Parisian women who take on the principal characteristics of Bécassine. This reversal of roles is complemented by a reversal of the ethnographic gaze as the Parisians themselves are presented as exotic and mildly ridiculous: travellers disappearing into Metro stations become 'des fourmis sous terre' (Calvez and Caouissin 1937, 74), a made-up woman is compared to 'une fouine qui vient de saigner une poule' (Calvez and Caouissin 1937, 75), and the Parisian tourist becomes the object of ridicule:

> Que diriez-vous si les Bretons s'amusaient à tourner publiquement en ridicule la Parisienne? [...] Il leur suffirait de peindre au naturel quelques-uns des spécimens qu'ils voient tous les étés sur les plages. (Calvez and Caouissin 1937, 71).

The suggestion that we are witnessing a mutually incomprehending exchange of gazes is significant. It is not so much the apparent stupidity of Bécassine as her distancing from a centralised, Parisian point of reference that is of interest here. The Brittany represented in the *Aventures de Bécassine*—whether it be that used as a backcloth to individual episodes, or that imagined by Bécassine herself—is (like the heroine's costume itself) generic, not reflecting the diversity of an individual culture, but rather presenting that culture as a monolithic difference. Brittany is subject to a process of internal exoticism—in Morvan Lebesque's terms, it is 'exotisée sur son propre sol' (Lebesque 1970, 62)—, a process whereby peripheral difference is isolated from its specific geographical and cultural context, recuperated towards the Parisian centre where it is used not only to titillate the public imagination, but also as a screen on which is projected the superiority of the centre. The Brittany of Bécassine is not only what Paris is not; it also depends on Paris even for self-articulation—for, in Alain Corbin's terms: 'La province n'existe pas par elle-même' (Corbin 1997, 2851).

The figure of the monolith is important, for it highlights the fixity of the vision of Brittany that emerges from this Parisian representation. The contrast between centre and periphery emerges in particular from the 1935 album, *Bécassine à Clocher-les-Bécasses*, in which the heroine leaves Paris to return temporarily to her home village. The name of the village itself—microcosm of rural Brittany—is striking: the implied stupidity of *Bécasses* is supplemented by the parochial introversion of *Clocher*. To a dynamic, mechanised, modern Paris is opposed a static, antiquated, traditional Brittany—and this inanimation is emphasised by the fact that the local population is never seen to be working, merely watching others or travelling to or from work. What is significant in this album is the implied slippage between Bécassine's vision of Brittany and the culture with which she is faced. Witnessing traces of modernity—the advent of tourism, the replacement of vernacular architecture with urban housing—, she projects a different, pre-existing version of Brittany. This difference is most obviously articulated in her clothing which sets her apart even from other Breton characters. She wears her distinctive, unchanging green dress, white apron and generic *coiffe* from the first album to the last, and it is this costume which distinguishes her—renders her exotic even—whether in Brittany or Paris, or on her foreign travels. Bécassine clings to her parodic version of a national dress as she clings to the vision of her culture which she has been conditioned to accept: a repeated refusal to wear any other clothing leads to recurrent visual humour, with a tram conductor's uniform (Caumery and Pinchon 1918, 15), an Alsatian headdress (Caumery and Pinchon 1916, 55), mountaineering gear (Caumery and Pinchon 1923, 41) placed precariously and temporarily on top of her national dress.

Morvan Lebesque describes how Breton servants in Paris were obliged to retain their *coiffes*:

> Les *Madames* françaises exigent de leur bonne bretonne qu'elle serve en coiffe. D'abord, pour le spectacle, quand on a des invités; ensuite et surtout, pour que cette fille n'oublie pas ses origines. Elle est servante *puisque* bretonne, renier son pays serait refuser sa condition; nous l'avons ramenée de nos vacances, sans nous elle pataugerait encore dans des gadoues avec ses cochons, elle nous doit de la gratitude; et puis, sa coiffe répond à ses vertus: tant qu'elle la portera, elle gardera un pied en Bretagne, ne s'émancipera pas, ne nous jouera pas le tour affreux de cesser de croire en Dieu et en nous. (Lebesque 1970, 112).

Lebesque's polemic seems to reveal a specific aspect of Bécassine's character: her difference in the albums is not merely to do with geography and her peripheral origins, but is also temporal—in his own terms: Brittany is 'à cent lieues et cent ans de Paris' (Lebesque 1970, 33). Accordingly, the representation of Bécassine depends on what the anthropologist Johannes Fabian has described as the 'denial of coevalness' (Fabian 1983). Fabian claims that in anthropology the uses of evolutionary time (in notions such as civilisation, evolution, development, modernisation, urbanisation, industrialisation) have epistemological and ethical underpinnings that suggest that all anthropological representations are rooted in historically established relations of power. It is the usefulness of this model in the field of exoticism which interests me, for it can be applied for an understanding of the internal exoticism in the *Bécassine* albums. Pinchon and Caumery assign a different time (pre-modern, pre-urban, pre-industrial) to their heroine, and use this temporal difference to distance her further from the society into which she has been adopted. Certainly, she remains an ambiguous figure: flying, driving, travelling at a time when these activities were far from everyday, especially for women, but she manages to carry out these activities unwittingly—almost despite herself. The humour of these episodes is not only rooted in their incongruity, but also in the innocence with which Bécassine undertakes them.

In terms of plot, Bécassine can indeed become Tintin, travelling across America, mixing with native Americans and overturning the cowboy-and-indian stereotypes she brings with her in order to become sensitive to the decline of their culture. *Tintin au Congo* echoes the earlier *Bécassine voyage* in several aspects: like Tintin, for instance, Bécassine serves as the bearer of Western medicine, much to the chagrin of the local witch doctor or medicine man. But whereas Tintin becomes the vehicle of Western civilisation in all its guises—education, language, mechanisation—, faced with American modernity Bécassine is like Hergé's Congolese. Her confused reactions to a folding bed (Caumery and Pinchon 1921, 17), a dictophone (21), a vacuum cleaner (53), and condensed milk (51) reveal not only an unfamiliarity with modernity, but also—as Lebesque explains—a resistance to it:

> Bécassine vit hors du temps et du monde, dans le cocon de sa dévotion à Mme de Grand-Air: ce cocon n'est autre que *sa* Bretagne qu'elle a transportée avec elle et qui la préserve des 'tentations'. L'extérieur est pour elle l'enfer, les trains, les bateaux, la grande ville, *ma doue beniguet*, l'épouvantent; toute rencontre lui inspire méfiance, elle ferme l'oreille à tout propos qui ne concerne pas son service domestique: quand la guerre de 14 éclate, elle demande à Firmin et à Zidore la signification du mot *boche* qu'elle n'a jamais entendu. (Lebesque 1960, 113).

Bécassine's exclusion from modernity is part of a more complex system of reinforcement of the division between centre and periphery explored above. As a result, the vision of rural France encapsulated in the albums is treated as humorous because: i) it is different from Parisian modernity whose standards it does not attempt to reach; and ii) even when a Breton attempts to imitate the Parisian, he or she fails dismally. The identity of the centre is safe on both counts. Again, this is particularly apparent in *Bécassine à Clocher-les-Bécasses* where the protagonist's cousin, Marie Quillouch, is the butt of ridicule because of her attempts to ape Parisians: she drinks tea (Caumery and Pinchon 1935, 37), she tries to 's'attifer en demoiselle de la ville, au lieu de porter notre joli costume breton' (35), she builds a *pavillon* instead of a traditional Breton house:

> Nous voilà repartis pour l'autre bout du pays, où est la maison que Louch s'est construite au temps de sa splendeur. Une drôle de maison, genre 'modern style', affirme mon nouveau cousin. Moi, je trouve que c'est surtout genre affreux style.
>
> Ça ressemble en plus laid aux sculptures en saindoux qu'on voit à la devanture de certains charcutiers. 'Oh ! curieux !' dit miss Mary. Elle fait jouer son kodak et ajoute: 'Sans la photo, jamais en Angleterre on ne croirait qu'il y a une maison tellement vilaine dans la France jolie'. Nous entrons... (46).

The aspiration to modernity is offered as no more than an illusory way out, as Breton culture is constantly brought back to the status of static museum object. Already, in *L'Enfance de Bécassine*, the heroine had been taken specifically to the Musée de Quimper where she fails to distinguish between the mannequins in Breton costume and her own neighbours. The humour of this case of mistaken identity is rooted in a process described by de Certeau in a well-known text whose title I have borrowed for the title of this article. In the second half of the nineteenth century, according to de Certeau, the threat of popular culture was transformed and assimilated, via folklore in particular, into 'un musée désormais rassurant' (de Certeau 1993, 53).

It is not my aim to explore the potentially self-destructive implications of de Certeau's article in which 'la culture populaire' is seen as inevitably corrupted by the contact of academic discourse— although his reflections have implications for anyone attempting to study the transformation of the BD into an object of scholarly attention. I am more interested in concluding that what de Certeau describes as an 'exotisme de l'intérieur' (de Certeau 1993, 48) has wide-ranging implications for a reading of Bécassine. In *La Culture au pluriel*, processes of exoticism are traced from a late eighteenth-century rusticophilia in which the French peasant is transformed into a 'bon sauvage de l'intérieur', through the mid-nineteenth-century policing and suppression of popular chapbooks, to the later nineteenth-century aestheticisation of popular culture, converted into an object of nostalgia and integrated into notions of national 'heritage' and of a cohesive, centralised geographical 'community'. Interpreters such as Pinchon and Caumery inherited Breton culture as a beautified corpse, fixed in the past, whose ressusciation in the BD can only produce a mirage. In *Les Aventures de Bécassine*, there is a suppression of the more disturbing or subversive aspects of popular culture: violence, sexuality, the threatening alterity of the child, and their replacement by a clearly temporal alterity which forces Breton culture into the past and links it to the ever-receding spectre of an authentically popular French origin. Bécassine would seem to illustrate de Certeau's principal point about such a strategic operation which, substituting for the practices of the vast majority of the population a static, stable set of representations, sets up a reassuring other as an inert body to be controlled by a centralising authority: '*Peut-on être breton?* demandait Morvan Lebesque. Non [...], sinon à titre d'objet "aboli" et nostalgique' (de Certeau 1993, 68).

\* \* \*

There is, however, a brief post-script to this conclusion: the late twentieth century saw a return to Bécassine and the re-publication in facsimile of the whole series of her adventures. The reaction to the later, updated appearances of Bécassine after the deaths of Pinchon and Caumery had proved similar to that triggered by Tintin's appearance in jeans as opposed to his regulation plus fours: 'Une Bécassine roulant scooter et s'exprimant à la manière de Spirou... C'était inadmissible!' (Forlani 1961, 14). In the light of this rejection of modernisation and in spite of the lack of technical sophistication of the *planches*, contemporary readers rediscover in the original Bécassine an exoticism of rural France which seems to be part of a myth of lost origins:

> Oubliés les préjugés, dépassés le racisme ordinaire, anachronique—ou presque—et la condescendance parisienne, Bécassine devient témoignage car la France tout entière est nostalgique et mélancolique. (Le Bourdonnec 1996, 43).

A new French ruralist myth emerging in particular since the 1970s—and of which the success of Per Jakez Hélias's *Le Cheval d'Orgeuil* is an important indicator—has led to the hallucination of a rural France by its urban counterpart. The role of Bécassine in this particular aspect of the contemporary *crise identitaire* would be the subject of another article. But it seems that the fixity and denial of coevalness which marked her initial appearance are no longer simply the source of superiority and even derision, but allow instead the comfort of a more complex fin-de-siècle nostalgia whereby a society mourns what it has changed irreparably.

## Bibliography

Amouricq, André 1992. *Le Petit monde de Pétassine*, Paris: Albin Michel.

Berger, Suzanne 1977. 'Bretons and Jacobins: Reflections on French Regional Ethnicity', in Milton J. Esman, ed., *Ethnic Conflict in the Western World*, Ithaca: Cornell University Press, 159-78.

Bertho, Catherine 1980. 'L'Invention de la Bretagne. Genèse sociale d'un stéréotype', *Actes de la Recherche en Sciences Sociales*, 35, 45-62.

Calvez, Léone, and Herri [sic] Caouissin 1937. *Bécassine vue par les Bretons*, Saint-Pol-de-Léon: Ronan.

Caumery, M. L., and J. P. Pinchon 1913. *L'Enfance de Bécassine*, Paris: Gautier-Languereau.

Caumery, M. L., and J. P. Pinchon 1916. *Bécassine pendant la Grande Guerre*, Paris: Gautier-Languereau.

Caumery, M. L., and J. P. Pinchon 1918. *Bécassine mobilisée*, Paris: Gautier-Languereau. [Dessins de Edouard Zier].

Caumery, M. L., and J. P. Pinchon 1921. *Bécassine voyage*, Paris: Gautier-Languereau.

Caumery, M. L., and J. P. Pinchon 1923. *Bécassine alpiniste*, Paris: Gautier-Languereau.

Caumery, M. L., and J. P. Pinchon 1935. *Bécassine à Clocher-les-Bécasses*, Paris: Gautier-Languereau.

de Certeau, Michel 1993. *La Culture au pluriel*, Paris: Seuil. [First published 1974].

Corbin, Alain 1997. 'Paris-Province', in Pierre Nora, ed., *Les Lieux de mémoire*, 3 vols, Paris: Gallimard, *Quarto*, II, 2851-88.

Dubost, Paulette 1992. *C'est court, la vie. Souvenirs*, Paris: Flammarion.

Fabian, Johannes 1983. *Time and the Other. How Anthropology Makes Its Object*, New York: Columbia University Press.

[Forlani, Remo] 1961. 'Le Roman vrai des bandes dessinées. En direct de Clocher-les Bécasses', *Pilote*, 85, 14.

Gaumer, Patrick, and Claude Moliterni 1994. *Dictionnaire Mondial de la Bande Dessinée*, Paris: Larousse.

Jando [scénariste], and Pablo [dessinateur] 1974. *La Naissance de Bécasexine*, [n.pl.]: MD.

Lacassin, Francis 1969. 'Bécassine ou le temps retrouvé', *Magazine littéraire*, January, 38-43.

Lebesque, Morvan 1970. *Comment peut-on être breton? Essai sur la démocratie française*, Paris: Seuil.

Le Bouronnec, Yannick 1996. *Le Miracle breton*, Paris: Calmann-Lévy.

Lehembre, Bernard 1992. 'Bécassine revendiquée par les Bretons', *Historia*, 552, 96-99.

Le Guen, Annik 1994. *La Trépidante histoire de Bécassine*, Port-Louis: La Fouesnardière.

Loselle, Andrea 1997. *History's Double: Cultural Tourism in Twentieth-Century French Writing*, New York: St. Martin's Press.

Lossouarn, Olivier 1969. *Les Bretons dans le monde*, Paris: Jean Didier.

Martin-Fugier, Anne 1979. *La Place des bonnes. La domesticité féminine à Paris en 1900*, Paris: Grasset.

Ory, Pascal 1979. 'La France de Bécassine', *L'Histoire*, 10, 82-83.

Pennacchioni, Irène 1982. *La Nostalgie en images: une sociologie du récit dessiné*, Paris: Librarie des Méridiens.

Prado, Patrick 1980. 'Le Va et le vient. Migrants bretons à Paris', *Ethnologie française*, 10.2, 191-96.

Vitruve, Raymond 1991. *Bécassine, œuvre littéraire*, Paris: La Pensée Universelle.

Viau, Robert 1998. *Les Visages d'Evangéline. Du poème au mythe*, Beauport (Quebec): MNH.

# BD Theory Before the Term 'BD' Existed[1]

## Laurence Grove
## University of Glasgow

Rodolphe Töpffer (1799-1846), the Swiss schoolmaster who composed and drew numerous caricatural narratives for the delight of his pupils, is generally accepted by current critics as the inventor of the bande dessinée. In the introduction to the catologue that accompanied the 1996 exhibition in honour of Töpffer, Thierry Groensteen is clear on the subject: 'Pour la bande dessinée, la question des origines ne souffre plus guère de discussion: Rodolphe Töpffer en est bel et bien l'inventeur' (Groensteen 1996, 13).[2]

Yet how did Töpffer and his contemporaries view his rôle as inventor of the bande dessinée? Moving beyond Töpffer, this paper will also consider the period from the 1920s to the 1950s, the era seen by many as the Golden Age of the BD (Gaumer and Moliterni, 1994). Our approach will not be that of retrospective analysis, but rather in terms of the phenomenon as viewed through the eyes of commentators of the time. The conclusion will then ask what these early attempts—or non-attempts—to define the form can tell us about the form itself.

To return therefore to the Töpffer question above, the short answer is that he and his contemporaries did not envisage the role of inventor of the BD. Works on Töpffer published in or around his lifetime are relatively scarce, the only book-length studies being Auguste Blondel's *Rodolphe Töpffer: L'Ecrivain, l'artiste et l'homme* (1886) and l'Abbé Pierre-Maxime Relave's *Rodolphe Töpffer: Biographie et*

---

[1] This paper is part of a larger project, *The Emblematic Age: Text/Image Mosaics in the Dawn of Technology*, to be published by Ashgate and for which I have received generous support from the British Academy and AHRB. Certain aspects of the paper have already appeared in 'Visual Cultures, National Visions: The Ninth Art of France,' *New Directions in Emblem Studies*, ed. Amy Wygant (Glasgow: GES, 1999), pp. 43-57.

[2] For a similar viewpoint, see also Groensteen 1998.

*extraits* (1899). In both these cases emphasis is very much on Töpffer's life, his work as a journalist, as a teacher and as a tourist. When his BDs, as we now know them, are mentioned, as for example on page VII of the 'Préface des Editeurs' of an early edition of the *Voyages en zigzag* (Töpffer 1846, see **Figure 1**), they are viewed not in terms of the originality of the text/image form, but rather with reference to the characterisation. In this example the 'BDs' are merely labelled 'histoires comiques' and the editors concentrate on the personalities and actions of M. Jabot, M. Vieux-Bois and M. Crépin.

More generally, the *Dictionnaire historique & bibliographique de la Suisse* (1932) has no entry for Töpffer, nor does the *Grande Encyclopédie* of circa 1890. The *Grand Dictionnaire universel du XIX siècle* (1876) does dedicate three columns to him, but once again these are largely biographical, underlining Töpffer's role as an artist. There is no mention of the notion of text/image interaction or of narration through pictures.

The nature of the original dissemination by Töpffer of work now classed as '*bandes dessinées*' also suggests that his standing was far different then than today. His hand-drawn pieces were generally circulated amongst a limited circle of family and friends, including Goethe (Kaenel 1996, 126). When Töpffer's works did go to print, his publisher and cousin Jacques-Julien Dubochet would often use Parisian artists such as Girardet, Francais, Daubigny or Cham for the final version of the *vignettes* (Kaenel 1996, 165). In the case of the 1840 edition of *Dr Festus*, Töpffer produced the text in a separate edition from that of the images (Kaenel 1996, 171-72).

In short, the view that modern bande dessinée studies present of Rodolphe Töpffer is very much a retrospective one, certainly not a reflection of the analysis of the time. Groensteen's summary of the beginnings of the BD, 'Töpffer en est bel et bien l'inventeur', might be contrasted with the 1886 view of things as presented by Blondel:

> En résumé, il ne faut pas chercher dans les albums de caricature de Töpffer autre chose que ce qu'ils étaient pour leur auteur, un passe-temps. (Blondel 1886, 118)

To what extent can the same be said of the bande dessinée in its twentieth-century development? The boom period of 1934-59 and, more specifically, 1947-50, have been well documented. Pascal Ory's 'Mickey Go Home!: La Désaméricanisation de la bande dessinée (1945-1950)' gives a particularly lucid analysis of changes that occured at the time, and a number of publications have considered the causes and effects of the 1949 law that introduced new censorship of children's publications

(Crépin 1999, Groensteen 1999, Crépin and Groensteen 1999). In short, it was a time when children's publications were vastly popular and it was in these that appeared what we would now clearly call bandes dessinées (see **Figure 2**, for an example).

Statistics vary according to the sources consulted, but a reasonable idea of the circulation figures in question can be obtained from Jacqueline and Raoul Dubois's *La Presse enfantine française* of 1957: they give *Le Journal de Mickey* as having a monthly press run of 511 000 and the total press run of all children's publications as being 19 823 910, with a monthly income of 480 000 000 FF.

Although much has been written on the parliamentary debate surrounding the 1949 law, critical reaction of the time has been less fully documented.[3] Nonetheless reaction was intense, as can been seen from a variety of publications—publications I have chosen because they provide interesting examples whilst remaining representative of a general trend—from the 1920s to the 1950s.

The immediately striking characteristic of such early commentaries was the emphasis on the publications' poor quality and, by extention, harmful effect.[4] Marie-Thérèse Latzarus in *La Littérature enfantine en France dans la seconde moitié du XIX siècle* of 1924 typifies this stance:

> Les illustrations des journaux d'enfants de notre époque sont grotesques par leurs couleurs, et de mauvais goût par leur inspiration. Elles reproduisent, fréquemment, des scènes d'ivrognerie ou des pugilats. Elles ridiculisent des difformités ou des disgrâces physiques. Il n'est pas rare d'y voir des écoliers, tirant la langue à leur maître, ou des enfants, jouant de bons tours à leurs parents. (Latzarus 1924, 158)

Nearly three decades later Jean de Trignon, in his *Histoire de la littérature enfantine de Ma Mère l'Oye au Roi Babar* (1950), was making the same type of comment:

> La Presse enfantine connut à partir de 1880 un double courant. D'une part, croissance en nombre, mais d'autre part, avilissement de qualité. (Trignon 1950, 166)

> On vit naître des hebdomadaires de formats variés, dont les textes hachés et presque inexistants se réduisent à des interjections, parfois même à un point d'exclamation, placés dans les phylactères. Des filles blondes et des cow-boys sortis de films américains émettent ainsi de sortes de nuages ou de banderoles

---

[3] One exception to this general rule is Groensteen 1999.

[4] This is one of the topics emphasised by Groensteen in the article cited in the previous footnote.

où s'inscrivent des mots sans suite. C'est le sabotage de tout art et de toute littérature. Une mise en page fiévreuse acheva de donner une impression de désordre et d'anarchie. (Trignon 1950, 174-75)

As late as 1957 the Dubois in *La Presse enfantine française*, were clear in their condemnation:

Car rien n'est plus affligeant que la bêtise générale des histoires racontées en images par les illustrés; aucune ne supporte une analyse un peu sérieuse. (Dubois 1957, 6)

To believe such critics—and they are typical—the effect of such *illustrés* on children could be devastating. Alphonse de Parvillez in *Que Liront nos jeunes?* of 1943 went to extremes in connecting such publications with violent crime:

A Juilly, deux petits bergers massacrent une famille de cinq personnes. On trouve dans leur chambre une abondante provision d'illustrés. (Parvillez 1943, 36)

The Dubois (*La Presse enfantine française*) were to imply the same sort of cause and effect, despite absolving the *illustrés* of total responsibility:

Nous savons tous que l'illustré ne porte pas seul la responsabilité du passage des jeunes devant le tribunal pour enfants... (Dubois 1957, 4)

L'enfant assis sur le rebord d'un trottoir n'emportera pas un livre: il lira facilement un illustré, si peu éducatif soit-il. (Dubois 1957, 4)

One of the more extreme cases was a tract by D. Parker and C. Renaudy, *La Démoralisation de la jeunesse par les publications périodiques* (1944) which includes 'les Petits Journaux illustrés' as 'littérature pornographique' (see **Figure 3**). The inside cover (see **Figure 4**) summarises areas of concern: 'publications périodiques' come after cinema, but before prostitution, 'immoralité dans les lieux de travail' and alcoholism.

Putting aside the general label of pornography, some commentators, more specifically, saw the *illustrés* as strong political weapons. Georges Sadoul, one of the leading figures in French Communist circles and *rédacteur en chef* himself of an *illustré* aimed at the children of workers, *Mon Camarade*, saw Mickey Mouse as a powerful fascist beast, stating 'C'est ainsi qu'une innocente souris peut cacher, dans son ombre, un grand fauve hitlérien' (Sadoul 1938, 15). At the other end of the political scale, Henry Coston was also aware of the publications' power. In *Les Corrupteurs de la jeunesse* of 1943, Coston

*Laurence Grove* 43

refers to the creators of *Mon Camarade* (i.e. Sadoul and his associates) as 'venus de la Jérusalem moscovite pour inspirer cet hebdomadaire illustré' (Coston 1943, 26). In the same tract, he expresses his worries concerning 'l'emprise néfaste de ces Petits Illustrés judéo-maçons' (Coston 1943, 26). It is interesting to note that Mickey Mouse, depending on one's viewpoint, could be Hitlerite or Jewish, Communist and Masonic!

The clear concern with the uses to which such 'bandes dessinées' are put overshadows the vague terms used to describe the phenomenon itself. Latzarus, again in *La Littérature enfantine...*, criticises children's publications in the following terms:

> [...] cette transformation de l'illustration est une des caractéristiques de notre époque. Jadis, certains livres d'enfants (les livres de Bertin, par exemple) s'ornaient de gravures en couleurs d'une grande finesse. Mais lorsque l'illustration, couvrant toute une page, fut complétée par les nombreuses vignettes empiétant sur les pages de texte, on ne vit plus guère que des gravures noires. (Latzarus 1924, 290)

What we now know as *cases* or 'frames' are described ('les nombreuses vignettes empiétant sur les pages de texte') rather than named. The same is true in the case of Sadoul, writing four years after *Le Journal de Mickey* had first appeared in France:

> L'invention *des histoires en petits carrés légendés* est pour l'avenir des lectures enfantines un événement considérable. Avec ce genre d'images d'Epinal naît, en effet, une forme de dessins en action dont l'évolution aboutira de nos jours aux dessins animés de Walt Disney. (Sadoul 1938, 5; my emphasis)

> Et certes un hebdomadaire comme l'Epatant ne représentait pas un grand progrès éducatif sur l'image d'Epinal. Huit pages du journal étaient occupées par *des histoires en images par petits carrés* dont la disposition reproduisait fidèlement les anciens petits carrés des images d'Epinal et certains de leurs thèmes. (Sadoul 1938, 7; my emphasis)

Similarly, in Trignon's *Histoire de la littérature enfantine de Ma Mère l'Oye au Roi Babar* cited above, the author provides an analytic description of what we now recognise as *bulles* or speech-bubbles: 'Des filles blondes et des cow-boys sortis de films américains émettent ainsi de sortes de nuages ou de banderoles où s'inscrivent des mots sans suite.'[5]

Critics are clearly aware of the technical advances taking place, they are aware of the form's content and application, yet they provide virtually no analysis of the form *per se*. Indeed Trignon, again in *Histoire de la littérature enfantine de Ma Mère l'Oye au Roi Babar*, appears ill-at-ease with any hybrid text/image form:

> Inclure un chapitre sur le théâtre et le cinéma dans un essai sur la littérature enfantine est chose malaisée, car si les limites ne sont pas nettes en ce qui concerne les autres genres, nous nous trouverons ici en présence d'une confusion encore plus grande. (Trignon 1950, 206)

Not only, therefore, do we find no analysis of the text/image interaction now seen as an inherent component of the bande dessinée, furthermore no mention is made of the terms, including 'bande dessinée', that we now take for granted. In short, the bande dessinée clearly exists and has made an impact, critics are aware of the importance of its uses, but there is no real awareness, so it would seem, of the form as a form.

Which raises the question as to when did the Mickey story of our second illustration become a bande dessinée? Alain Rey in his *Dictionnaire historique de la langue française*[6] gives the term 'bande dessinée' as existing from 1940 in Paul Winkler's contracts. The *Trésor de la langue française* (Imbs 1975) strangely gives it as being synonymous with 'dessin animé'. The *Nouveau Petit Robert* gives the initial date of 1929. I would like to suggest, however, that the instances Rey and Robert have picked are in fact of the noun 'bande' being qualified by the adjective 'dessinée' and that 'bande dessinée' as a semantic unit did not exist until the end of the 1950s. Indeed, the *Robert* of as late as 1969 gives no mention of the term despite providing more than a full column on the word 'bande' and associated phrases ('bande de fer', 'bandes de billard', 'plate-bande', 'bande d'idiots'...). The subject catalogue of the Bibliothèque nationale de France does not include 'bande dessinée' before the 1960s.

The first self-conscious analysis of the workings of the bande dessinée in terms of its text/image interaction appears to be by Elisabeth Gerin in *Tout sur la presse enfantine* (1958, see **Figure 5**). Here, Gerin

---

[5] It is interesting to note that in the same passage Trignon appropriates the term 'phylactères', one generally used to describe the frame given to Egyptian hyroglyphics. The word has since become the accepted scholarly expression for *bulles*.

[6] Rey is also the author of a work on the theory of the bande dessinée, *Les Spectres de la bande*.

gives examples of cases in which the text explains the image or, conversely, of the 'triomphe de l'image', as well as analysing the different uses and presentations of text (e.g. 'ballons') in terms of the narration. The first self-conscious historical analysis of the 'BD' as a genre *per se* seems to be a series that appeared from 1961 at regular intervals in *Pilote*. In the first episode of the series, 'Le Roman vrai des bandes dessinée' (see **Figure 6**), the project is described as 'une histoire qui n'avait jamais encore été écrite', an epithet that to all intents and purposes appears accurate. It is interesting to note, however, that for Remo Forlani, the named author of the series, the 'inventor' of the modern bande dessinée is R. F. Outcault, the creator of Yellow Kid (1895), with Rodolphe Töpffer receiving no mention.

The return to Töpffer—or absence thereof—allows us to draw our first conclusion from these findings. We should be aware that there is a considerable difference between the way modern critics—in addition to those already cited, Henri Filippini (Filippini 1979) and Claude Moliterni (Moliterni 1989)[7] are but two examples—describe the modern bande dessinée and the way it was viewed at the time. To the modern eye, the *Mickey* story of our second illustration looks very much akin, in terms of format and genre, to any recent *Astérix et Obélix* album. Nonetheless, attitudes to *Mickey* in 1934 were very different from our current awareness of the bande dessinée's national and international traditions. In short, the form was used to promote, or at least was seen as promoting, certain ideas long before being defined or labelled.

Why or how is the bande dessinée different, in this respect, from other developing genres? In the case of genres that existed in Ancient times (e.g. theatre or poetry) there is always a tradition to which to relate, and as a result the form is inevitably self-conscious. In the case of the BD this is not so. How can one summarise BD theory before the term 'BD' existed? In short, there was not really any *per se* and, furthermore, the term bande dessinée is a relatively recent coinage.

Nonetheless one interesting and unusual example from the turn of the century is worth citing, that of John Grand-Carteret, a writer with an uncommon interest in the analysis of text/image relationships. Grand-Carteret (1850-1927) was a journalist who worked, amongst other things, on the 1883 Rousseau exhibition, showed a particular interest in caricatures, and, in 1893 founded *Le Livre et l'Image*.[8] In the preface to this new *revue* (Grand-Carteret 1893) he shows a rare awareness, at the

---

[7] Interestingly Claude Moliterni was a leading figure in *Phénix* publications, a journal that played an important part in the popularisation of the BD.

[8] For further information on John Grand-Carteret, see the appropriate entry in Prévost, Roman d'Amat and Tribout de Morembert 1985.

time of the 'proto bandes dessinées' such as those of *Le Rire* (see **Figure 7**),⁹ of the workings of text/image interaction:

> Le Livre et l'Image! C'est-à-dire ce qui se lit et ce qui se regarde; ce qui parle à l'imagination, ce qui s'adresse aux yeux; la langue littéraire et la langue graphique. (Grand-Carteret 1893, 1)

> Des études littéraires présentent, en quelques pages, la caractéristique d'une idée ou d'une période; des images viennent éclairer le texte, restituant sous leur forme réelle et tangible les objets dont on parle. (Grand-Carteret 1893, 1)

Grand-Carteret shows incredible foresight:

> [...] aujourd'hui, le document triomphe, et l'on peut affirmer que le XXe siècle verra se réaliser la grande révolution dont nous voyons les premiers germes: la langue graphique, l'Image, marchant de pair avec la langue littéraire, l'Ecriture. (Grand-Carteret 1893, 2)¹⁰

It seems that it is precisely this hybrid nature, the notion that the BD consists of component parts 'marchant de pair', that distinguishes it from other non-ancient forms, such as the novel.

A natural result of the practicalities of such status is the question of control, or lack thereof, through technology. A writer of novels, for example, may not control the distribution or censorship of his or her output, but he or she does have total control over the work that is initially produced. The same is not true in the case of hybrid visual forms. The final product is an amalgam of the author or authors' work, the printer's expedients and the decisions of the production team, and in the case of the bande dessinée the producers were prey to a fast-changing technology. The early-twentieth century saw the development of linotypes, photomechanical processes, helio-cylinders and offsets,¹¹ as well as the ever-growing influence of photography, cinema and television.

---

⁹ Although the first number of *Le Rire* did not actually appear until 1894, it is typical of the style of publications available when *Le Livre et l'Image* was launched.

¹⁰ Grand-Carteret also provided a 1906 edition of *Le Centre de l'amour* (Grand-Carteret 1906), an anonymous emblem book from approximately 1687. In the introduction he points to the way in which the component parts of the emblem interact, providing different elements of a completed whole. Interestingly, the (non) history of emblem theory in the early decades of the form's development has much in common with that of the BD. For references to work in which I explore this notion further, see note 1.

¹¹ For the technical aspects of printing in the Early-Modern period, see Martin and Chartier 1982 and 1986.

Like the internet of the 1990s, the post-war 'bande dessinée' was an easily recognised form, a tool of high potential attracting frequent attention and a form of expression in constant evolution. When the creator is not wholly in charge of the creation but technology dictates certain of its aspects, that makes for an interesting and thus powerful weapon, but not a definable one.

## Bibliography

Blondel, Auguste 1886. *Rodolphe Töpffer: L'Ecrivain, l'artiste et l'homme*, Paris: Hachette.

Couton, Henry 1943. *Les Corrupteurs de la jeunesse*, Paris: Bulletin d'Information Anti-Maçonnique.

Crépin, Thierry 1999. '1950-1954: La Commission de surveillance entre intimidation et répression', *9e Art: Les Cahiers du Musée de la Bande dessinée*, 4, 21-27.

Crépin, Thierry, and Thierry Groensteen (eds). 1999. *«On Tue à chaque page»: La Loi de 1949 sur les publications destinées à la jeunesse*, Paris: Editions du Temps.

*Dictionnaire historique & bibliographique de la Suisse* 1932. Neuchatel: Administration du Dictionnaire Historique & Bibliographique de la Suisse.

Dubois, Jacqueline, and Raoul Dubois 1957. *La Presse enfantine française*, Paris: Editions de Franc et Franches-Camarades.

Filippini, Henri et alii 1979. *Histoire de la bande dessinée en France et en Belgique des origines à nos jours*, Grenoble: Glenat.

Forlani, Remo 1961. 'Le Roman vrai de la bande dessinée'. Series that appeared in *Pilote* from 1961 onwards.

Gaumer, Patrick, and Claude Moliterni 1994. *Dictionnaire mondiale de la bande dessinée*, Paris: Larousse.

Gerin, Elisabeth 1958. *Tout sur la presse enfantine*, Paris: Centre de Recherches de la Bonne Presse.

Grand-Carteret, John 1893. 'En Manière de Préface', *Le Livre et l'Image*, 1, 1-2.

Grand-Carteret, John (ed.) 1906. *Le Centre de l'amour*, Paris: Albin Michel [original work of unknown authorship, c. 1687].

*Grand Dictionnaire universel du XIX siècle* 1876. Paris: Administration du Grand Dictionnaire Universel.

*Grande Encyclopédie* c. 1890. Paris: Société Anonyme de la Grande Encyclopédie.

Groensteen, Thierry 1998. 'Töpffer, The Originator of the Modern Comic Strip', in Charles Dierick and Pascal Lefèvre, eds., *Forging A New Medium: The Comic Strip in the Nineteenth Century*, Brussels: VUB University Press, 107-114.

Groensteen, Thierry 1999. 'C'était le temps où la bande dessinée corrompait l'âme enfantine....', *9e Art: Les Cahiers du Musée de la Bande dessinée*, 4, 14-19.

Groensteen, Thierry (ed.) 1996. *Rodolphe Töpffer: Aventures graphiques*, [Genève]: [Musées d'Art et d'Histoire].

Imbs, Paul, ed. 1975. *Trésor de la langue française: Dictionnaire de la langue du XIXe et du XXe siècle (1789-1960)*, 16 vols., Paris: CNRS.

Kaenel, Philippe 1996. *Le Métier d'illustrateur 1830-1880: Rodolphe Töpffer, J.-J. Grandville, Gustave Doré*, Paris: Messene.

Latzarus, Marie-Thérèse 1924. *La Littérature enfantine en France dans la seconde moitié du XIX siècle*, Paris: PUF.

Martin, Henri-Jean, and Roger Chartier (eds) 1982. *Histoire de l'édition francaise: Tome I: Le Livre conquérant: Du Moyen Age au milieu du XVIIe siècle*, Paris: Promodis.

Martin, Henri-Jean, and Roger Chartier (eds) 1986. *Histoire de l'édition francaise: Tome IV: Le Livre concurrencé: 1900-1950*, Paris: Promodis.

Moliterni, Claude, ed. 1989. *Histoire mondial de la bande dessinée*, Paris: Horay.

*Nouveau Petit Robert* 1994. Paris: Robert.

Ory, Pascal 1984. 'Mickey Go Home!: La Désaméricanisation de la bande dessinée (1945-1950)', *Vingtième Siècle*, 4, 77-88.

Parker, D. and C. Renaudy 1944. *La Démoralisation de la jeunesse par les publications périodiques*, Paris: Cartel d'Action Morale.

Parvillez, Alphonse de 1943. *Que Liront nos jeunes?*, Paris: Les Editions du temps Présent.

Prévost, Michel, Jean-Charles Roman d'Amat, and Henri Tribout de Morembert (eds) 1985. *Dictionnaire de biographie française,* 18 vols., Paris: Letouzey et Ané.

Relave, L'Abbé Pierre-Maxine 1899. *Rodolphe Töpffer: Biographie et extraits*, Lyon: Emmanuel Vitte.

Rey, Alain 1978. *Les Spectres de la bande*, Paris: Minuit.

Rey, Alain 1998. *Dictionnaire historique de la langue française*, Paris: Robert.

*Le Robert: Dictionnaire alphabétique et analogique de la langue française* 1969. Paris: Société du Nouveau Littré.

Sadoul, Georges 1938. *Ce que lisent vos enfants*, Paris: Bureau d'Editions.

Töpffer, Rodolphe 1886. *Voyages en zigzag*, Paris: J. J. Dubochet [facsimile reprint by Slatkine of Geneva, 1996].

Trignon, Jean de 1950. *Histoire de la littérature enfantine de Ma Mère l'Oye au Roi Babar*, Paris: Hachette.

*De nouvelles formes naissent*:
Le Corbusier and the bande dessinée

**Judi Loach**
**University of Cardiff**

> Nous voyons par le monde fourmiller des puissances énormes, industrielles, sociales; nous percevons, sorties du tumulte[,] des aspirations ordonnés et logiques et nous les sentons coïncider avec les moyens de réalisation que nous possédons. De nouvelles formes naissent; le monde crée une nouvelle attitude. Une époque neuve commence et des faits nouveaux surviennent. (Le Corbusier 1929, 97)

## Introduction

Strange as it may at first seem, relating certain graphic formats developed or exploited by the great Modernist architect Le Corbusier to such a popular and popularist medium as the bande dessinée can prove illuminating. There are unquestionably parallels inherent in the ways in which architects conventionally present their schemes and the way in which the bande dessinée operates: architects have always been trained to communicate primarily through drawings yet have never been able to express their ideas satisfactorily without simultaneous recourse to words; in their technical drawings words therefore necessarily intrude within the pictorial space, in the form of annotations, clarifying functions and materials, or precisely defining dimensions. Moreover, architects cannot fully convey any scheme through a single such image-word amalgam, since our understanding of architectural space depends upon our experience of being in and moving through it; they are therefore obliged to produce a series of drawings, representing different visual perceptions of the space(s), in order to construct a representation of the building as a whole. Yet, despite the exceptional potential of the bande dessinée format for communicating architecture through graphic means, architects have exploited it much less than one might therefore expect.

Le Corbusier's work, however, offers several instances which resemble the bande dessinée. The most explicit example is probably his so-called 'Lettre à Madame Meyer', of 1925, which comprises a sequence of hand drawn scenes, each accompanied by a caption, usually placed immediately beneath the image (**Figure 8**). This caption is sometimes contained within a rather cartoon strip-like bubble, which in a couple of cases actually invades the pictorial space, for instance taking the form of a cloud in the sky. The 'letter' as a whole constitutes a continuous narrative, in which a building—a villa designed by the architect for his putative client Mme. Meyer—assumes the role of the central character.

The question immediately raised is why Le Corbusier exploits this format whereas his colleagues do not. In turn this leads to the question as to whether he is knowingly invoking such a popularist medium as the bande dessinée, or whether this resemblance is unconscious, or even merely coincidental. To answer these questions, one needs to take account of the historical circumstances in which Le Corbusier was working. In the teens and 'twenties of the twentieth century, the bande dessinée had not yet been defined as a genre. On the one hand, its employment had thus not yet been prescribed as narrowly as it is today, with the result that it was used for a wider range of purposes than we might anticipate. On the other hand, during these years, Le Corbusier was not necessarily imitating bande dessinée format, but could equally well have been working in parallel with those developing the genre, drawing on the same sources as them. An understanding of his particular usage of formats evoking bande dessinée thus casts light on how that genre was more broadly perceived, at that moment when it was first becoming recognised as such; it also illuminates wider aspects of the genre's early development.

### 'Le monde crée une nouvelle attitude'—*L'Esprit Nouveau*

Although bande dessinée formats had been used earlier, it only became defined as a genre in the 1930s. The period of its definition and recognition—the preceding two decades—thus coincided with an explosion of avant garde activity in the arts in Paris: painting and sculpture moved from Cubism through Dada to Surrealism; poetry witnessed equally radical experiments, from Cendrars' free forms and Apollinaire's 'Calligrammes' to Schwitters' *merz*; music produced similarly innovative forms, with radical departures in classical composition—Satie, Stravinsky et al.—which were, however, overshadowed by the rise of jazz; dance perhaps attracted the most attention, thanks to the controversial productions of the Ballets Russes and the Ballets Suédois, and was certainly the most pervasive promoter of modernity, through eurhythmics and other forms of lyrical physical exercise, and the vogue for tango and fox-trot. In all these fields artists, in an often painful awareness of the social and cultural dislocation induced by the urban reality of industrial society—the 'profond bouleversement de l'époque machiniste', as Le Corbusier called it (1929, 60)—expressed their dissatisfaction with the preferred subjects and forms alike of their academic masters, as these seemed wholly irrelevant to the new conditions.

Their consequent commitment (often naive) to a progressive social agenda and the material context of their rejection of academic tradition together explain why an avant garde intent upon promoting an industrialised form of modernity turned to the popular culture of the day, both for its subject matter and for appropriate media and formats through which to communicate their ideas in visual form (see Weiss 1994). In their still lifes, objects drawn from the everyday life of working class people predominate: bottles and glasses; pipes, cigarettes and matches; newspapers, posters and playing cards; guitars or mandolins and sheet music. This is perhaps made most explicit in Purism, the artistic movement developed by Le Corbusier and Amédée Ozenfant, premised as it was on a belief in the status of everyday household objects— notably the bottles, glasses and bowls most commonly used in artisan class cafes and homes—as classic *types*, the results of a selection process operating in the domestic realm equivalent to that of natural selection in the jungle (see Green 1976). In other words, the avant garde worked with, and reworked, objects from everyday, artisan class life, rendering them eye-catching, even provocative, through changing their context or juxtaposing them in unexpected ways. This avant-garde attitude, epitomised by Dada's ready-mades, thus paralleled practices common in popular culture, such as the music hall's appropriation of actuality (see Weiss 1994, 45).

Likewise avant-garde artists displayed a preoccupation with those genres of artisan class entertainment in vogue at the time, circus and music hall. Le Corbusier's personal involvement in these is proven by his marriage to a music hall dancer, and '50 aquarelles de Music-Hall ou le QUAND-MEME des Illusions', the collection of fifty watercolours depicting music hall and circus which he produced in 1926. *L'Esprit Nouveau*, the magazine founded in 1920 by Le Corbusier (or rather Charles-Edouard Jeanneret, as he was still called at the time) along with other members and supporters of this avant-garde, even included rubrics covering music hall, cinema, circus and sport in each issue (see, for example, Bizet 1921). An essay published in it, tellingly entitled 'Le Cirque, art nouveau', extolled the circus as 'une spectacle faite de réalités', at the expense of theatre, which 'ne vit que de fictions' (Arnauld 1920); the former constituted a 'présentation' of modern life, whilst the latter could offer no more than a 'représentation' of it. Moreover, a Roman heritage was claimed for the circus, but not for theatre; and, in keeping with hygienist preoccupations of the time, the circus was further commended for its 'liaison intime avec le sport'.

Simultaneously the avant garde availed itself of layouts and graphic techniques culled from the media—more precisely, the mass media—developed by modern, industrialised society: newspapers, posters and other publicity material, packaging. The rapid production and intrinsic ephemerality of these media endowed them with a sense of topicality and urgency, which was enhanced by their subject matter, including cartoon and caricature (echoing the revue in the music hall). It is significant that Le Corbusier had trained in industrial design rather than fine arts, and had done so in a school of decorative art, virtually set up by the local chamber of commerce of a modern industrial town (La Chaux-de-Fonds). He seems to have collected trade catalogues, manufacturers' brochures, mail order catalogues and technical journals expressly to provide the material for illustrating his own essays (as can be seen in *L'Esprit Nouveau*). Likewise he ransacked this commercial milieu for the stencils with which to letter and number his designs.

Although 'l'esprit nouveau' was an optimistic slogan much bandied around throughout the First World War, its appropriation for this magazine's title seems indebted to Apollinaire's particular use of it in a 1917 essay on the ballet 'Parade', entitled '"Parade" et l'Esprit Nouveau'. Commissioned by Serge Diaghilev for his Ballets Russes, this ballet had combined the creative energies of Cocteau (librettist), Massine (choreographer), Picasso (designer) and Satie (composer), and in his essay Apollinaire eulogised it as a 'herald of new, more comprehensive art'. In this context *l'esprit nouveau* demands artists' mutual collaboration, as the only way of producing art works capable of reflecting the complexity and dynamism of modern industrial society. Such an attitude again parallels music hall and circus, which both relied upon bringing together a variety of different artists. The belief in synthesis as the prerequisite for creating modern art would continue to underpin a certain sector of the avant-garde throughout the following decades, with Le Corbusier and Matisse founding the Association pour une Synthèse des Arts Plastiques in 1949.

It is therefore not surprising that existing media were recombined to create new hybrid forms, or were at least transposed for new usages, collage becoming the exemplar of such formal innovation. Through the collaboration of writers with visual artists the relationship between word and image was re-examined (see Peyré 2001); this led both to new juxtapositions of the two, inspiring radical layouts, and to the graphical treatment of textual material, with a renewal of interest in typography and the use of words or letters as images in their own right. The first issue of *L'Esprit Nouveau* magazine explained its title as standing for 'un esprit de construction et de synthèse guidé par une conception claire'. As such it embodies the spirit of the age, that which now pulses through most human activity, in the arts and sciences (and thus industry), and indeed society as a whole, even if it had not yet permeated all artistic output. Centuries of ferment and disorder had now led to the release of terrific forces which had been channelled together into this communal effort, in turn bringing about the rise of a truly great era: 'Une grande époque vient de commencer, car toutes les formes de l'activité humaine s'organisent enfin selon le même principe'.

The newly (re)awakened 'esprit de construction et de synthèse', 'd'ordre et de volonté consciente', was as essential for the arts as for the sciences or philosophy, as necessary for creating paintings or poetry as for designing bridges. Hence all creative people need ordering systems appropriate to their art, 'des systèmes esthétiques':

> L'art, comme la science, comme la philosophie, c'est l'ordre mis par l'homme dans ses représentations. Il n'y a pas d'oeuvre d'art sans système esthétique plus ou moins conscient, plus ou moins élaboré chez celui qui l'a créée, comme il n'y a pas de travail scientifique ou philosophique auquel n'ont présidé des conceptions systématiques plus ou moins avouées, des hypothèses plus ou moins dégagéees. Les systèmes esthétiques, scientifiques, philosophiques sont des édifices, des constructions qui mettent en œuvre des matériaux déterminés. La réflexion du créateur doit porter tant sur la construction qu'il veut élever que sur les matériaux qu'il veut mettre en oeuvre. (Arnauld, 1920)

Consequently the arrangement of elements to form the overall composition assumed as important a part in its design as did the choice or design of those individual elements. Since Le Corbusier saw *L'Esprit Nouveau* less as a collection of academic essays than as a propaganda tool, it is not surprising that his magazine layouts expressed these beliefs in literally graphic form.

A few years later (1925), in an essay defining 'sentiment moderne', Le Corbusier elaborated this 'sentiment' in terms of the avant garde's reaction against the Beaux Arts' inherently romanticist vision of the artist as heroic individual:

> A l'individualisme, produit de fièvre, nous préférons le banal, le commun, la règle à l'exception. Le commun, la règle, la règle commune, nous apparaissent comme les bases stratégiques du cheminement vers le progrès et vers le beau.

Le beau général nous attire et le beau héroïque nous semble un incident théâtral.

The new means made available by technological progress and industrialisation enabled greater precision than before and implied a new sense of order. Consequently the 'sentiment moderne' was to be defined by: 'un esprit de géométrie, un esprit de construction et de synthèse' (*L'Esprit Nouveau*, 1; reprinted in Le Corbusier 1929, 97). As before, the ideas enunciated within the pages of *L'Esprit Nouveau* influenced the manner of their presentation there. This time the text's praise of the beauty inherent in anonymous, industrialised and mass-produced objects was reflected in its columnar arrangement on the page, its dependence on photographs or line drawings alone for illustrations, and the regular sizing and framing of the images used; taken together, these features alluded to the most common form of industrialised publishing, namely the newspaper.

Within this perspective *L'Esprit Nouveau* had already taken 'tous les arts plastiques' as sharing a common ground, comprising certain universal 'formes que les yeux voient', across all historic periods and geographic ranges. The vehemence of Le Corbusier's outcry here against 'Les yeux qui ne voient pas'—the eyes of the establishment blind to the contemporary manifestation of such universal forms through the new products of industry—is explained by the magazine's primary aim, stated as making such forms visible. This in turn dictated the form(at) of the magazine: 'clarté de lecture, clarté de conception'. Hence its highly innovative layout: the adoption of innovative, eye-catching juxtapositions of word and image, both to effect an immediate impact on the reader and ensure that these messages stuck in the memory; the exploitation of unexpected typefaces or scales of type, treated with the degree of care usually reserved for images; the superimposition of different genres of image (notably drawing and photograph) or of word and image; and, most relevant to the present argument, the highlighting of key material by its arrangement in *bandes* of *cases* (Le Corbusier 1929, 33). That the result more closely resembles propagandist tracts than conventional art magazines is due to a commonality of aim—namely action—as it sought to persuade the widest possible audience not merely to concur with the ideas presented but to act on them.

Le Corbusier's views on architecture and planning, as first expressed through the pages of *L'Esprit Nouveau*, would reach a much wider, and longer lasting, audience through their subsequent republication in book form as *Vers une architecture* (first published in 1923). In 1925, the year of his 'Lettre à Mme. Meyer', the magazine appeared at the Exposition Internationale des Arts Décoratifs, in pavilion form. The inherent ambiguity between media, engendered by the avant garde's 'synthesis of the arts' is most poignantly demonstrated by perhaps the most widely reproduced image of this publisher's exhibition pavilion, the photograph of part of its front elevation, taken so as to simulate the magazine's cover (**Figure 9**). This image equally served as the cover for a book published by Le Corbusier in 1925, *L'Almanach de l'Architecture Moderne* (**Figure 10**; see also Le Corbusier 1929, I, 215), which he in turn presented as the *livre d'or*—effectively souvenir programme—for the pavilion.

Designed by Le Corbusier, this pavilion translated into tangible reality his theoretical prototype for a single dwelling 'cell', this term being chosen to prompt, simultaneously, biological and industrial allusions. This 'Citrohan house'—so-called in order to evoke the homophonous car—was to be produced on a conveyor belt, like a car, thus reducing costs in order to extend the availability of healthy modern homes to all social classes. The pavilion was therefore intended as a persuasive demonstration:

> ...Montrer que l'industrie créée par selection (par la série et standardisation) des objets purs ...
> ...Montrer qu'un appartement peut être standardisé pour satisfaire aux besoins d'un homme 'de série'. La cellule habitable pratique, confortable et belle, véritable machine à habiter, s'agglomère en grande colonie, en hauteur et en étendue. (Le Corbusier 1929, 98)

The *immeuble-villas*, his proposed solution to both the housing crisis and the urban chaos of the day, stacked terraces (called 'bandes' in French) of such houses, each with its own private garden, on top of one another; in this way he effectively translated the two-dimensional 'bande des cases' into three-dimensional material form. Le Corbusier uses a variety of different sorts of image in order to illustrate his concept of *immeuble-villas*, as if attempting to communicate with a range of audiences at the same time. One image, however, is particularly innovative, perfectly collaging a drawing (a perspective view) of this project with a photograph of the scaffolded Bon Marché department store (**Figure 11**), and doing so explicitly so as to convey a sense of the scale of his housing block; he had probably taken this presentational technique from advertisements for building materials or contractors, as appeared in professional or technical magazines.

Le Corbusier used his Pavillon de l'Esprit Nouveau as the platform from which to launch his 'Appel aux industriels'. This urged them to undertake the mass production of a single kind of window as the basic 'élément type', dimensioned according to a 'module anthropocentrique', from which all buildings would be developed. He chose to focus on the window as the 'élément mécanique type de la maison' because it constituted the single constructional element most revolutionised by the invention of the reinforced concrete structural frame. What he had in mind was therefore a sliding strip window, which simultaneously maximised the entry of daylight and the internal space (hitherto invaded by inward opening casements) (Le Corbusier 1929, 77). In his graphical presentation of this concept in the *Almanach* (subsequently reproduced in his *Oeuvre Complète*) the band of strip windows—like the 'cells' in the *immeubles-villas*—approximates in formal terms to the *bande* of *cases* in a bande dessinée—just as the individual villas had done in his 'immeubles-villas' project. This parallel may be explained by reference to common factors underlying these two—at first sight unrelated—phenomena of the early twentieth century. First, in both instances the rigorous orthogonality and modularisation inherent in each of the boxes derives from constraints imposed by its mechanical production, whether that be in terms of metal extrusion presses or printing presses. Second, again in both instances, the rectangular frame delineated by the spare line serves to enclose a view, or at least a potential view, either a view out from the home or a scene in the narrative recounted through the cartoon strip.[1]

It is at this point in developing his theories that the 'Lettre à Mme. Meyer' first appears. Specifically, it is presented within the pages of the *Almanach*; it thus appears within a context directly drawing parallels between the modern lifestyle to be made possible by the *immeubles-villas*, now experienced through visiting the Pavillon de l'Esprit Nouveau, and the ideological argument underpinning it, as enunciated within the pages of the *Almanach*.

## 'Aspirations ordonnés et logiques' and their 'moyens de réalisation'—a 1920s vision for modern homes

Le Corbusier dedicated the *Almanach* to the wealthy industrialist Henri Frugès, and did so most obviously in thanks for his generous contribution towards the construction costs of the *L'Esprit Nouveau* pavilion. Yet this dedication also, and no less importantly, acknowledged his role in first enabling the architect to realise his vision for 'La Maison Standardisée'; for it is thus that Le Corbusier captioned a picture of Pessac, the housing estate outside Bordeaux, aptly named 'Quartiers Modernes', which was being erected by Frugès to the

---

[1] Le Corbusier seems to have always perceived the window as framing a view out; see, for instance, his description of his first Purist house, for Raoul La Roche: 'les baies ouvrent des perspectives sur l'exterieur' (1929, 60).

architect's designs at the same time as both the pavilion and its accompanying *Almanach* appeared.[2] Here 'le plan standardisé' had led to a 'construction rationelle par cubes' (Le Corbusier 1929, 69), so as to afford optimum diversity of individual units (**Figure 12**). Pessac thus constituted the first built demonstration of his ideas:

> le but: le bon marché
> le moyen: le ciment armé
> la méthode: la standardisation, l'industrialisation, la taylorisation.
> (Le Corbusier 1929, 80)

Here the *bandes* of *cases* representing the industrialised and mass-produced windows (shown in the top right hand corner of the page) are translated from two dimensions to three, in order to represent the similarly industrialised and mass-produced houses; this message was conveyed tacitly, through the continuity in means of representation. The adoption of a means of representation commonly found in construction handbooks implies that this message is primarily directed—as indeed it was—towards builders, or developers.

For Le Corbusier the introduction of reinforced concrete structures, far from narrowing the variety of building designs, greatly increased the possibilities for architectural expression, by liberating designers from the constraints hitherto imposed upon them by load-bearing masonry walls. The columnar grid now enabled facades to be opened up, exploiting the horizontal sliding window, an industrially mass-produced element. One of the essays in his *Almanach*, 'Construire en série', spelt out this concept of composing a building from standardised elements (Le Corbusier 1925, 77-82); significantly, this was illustrated by a single element from the *L'Esprit Nouveau* pavilion, namely its tubular steel staircase (see also Le Corbusier 1929, 102). Another essay in the *Almanach*, 'Un tournant', further described the revolution which mass-production, achieved through Taylorisation, could bring about in the construction industry (Le Corbusier 1925, 73-76). Yet another essay in it, tellingly entitled 'La liberté par l'ordre', expounded the biological metaphor of standard cells building up to form organic structures (Le Corbusier 1925, 121-28).

Evidently the graphical means traditionally used by architects to present their work—plans, sections and elevations—had proved inadequate for the purposes of modern architects such as Le Corbusier. Their principal interest no longer lay in presenting any single finished

---

[2] A further link between these two projects is provided by their both being officially opened by the same minister, Anatole de Mongie (of particular significance since neither was financed by the government).

design so much as in communicating a concept as to how one might design and construct buildings in general, specific buildings now serving as exemplars to illustrate their new approach. Moreover, they wanted to communicate with a wider public—or rather publics—than their profession had usually addressed, and therefore needed to exploit a wider range of graphic and textual media, in particular encompassing media accessible to those not accustomed to reading architectural drawings. The unconventional format of *L'Esprit Nouveau* engendered that of Le Corbusier's ensuing books, from *Vers une architecture* and the *Almanach* onwards, and most clearly in the progressive publication—volume by volume—of his *Oeuvre Complète*, whose content and layout he personally supervised. Texts are complemented throughout by diagrams explaining either theoretical ideas or practical construction, and by photographs portraying the experience offered by a building; often the balance is reversed, with text reduced to explanatory captions serving the images.

By this means Le Corbusier was able to enunciate his key message, beginning with his Maison Domino first devised in 1915: here the new structural system frees up the plan, whilst the deployment of 'éléments standards, combinables les uns avec les autres' can actually 'permet[tre] une grande diversité' (1929, 23), notably within a single housing estate. The same message is then reiterated through his subsequent schemes. For instance, a seaside villa (1916) was conceived like an industrial building, 'construite en éléments de série' yet aesthetically pleasing (partly due to the aesthetic of its 'unité modulaire', partly because of the greater space affordable thanks to the economies of industrial production). The Citrohan House (1920 onwards), developed as a 'type' for mass production on an assembly line, was designed as a minimum dwelling unit like a liner cabin, its dimensions carefully researched (including analysis of railway sleeping cars—see Le Corbusier 1929, 150) in the quest for 'standardisation systématique' (Le Corbusier 1929, 31 and 45). Finally, in 1925, the year of the *L'Esprit Nouveau* pavilion and the 'Lettre à Madame Meyer', the Maison Monol, yet another design for a mass produced house, is presented as demonstrating how 'L'unité des éléments ... est une garantie de beauté' (Le Corbusier 1929, 30).

Le Corbusier applied the same theories of standardisation to town planning, first exhibited in 1922 as his project for a 'Ville Contemporaine de 3 millions d'habitants', at the Salon d'Automne (Le Corbusier 1929, 34-35). His intention in moving into town planning was to instigate organic relationships between the individual ('homme tout seul rentrant chez lui') and the 'grande ville' ('homme en collectivité'). Still employing the metaphor of the cell for the family unit's standardised and mass-produced dwelling, he now evoked monastic as well as biological allusions; his prime model for his block of 'immeubles-villas', an assembling of individual homes into an integrated whole so as to achieve the optimum balance between community and privacy, was the Carthusian monastery he had visited at Ema, in Italy, within which each monk had his own house with associated garden. Le Corbusier's block translated the mediaeval monastic model into a modern industrial language: for instance, modern technology, notably advances in services, such as refrigeration, lifts and telecommunication, enabled one to order meals from the block's communal kitchen, to be delivered direct to one's front door (just as the Carthusian's meals were delivered through a hatch by his cell door from his community's kitchen). The rooftop running track and solarium (made possible by the reinforced concrete structure) would bring about a healthier form of living at higher densities of development than before, enabling a new form of socialisation whilst still assuring the privacy of individual families (Le Corbusier 1929, 40).

These parallel, yet distinct, concerns—for homes designed to ensure familial privacy and cities designed to induce communal activity amongst citizens—are perhaps most vividly illustrated by the Pavillon de l'Esprit Nouveau. For whilst one half took the form of a full-scale mock-up of a single 'cell' from an *immeubles-villas* block, the other half comprised a 'Pavillon des Dioramas', an exhibition gallery dedicated to expounding Le Corbusier's town planning theories. This focused on his abstract scheme of a 'Ville contemporaine' enunciated three years earlier for construction anywhere, and a new scheme, his 'Plan Voisin', in which the same principles were applied to the redevelopment of a real and well known site, nothing less than the entire heart of Paris (Le Corbusier 1929, 108-21). Although Le Corbusier, in his own descriptions of this scheme, justified its title as acknowledging Gabriel Voisin's role as co-sponsor (with Frugès) of the pavilion, his explanatory epithet—'du nom des célèbres constructeurs d'avions et d'automobiles'—confirms how he intended such use of Voisin's name to colour one's reading of the scheme. For this well known pioneer of aviation was also an established industrialist manufacturing aeroplanes and cars, thus epitomising the modern man for whom the *immeuble-villas* and this redeveloped city centre were designed. Voisin had even prefigured Le Corbusier's housing 'cells', by producing a prefabricated house, to be delivered by lorry fully furnished, right down to the curtains hanging at the windows, an icon of modernity which Le Corbusier had already published in the second issue of *L'Esprit Nouveau* in 1920.

Le Corbusier's theoretical writings advocating the implementation of standardisation and industrialisation in the production of homes and the wider built environment were always presented in formats which complemented, and even dramatised, his ideas. It was surely within such a perspective that, perhaps unconsciously, he depicted the terraces of 'cells' constituting his *immeubles-villas* in such a way that they resembled the *bandes* of *cases* characteristic of bandes dessinées (**Figures 13 & 14**), a graphic format lifted from artisan class culture (Le Corbusier 1929, 43).

## The *Lettre à Mme. Meyer*

At the same time Le Corbusier was also using a series of commissions—or potential commissions—for private villas as opportunities for exploring the degree of variation achievable for individual family 'cells'. Here he was very evidently working as an artist, directly translating his Purist (Post-Cubist) theories from the two dimensions of the painted canvas into the three dimensions of architectural form and space. His first major commission in this field (from 1922 onwards) was a pair of semi-detached houses in the Paris suburb of Auteuil, for the Swiss banker and art collector Raoul La Roche and for his own brother, the avant garde composer and eurhythmics teacher, Albert Jeanneret (Le Corbusier 1929, 58, 60 and 61).

It is in this context that Le Corbusier first illustrates a project using—albeit separately—the layouts and graphic techniques which he will combine together just a few years later to form his presentation most strongly resembling a bande dessinée, his 'Lettre à Madame Meyer'. He opens by offering us a series of fluid sketches, unframed views of uniform size, depicting the external and internal spaces of a single house, thus prefiguring in style and content the individual images from which the 'Lettre' will be composed. In his presentation of these first two houses, however, the images are wholly uncaptioned, a solid block of text filling the left hand column, running continuously from top to bottom of the page. Then, after presenting some early stages in the project's development—plans for the Villa La Roche and sketch perspectives of the entire development (here comprising three, rather than two, houses)—Le Corbusier proceeds to offer two double-page spreads of views of the internal and external spaces of the two houses as built (interpolated by a double-page spread of plans and photographs of exteriors) (Le Corbusier 1929, 62-63 and 66-67). This time, however, these views are presented in the form of photographs or of framed sketches.

On the one hand, the individual images—corresponding to *cases* in a bande dessinée—are not yet arranged to form a continuous sequence, taking us through and around the entire house(s) in a predetermined order. On the other hand, the accompanying text introduces the theoretical concept, namely that of 'promenade architecturale', which will underpin—and indeed engender—such a layout. Like a landscaped park in eighteenth century England, the Villa La Roche has been designed around a route contrived so as to offer a sequence of contrasting and carefully framed views ('perspectives'), revealed in turn as one follows the prescribed itinerary; here scenes of privacy and intimacy are framed by walls or columns, scenes of untamed nature by window openings ('baies'). Le Corbusier's explanation recalls Picturesque theory: 'On entre: le spectacle architectural s'offre de suite au regard; on suit un itinéraire et les perspectives se développent avec une grande variété' (Le Corbusier 1929, 60).

As in the Picturesque tradition, the intention is not to lead the visitor directly from entrance to exit, but to zigzag around the house, moving through it so as to reveal set pieces en route, and only gradually disclosing how the whole fits together; it functions just like the narrative of a novel, or indeed of a bande dessinée. Paradoxically, this 'machine for living in' is expressly designed so as to draw one around it in an indirect way, to ensure that one takes time to appreciate each space and view before moving on.

Architecture is certainly not considered as anything static but dynamic, 'spectacle' being understood here in the sense of a theatrical experience. The final paragraph provides further hints that the building is no longer merely serving as a backdrop against which a drama will be acted out, but rather that it has now become the subject of the tale which will unfold as we, its spectators, move through this carefully orchestrated sequence of spaces: the features characteristic of Le Corbusier's model machine for modern living—pilotis, strip windows, roof garden and free facade (here called a 'façade de verre', glazed facade)—are referred to as 'évènements architecturaux'. The new techniques and spirit, born alike of the 'profond bouleversement de l'époque machiniste', impose new truths, which unfold 'fatalement', the narrative of modern architecture embodied in this building proceeding as ineluctably as a Greek tragedy.

Le Corbusier's presentation of his Villa Meyer project, in the form of a letter to his putative client, is the first occasion on which the format most appropriate for illustrating a 'promenade architecturale'—effectively a *bande* of *cases*—is constructed from freehand sketches recording each of the sequential views. The layout adopted thus recalls some well-publicised attempts to record movement in static form, by reducing it to fit within a series of identical frames, the experiments in chrono-photography pioneered by Muybridge and Marey. Such work—straddling art and technology—would have appealed to Le Corbusier, as indeed it did to the wider Parisian avant garde (witness, for instance, its influence on Duchamp).

The 'Lettre à Mme. Meyer' also marks the first occasion where Le Corbusier breaks up the text, effectively into separate captions, each relating to a different scene, thus further evoking a bande dessinée. In his presentations of his Purist villas, Le Corbusier always describes each space in terms of the activities he envisages being performed within it. The series of domestic episodes thus depicted turn his account of any house—including that proposed for Mme. Meyer—into a narrative, in which the building acts out the principal role. In the 'Lettre', as in the bande dessinée, the storyline is primarily carried by means of a series of images, and specifically those of the narrative's principal character.

Le Corbusier exploits a format resembling bande dessinée here as a means of leading his potential client into and through the house which he proposes to build for her. Instead of beginning from the front gate or the front door, the first frame opens the narrative with a more abstract contextualisation of the house as a whole, accompanied by a bird's eye perspective view of it within its physical context, mature trees along the property boundaries excluding the buildings around from sight. This frame thus plays a role equivalent to the introduction in a literary work. One glimpses at the outset the building's simplified form and sleek finish, so as to best appreciate its 'belle proportion'; the designer emphasises here how it will 'sonne' well 'sous la lumière', and stand out 'nobly' against the 'tumulte d'alentour'.

The second frame then introduces an element of surprise, by leading the client around to the principal entrance, which is now revealed to be not at the front of the house, as was expected, but instead at the side. The following frame whisks her through the ground floor hall (unillustrated) to the high-ceilinged sitting room at first floor level. Although the entrance hall had been lauded in the previous frame as 'grand, inondé de lumière', it is now implicitly deprecated, in that the sitting room is described as having been placed above it explicitly so as to be 'hors de l'ombre des futaies'; the accompanying image is designed to convince Mme. Meyer that, thus situated, the sitting room will not only benefit from sunlight flooding in but also from the opening up of extensive views out: 'la magnifique vue sur les feuillages' and the opportunity to 'voir davantage le ciel'.

The service areas accommodated within the ground floor—kitchen, laundry, garage and so on—pass unmentioned in the captions and are equally invisible in the images; presumably this is because neither Mme. Meyer nor her guests will encounter these on their tour through the house. The absence of illustration for the hall helps to focus attention on the positive advantages of the sunny sitting room, so that one will overlook the hall's dank atmosphere, overshadowed as it is by the tall trees necessary to assure the residents' privacy from their (close) neighbours.

Since the large, free-flowing space of the sitting room (which occupies virtually all the principal storey of the house) embodies, and makes manifest, the essential character of the house, Mme. Meyer must be encouraged to linger there before moving on. Accordingly the next frame remains in the sitting room, drawing the visitor further in, and offering a different view of it; this is accompanied by a further complementary caption, image and text serving together to reinforce the impression conveyed so far, for here 'on domine donc, la lumière afflue'. The bay window can accommodate a conservatory or even aquarium between its two glass walls. A French window opens onto a footbridge leading to a shaded terrace, an outdoor dining room where Mme. Meyer will lunch and dine.

The next frame continues to lead us around the open plan space of this principal floor, which is now revealed to serve as library as well as lounge and dining room. Here Mme. Meyer will sit and read. She is then directed to look up across to the dressing room on the mezzanine above. In the following frame this is revealed as looking out over the treetops, and back down to the dining terrace. The act of dressing is explicitly dramatised: Le Corbusier suggests that, by doing so here, Mme. Meyer will star in a drama which only this theatrical house will let her perform. He then proceeds to incite her to exploit this room's potential as an inverted balcony, by appearing on it before an audience gathered in the garden below; conversely she could treat the garden as a stage onto which she can descend via either one of two staircases seemingly provided for this purpose alone.

The penultimate frame opens, however, with an alternative invitation, to ascend, to the culmination of the *promenade architecturale*, the roof garden with its pool and solarium, and behind these the breakfast terrace: 'l'herbe [...] pousse contre les joints des dalles. Le ciel est dessus. Avec les murs, autour personne ne vous voit. Le soir on voit les étoiles et la masse sombre des arbres... Avec des écrans coulissants on s'isole complètement'. As with a bande dessinée, the reader is drawn in to share the characters' feelings, and in this case virtually to empathise with the building which plays the principal role in this drama.

Evidently the *promenade architecturale* is not merely functional in intent, moving us on from one place to another, but also ritual, inviting our initiation into a new state of consciousness, to be attained by obediently following the set route. In his study of Le Corbusier's villas, Tim Benton notes that the promenade always leads the visitor upwards, so as to culminate at a high point, in a metaphysical as much as physical sense. It leads to a place of contemplation, where the mind or spirit is catered for as much as the body. It can lead to risk—a parapet-less flat roof, often only accessible by a ladder or precarious spiral stair—so as to force one to face one's inner self (Benton 1987, 10). It usually leads to a place of escape from the mundane and pragmatic, where one can come into direct contact with the sky, be surrounded by fresh air, and where greenery obliterates all sight of human artifice. Thus the promenade culminates in a reunion with nature, a quasi-Rousseauesque idyll.

Within this context one appreciates why the final frame no longer depicts the house itself, but instead looks outwards from this endpoint of the route; the caption, comparing the view with a Carpaccio painting, discloses that the villa's garden is not so much confined within the rooftop terrace as viewed from it, extending as far as one can see from here all around, drawing the Bois de Boulogne into the private dwelling: 'Ce jardin n'est point à la française mais est un bocage sauvage où l'on peut se croire loin de Paris'.

Each of the *cases* is filled with a view rendered in free hand sketch technique, reminiscent in style of contemporary cartoon(strip)s or caricatures. The cartoon deliberately contrasts with the collage, which Le Corbusier had exploited in his avant garde propagandist works, and most notably in *Vers une Architecture*, in that it is manifestly hand drawn, and thus most closely resembles handcraft or the work of an individual artist, as opposed to the mass-produced imagery obtained from any mechanical process, such as printing or photographic reproduction. It thus inherently implies a sense of intimacy, of personal communication. By adopting this sketchy, hand-drawn feel, Le Corbusier inevitably reinforces the sense implicit in his title here, that of 'letter'. By evoking the bande dessinée, which often narrates romances, he also hints discreetly at the possibility that the tale he is recounting here might equally be, or become, a romantic one: 'Ce projet, Madame, n'est pas né d'un coup sous le crayon hâtif d'un dessinateur de bureau, entre deux coups de téléphone. Il a été longuement mûri, caressé, en des journées de calme parfait en face d'un site hautement classique.' The implied *sous entendu*, the hint of confidences shared, reinforces that sense of secrecy introduced through the concept of an initiatory route.

The communication here appears to be private, between architect and potential client. The client is led through such messages implied by the very genre adopted—the one-off communication, the quasi-secret letter—to feel special, privileged, the object of the particular attention of this professional; she is treated as his intimate and trusted confidante, the beneficiary of a special relationship (with even an implication of possibly instigating an intimate relationship). Although one might cynically read it as a highly refined piece of salesmanship, tailored specifically for its addressee, it was certainly written with genuine sympathy for that particular individual in their current stage of life. For Le Corbusier was writing here to someone who, like himself, had married relatively recently. Furthermore he was doing so at the moment when his main preoccupation was building a pair of semi-detached villas—the Villa La Roche-Jeanneret—one of which was destined as the family home for another couple, his own brother Albert Jeanneret and his wife Lotti Raaf, who had married in 1923 and, like the Meyers, were now wanting to settle in Paris in a place suited to raising a family.

In fact this approach by Le Corbusier to the Meyers proved unsuccessful. In April 1925 he had written to Pierre Meyer with details of two sites he had found in Neuilly, then a fashionable Western suburb of Paris, both of which seemed ideal for building a villa on. A month later Le Corbusier wrote to Meyer's wife, presumably because her husband had failed to reply; in order to predispose her to build (and thus to engage him as her designer) he claimed that he had now found another client willing to share one of these sites, which he seemed to have realised was rather large for a single villa. The Meyers, however, would then plump for the other site. Le Corbusier continued in appealing to Mme. Meyer, perhaps feeling that she could be more easily persuaded, or perhaps now aware that the money required to build this house was to come from her mother, Mme. Hirz. The architect presented his vision to Mme. Meyer in the form of the illustrated letter, which he sent in the October of that year. She failed to respond, perhaps because she was by this time pregnant with her first child; but Le Corbusier continued to develop the scheme, with his cousin Pierre Jeanneret. In May 1926, however, Mme. Hirz wrote to explain that a financial crisis meant that she was now unable to pursue the project. Although hope was not entirely abandoned at this stage—the architect's last drawings (for a variant project) dating from the following month—no fees were ever paid and the house was never built (Benton 1987, 142-49 and 221-23).

A few years later, however, Le Corbusier published this 'letter' within his *Oeuvre Complète,* thus opening it up to us, as flies on the wall. Just as we follow the narrative of lovers unfolding through a cartoon strip, so here we observe, as a third party, the gradual disclosure of the building's 'romance', thus virtually endowing that building with the status of a person, inviting us to empathise with it as much as with a fellow human being. By these means the 'letter' is intended to act as persuasively as before, despite the change of context and therefore of intended readership—from an identifiable patron with whom the writer was personally acquainted to unknown, indeed unknowable, readers.

Now, however, it is intended to convince its readers of the virtues of this kind of modern architecture in general, rather than of the need to build any house in particular.

## Conclusion

On settling in Paris towards the end of the First World War, Le Corbusier had joined an artistic and literary avant garde painfully aware of how industrialisation had overturned the previous social order. Consequently not only the subjects and forms prevailing in conventional art (and literature) but also the very concepts of fine art and decorative arts alike now seemed irrelevant. Sharing this viewpoint, these artists believed that any art appropriate to the new world in which they found themselves could no longer serve wealthy elites but rather should exploit industrialisation to render artists' work affordable to all sectors of society. Recognising that such a radical aim could only be attained through collective effort, these artists proclaimed a synthesis of the arts, whose aesthetic would thus inevitably reflect its underlying social ethic. Reacting against the accepted norms promoted by an artistic establishment oriented towards the conservative markets of the bourgeoisie and upper classes, the avant garde cultivated its fascination with the culture of the lower social classes, from which it drew inspiration in terms of subject matter and form alike.

In *L'Esprit Nouveau*, however, the Purists Jeanneret (Le Corbusier) and Ozenfant suggest that the hallmark of the 'art of today' will consist less in a new synthesis of the various arts than in the rediscovery of a timeless essence intrinsic to them all, one of the mathematical principles inherent in the underlying structures of their products. Since these principles were believed to derive in turn from nature, a parallel was implied between the objects of biological and cultural creation, leading to the application of the concept of natural selection human production. Within the context of modern society, industrially produced objects which have attained the status of everyday classics—such as those designs of glass or bottle most commonly found in artisan class cafes—are considered as equivalent to those biological species which win out in evolution's survival of the fittest. *L'Esprit Nouveau* proclaimed the task of the artist no longer to be that of creating works of art whose value derives from their uniqueness but, on the contrary, of designing such universal *types*, or models, for mass production; as industry had already demonstrated, economies of scale would bring down costs so as to enable their acquisition by all members of society, whilst functionality would ensure the survival of those fittest for their purpose.

Architecture, at once the necessary framework for everyday life and the mother of the arts, embracing all others, becomes the ultimate site where this aesthetic strategy is to be put into action. The modern home is to be designed as an elemental cell, for industrial mass production, so as to make healthy housing available to all sectors of society. Its industrial origin, however, is simultaneously an issue of functionality and aesthetics; for if 'form follows function' (as a Modernist dictum ran), the very appearance of such industrially mass-produced works would necessarily articulate this polemical message.

In this context the architect, as archetypal designer, should no longer present a particular scheme to an individual client but, like industrial manufacturers, sell a model to a mass market. To make large scale production viable s/he needs to win over large numbers of customers, and to do so those genres of mass media developed by industrial manufacturers will have to be exploited. In his architectural essays written for *L'Esprit Nouveau*, and subsequently republished in *Vers une Architecture*, Le Corbusier does precisely this, experimenting with a variety of formats lifted from the commercial sector (including the *bande* of *cases*); in the process his publications automatically acquired a mechanistic imagery which appropriately expressed his ideas. That *Vers une Architecture* contrasted so starkly with contemporary architectural publications was directly due to the sharp divergence of aims in both intended audience and message, Le Corbusier aiming to sell a concept to as wide a public as possible, rather than a single building to an individual client.

At the same time, outside this artistic avant garde (and indeed the art world in general), publishers were experimenting with the same formats (including the *bande de cases*), again adopted from commerce, and again with maximising circulation in mind, doing so by targeting a predominately lower class audience. The bande dessinée developed in this context, being cheaply printed, in newspapers and the like. It not only depended upon a modern machine—the high speed printing press—for its production but equally provided visible expression of industrialisation's repetitive and mechanistic ethos, through its regular series of orthogonal frames.

It seems highly likely that all of these users of a *bande de cases* format—from the most ideological wing of the avant garde to the simply commercial popular press—were drawing on earlier printing traditions, and in particular on one of the earliest aiming specifically at the popular mass market, that of the *imagerie d'Epinal*.[3] This was the French version

---

[3]    The classic text on specifically Epinal images was Perrout 1923, but this has now been superseded for woodcut production by Garnier-Pelle 1996, a catalogue

of the British 'penny plain, tuppence coloured' tradition of cut outs and illustrated broadsheets. Anyone growing up in late nineteenth-century France or Switzerland would have been familiar with this from childhood onwards. Through it they would have imbibed such habits as making collages from cut-outs and reading tales recounted through a series of framed images with complementary captions, in other words virtually in the form of bandes dessinées. Further investigation of this source's potential influence must await a further essay, but it is worth noting in passing the particularly didactic and moralising character of much of this production, since this would have subconsciously qualified contemporary readers' interpretation of material presented in bande dessinée format; in this context Le Corbusier's usage of such formats for propagandist purposes was singularly apposite.

It seems more probable that Le Corbusier and early *bédéistes* drew on the same graphic conventions (in particular *bandes de cases*) originally developed for mass publication than that the architect was generally influenced directly by the nascent but yet to be undefined genre of the bande dessinée. In his 'Lettre à Madame Meyer', however, Le Corbusier uses the *bande de cases* format in such a way as to suggest that he may be intentionally prompting allusions to early examples of this specific genre. For here, to recount a narrative about a static and unfeeling object he chooses a format which is tacitly imbued with two sensibilities commonly found in bandes dessinées, namely adventure and romance. In inviting Madame Meyer on an exploration of a strange house, Le Corbusier implies that building such a home would be an adventure. In drawing her along its initiatory route and sharing intimate confidences with her along the way a romantic element is introduced. In using this format to communicate with an individual, and moreover a cultivated one from a higher social class, Le Corbusier demonstrates how this format, developed by industry for mass production for a lower class audience, was now being consciously appropriated by artists in the Parisian avant garde of *entre deux guerres*.

---

raisonné of over 2,000 such images d'Epinal, from the seventeenth to nineteenth centuries, preceded by brief essays on the origins of the genre in the seventeenth century, an analysis of the prints produced by the Pellerin company in the eighteenth and nineteenth centuries, and the production of its (short-lived) rival, Pinot & Sagaire, in the nineteenth century.

## Bibliography

Arnauld, Céline 1920. 'Le Cirque, art nouveau', *L'Esprit nouveau*, 1, 97-98.

Benton, Tim 1987. *The Villas of Le Corbusier: 1920-1930*, New Haven: Yale University Press.

Bizet, René 1921. 'Dialogue sur l'Esthétique du Music-Hall', *L'Esprit nouveau*, 6, 675-78.

Garnier-Pelle, Nicole (ed.), with Maxime Préaud 1996. *L'Imagerie populaire française*, vol. 2 (*Images d'Epinal gravés sur bois*), Paris, Réunion des Musées Nationaux.

Green, Christopher 1976. *Léger and the Avant-Garde*, London: Tate Gallery.

Le Corbusier 1925. *L'Almanach de l'architecture moderne*, Paris: G. Crès.

Le Corbusier 1929. *Le Corbusier et Pierre Jeanneret: Oeuvre Complète*, ed. by W. Boesiger, vol. 1, Zurich: Artemis.

Perrout, R. 1923. *Trésors des images d'Epinal*, Paris: Barembach. [Reprinted 1985.]

Peyré, Yves 2001. *Peinture et poésie, le dialogue par le livre*, Paris: Gallimard.

Weiss, Jeffrey 1994. *The Popular Culture of Modern Art: Picasso, Duchamp and Avant-Gardism*, New Haven: Yale University Press.

## *Le Grêlé 7/13*:
## A (Communist) Children's Guide to the Resistance

### Laurent Marie
### University College Dublin


*Le Grêlé 7/13* is both the title and the hero of a bande dessinée that first appeared in *Vaillant* in June 1966 and last in *Pif-Gadget* in May 1971, although there was also a short-lived eponymous quarterly in 1973. Created by the script-writer Roger Lécureux and the illustrators Lucien Nortier and Christian Gaty, it narrates the adventures of a young Parisian who flees Nazi-occupied Paris to go to Campagnac in the South-West of France, where he becomes the leader of the local maquis. *Vaillant*, which became *Pif-Gadget* in 1969, was intimately and financially linked to the French Communist Party (PCF). The portrayal of the French Resistance in *Le Grêlé 7/13* constitutes, if necessary, a confirmation of the Communist sponsorship of the journal, since the Resistance period represents one of the high points of French Communist history and can be regarded as one of the main sources of the PCF's post-war prestige. This article will examine the place of *Le Grêlé 7/13* in the PCF's own relationship with its involvement in the clandestine struggle against Nazi Germany.

Before exploring the BD itself, it is helpful to look at both the origins of *Vaillant* and the Resistance heroes that this publication hosted prior to *Le Grêlé 7/13*. *Vaillant* was born out of the Resistance movement. It originated as *Le Jeune Patriote, organe des Jeunes du Front National* which emerged from underground publication in October 1944.[1] It became *Vaillant* with its n°31, keeping its subtitle '*Le jeune patriote*' for twenty-five issues until it was replaced by the child-friendly motto '*Le journal le plus captivant*' in May 1946. As could be expected,

---

[1] *Le Jeune Patriote* was published by the Comité de la jeunesse du Front national pour l'indépendance de la France. Its first clandestine issue was released in January 1942.

during the first years of publication, the journal contained a number of stories recalling the activities of well-known young Resistance heroes whether in the form of short biographies, often accompanied by illustrations, or in the form of BDs based either on fictional or real-life characters.

The first one, *Fifi gars du maquis*, published between June 1945 and November 1947, should be mentioned for at least two reasons. First, it bears testimony to the confusion reigning at the time. The hero, Fifi, is a young worker turned *maquisard* who is a member of the *Francs-tireurs-Partisans de France*, a mostly Communist organisation (Plas 1986-87, 21). Yet its illustrator, Auguste Liquois, was an ex-collaborator of the pro-German/pro-Vichy journals *Le Mérinos* and *Le Téméraire*. In the former, Liquois under the name of Robert Ducte, was responsible for the anti-Resistance BD, *Zoubinette*, which depicted *résistants* as lecherous drunkards, and in the latter, he drew *Vers les mondes inconnus* with its portrayal of the white race as superior to any other. In view of the ardently racist and pro-Vichy tone and discourse of these strips, it is difficult to agree with BD historian Henri Filippini who claims that some of these collaborations with pro-Nazi journals happened involuntarily (Filippini 1988, xiv). It is even more surprising then that the creators of *Vaillant* did not apparently know that Liquois had worked for publications sympathetic to the Germans, or, if they did, that they should turn a blind eye. Nonetheless as soon as the blunder was discovered Liquois was fired and Cazenave took over the illustrations.

*Fifi* is significant also for the reason that it was Roger Lécureux who twenty years later would write *Le Grêlé 7/13* and who replaced Michel D'Eaubonne (or Debonne) as *Fifi*'s script-writer (Birkan 1986, 16). Fresh from the real events, *Fifi* did not shy away from some of the more serious aspects of the Resistance and the Occupation: one strip vividly depicted a scene of torture, and another calls one of the *résistants* 'an enemy of Franco-German collaboration' (**Figure 15**). While many stories related the heroic deeds of well-known *résistants*, their political affiliation—i.e. their mebership of the PCF or organisations close to the Party—was never made explicit. For example, Charles Debarge, whose *Cahiers* of 1940-42 were adapted by Souriau into the BD *Combats dans l'ombre*, le colonel Fabien, whose biography was illustrated by Liquois, Guy Moquet and Danielle Casanova, about whom *Vaillant* also ran strips, were never explicitly defined as Communists (Plas 1986-87, 21 22). Whether this can be read as a sign of the journal's independence from the Party, as Gilles Plas argues, remains unsure. These martyrs ranked very high in the Party's own pantheon and their political affiliation would have been known to the readers' parents and probably to the readers themselves. In addition to these 'BD biopics' there were also other *bandes*, such as *Jean et Jeannette* and *Trois camarades,* whose direct subject matter was the Resistance (Filippini 1978, 54). Between the mid-1950s and the first episode of *Le Grêlé 7/13* in June 1966, strips focussing on the Resistance disappeared from *Vaillant* and *Vaillant le journal de Pif*, although there were a number of references made to the period: anniversaries of *resistants*' acts of courage, martyrs' deaths or historical dates, such as the liberation of Paris, are mentioned (Plas 1987, 36).

The fact that there was no *maquisard* hero in *Vaillant* for such a long time should come as no surprise. It corresponds to a period in the post-war history of the PCF when the Resistance was not at the top of the Party's agenda. According to Stéphane Courtois, as one might expect it was the 1939-1945 period that was of greatest significance for the PCF. First, it allowed the PCF to position itself at a national level in relation to the other parties, namely the Gaullists and the Socialists, but also at an international level, where the PCF was recognised as one of the agents of the anti-fascist struggle. Within the Party, the post-1945 attitudes to the resistance period revealed diverging viewpoints on these key years. What was at stake for the PCF was the respective importance that would be given, on the one hand, to the Resistance and, on the other, to the policy advocated by the Party before it engaged wholeheartedly and courageously in clandestine war. Courtois claims that after Maurice Thorez's return from the USSR, the Party's involvement with the Resistance was played down, while the policy the Party followed in 1939-40, as a direct result of the pact between Germany and the USSR, was repeatedly defended. Divisions ensued in the Party. Thus, while the PCF leadership praised its pre-1941 stance, the association 'Les Amis des FTP' (*Francs-Tireurs Partisans de France*) published a collection of fortnightly booklets, entitled *Jeunesse héroïque*, which 'recounted in a lively and popular fashion the partisans' feats of arms' (Courtois 1983, 8).

By 1945 the PCF had undergone a massive change with which Thorez could not come to grips. A new Party had emerged thanks to the new generation (16-25 year olds) that had come together as a result of the collective experience of the clandestine and highly dangerous armed struggle (Courtois 1983, 9-10). In other words, there was a split between the leadership that followed the rules dictated at an international level (i.e. by Moscow) and those new members who joined the Party thanks to its Resistance activities. The Cold War led to a marginalisation of those in the Party who opposed the leadership's discourse. For almost fifteen years, between 1951 and 1966, the Resistance was more or less a taboo subject. Whereas French Communists produced very few books on the Resistance during this period, there was, in the aftermath of Thorez's death in August 1964, a wave of PCF publications dealing with the period. These started in 1967 with an official history of the party's participation in the Resistance, to be followed by forty books over the next ten years. Echoing the Resistance revival that took place in the 'grown-up' Communist press, references to the period occurred more frequently in *Vaillant* in the years 1961-1965. In October 1961, *Vaillant* commemorated the Châteaubriant hostages and Guy Moquet (Plas 1988a, 40). In 1962, letters from readers' parents under the title 'escapees' letters' were published, and in Spring 1963 a page celebrated the 'groupe Manouchian', which was composed mostly of immigrant resisters (Plas 1988b, 41). This revival culminated with the release of *Le Grêlé 7/13*.

It was only in June 1966 that the first full-time Resistance hero since Fifi appeared in *Vaillant*. *Le Grêlé 7/13* came out at a time when the Resistance period was enjoying a new popularity in the realm of French entertainment. René Clément's 1966 film *Paris brûle-t-il?* was a box-office hit, thanks to the considerable amount of political manœuvering it provoked from the Communists and the Gaullists (Lindeperg 1997, 342-56). Later on in the year, film director Gérard Oury released *La Grande Vadrouille*, which would prove a lasting popular favourite. Specifically relating to the Party, the history of the PCF in the Resistance could be found in the *Histoire du PCF (manuel)*, published in 1964, a work which Georges Lavau defines as 'un étonnant phénomène d'inertie' and 'un parfait specimen d'écriture stalinienne' (Lavau 1978, 125). Indeed the chapters devoted to the Second World War stress the leading role played by the PCF and the reluctance of the Gaullists to participate fully in the Resistance movement (PCF 1964, 368-445). These pages end with the following paragraph:

> Aucun parti, aucun autre groupement de la Résistance ne consacra autant d'efforts, autant de militants, que le Parti communiste français, à la cause de la libération de la patrie. On l'appelle le Parti des fusillés. C'est un titre de gloire que personne désormais ne pourra faire oublier (PCF 1964, 455)

Significantly, the depiction of the *France résistante* offered by *Le Grêlé 7/13* succumbs to the Party's particular brand of *images d'Epinal*.

According to the prevailing Communist myth of the Occupation and the Resistance, the whole of France was *résistante*. *Le Grêlé 7/13* exemplifies this idealised Resistance narrative in three ways. The togetherness of the '*France résistante*' was described in geographical, social, and, more disturbingly, ethnic terms.

While most episodes of *Le Grêlé 7/13* take place in Campagnac, a small country town in the South-West of France, their eponymous hero is a blow-in from the French capital. There are few episodes in which references to his Parisian origins are not made. When interrogated by the German police in the first episode, Le Grêlé proudly gives his identity: 'Jean-Pierre Gavroche, Ménilmontant, Paris XXème, France' (**Figure 16**). Forced to leave Paris, he arrives in Campagnac—the transparency of this name with its similarity to *campagne* is hardly worth underlining— where he soon becomes leader of the *maquis*. On regular occasions Le Grêlé reminds his indigenous friends of his origins, often using Parisian idioms and adding *'comme on dit à Ménilmuche'*. It is therefore impossible for the readers to dissociate the Resistance outside Paris from the Resistance within. Indeed it is as if the people of Campagnac would have been unable to fight effectively without the presence of the young Parisian, although at the beginning some villagers call him by the derogatory nickname 'Le Parigot'. It is only after his first feat of arms that he becomes 'Le Grêlé' and befriends a young man, L'Ermite, his local double, who will accompany him throughout his adventures (**Figure 17**). On the one hand, this conveys the idea that France was at one—city and country, capital and provinces—in the struggle against the Nazis. On the other, the dependence of the provincial village on a Parisian leader can also be seen as a means to hide the divisions that occurred at the Liberation between Paris and certain provincial *maquis*: some local leaders (in the Limousin and Toulouse regions for instance) disapproved Thorez's decision to call for 'one State, one army, one police' and were later expelled from the Party (Robrieux 1981, 35-42, 83-84).[2]

At one territorially, France was united socially as well in her fight against Nazism. In *Le Grêlé 7/13* every social category supports the Resistance including workers, peasants, small shop-keepers, and the bourgeoisie (**Figure 18**). The working class is nevertheless depicted as the most naturally inclined to engage in, and lead, the struggle: Le Grêlé himself was a worker before arriving in Campagnac. The French railroad workers' courage and sacrifice are commemorated in one episode of the strip, 'Le Grêlé tient parole' (*Vaillant*, n°1123 to n°1130), that is inspired by René Clément's 1946 film *La Bataille du rail*. A *passage obligé* of the Communist discourse on Resistance, the *cheminots* are readily acknowledged as heroes of the Liberation of France. L'Ermite's suggestion, in Vaillant n° 1126, that a *cheminot* might be tempted by a financial reward which is two hundred times his salary meets with a rare if not unique rebuff on Le Grêlé's part:

---

[2] Robert Hue also refers to this episode of the PCF's history in an interview with Georges Guinguoin published in *L'Humanité* of 13 February 1998.

> Pour la première fois depuis qu'ils se connaissaient, le Grêlé toisa son compagnon avec colère:
> 'N'insulte pas les cheminots, L'Ermite'

Echoing Clément's film, the management and the white collar workers are also patriots, an example being the chief-accountant, M. Duval, who is a *résistant* (*Vaillant* n° 1127). In another episode, 'Mauvaise année Colonel Hartz' (*Pif-Gadget* n° 1285), Le Grêlé finds refuge in the apartment of a visibly well-off family which is hosting a dinner-party. After the hosts and guests act terrified when the German police tell them that 'terrorists' might be hiding in the building, thus fending off the patrol, they express their concern for the safety of the *résistants* (**Figures 19a-19b**). Le Grêlé, who earlier expressed his fear that one of the guests might say something, replies: 'Nous savons que la Résistance a l'appui de la population... Mais cette unanimité est merveilleuse...', making clear therefore that this unity may in fact not be entirely natural.

In view of the special place of the *femmes résistantes* in the French Communist movement—for instance in the 4 May 1957 issue of *Heures Claires*, Danielle Casanova is compared to Jeanne d'Arc— women are certainly underrepresented in *Le Grêlé 7/13*. In 'Le Grêlé perd la mémoire' (*Vaillant* n° 1139 to n° 1143), a nurse, Justine Laurat, helps Le Grêlé escape from a German hospital and then a series of frames shows the whole village helping him to get away. In 1969, there is a further episode, 'La Belle et la Belle' (*Pif-Gadget* n° 1250), where women have the central role: a number of women working in a canteen save the *résistants* by throwing dynamite at the Germans. Although Eliane Morel is clearly defined as a hero, it is Le Grêlé who gets the reward and is kissed by Eliane: *Le Grêlé 7/13* is no avant-garde work (**Figure 20**). This relative female absence points to the likely overwhelmingly male readership of BDs set in war time.

What unites the characters of different territorial, social and, to a lesser extent, gender origins is the defence of the country against the Nazi *occupant*. *Le Grêlé 7/13* is unequivocally a portrayal of the Resistance in *France* by *French* people. The nationalistic angle is pushed to the extreme. Thus the French allies are mentioned only very occasionally. 'Les Cow-boys du ciel' (*Vaillant* n° 1147 to n° 1152) mentions the Royal Air Force and the installation of a V1 launching base, but hints at the difficulties between the Free French in London and some *maquis*: when Le Grêlé declares, 'Et comme il est dommage que les bombardiers anglais n'aient pas détruit cette base cette nuit', L'Ermite answers that they probably did not know it was there in the first place. Later on the Americans discover the French resistance as the partisans find a lost American soldier, Lieutenant John Turker of the

United States Air Force. Turker is surprised by the fighting spirit of the *résistants*: 'C'est donc ainsi que vous menez la guerre en France', which somehow puts the American soldier and the *résistant* on an equal footing. The American is in awe of those young men:

> 'Si, les cow-boys comprennent très bien, surtout qu'ils ont affaire aux meilleurs, aux plus courageux jeunes gens qu'ils ont jamais connus'

Such a portrayal of a united, courageous France, second to none, was bound to leave little room to a truthful depiction of Franco-German collaboration. While the scarcity of references to this aspect of the Second World War was by no means unique, but indeed the norm in mid-1960s France whatever one's political affiliation, the way it was dealt with in *Le Grêlé 7/13* raises its own questions. Vichy France is hardly ever mentioned in the strip. In 'Merci colonel Von Hartz' (*Vaillant* n° 1154) a discreet reference is to be found in one frame, where 'Travail-Famille-Patrie' is written on the gable of a house. There are few instances of collaboration, but when French people act against the Resistance, they are only seen as helping the Nazi military with no mention of French collaboration at State level. Therefore they are only described as informers and traitors, as in 'Le tireur d'élite' (*Pif-Gadget* n° 1309) where the traitor is called Denis Mouchard (*mouchard* meaning informer).

While in this example the name of the character is enough to distinguish him from the others, the creators of *Le Grêlé 7/13* have resorted, in their willingness to show the French people in an entirely positive light, to differentiating the 'bad' from the 'good' by the characters' physiognomic traits. Clearly, if Le Grêlé, L'Ermite, the young *résistants*, and the good people of Campagnac are compared with the two traitors—Barnier, a traditional French name, and the informer in 'La Caverne d'Ali-Baba' (*Vaillant*, n° 1157 to n° 1163)—the only way for the readers to distinguish them is through their physical appearance, and particularly their faces (**Figures 21a-21b**). While Le Grêlé is French born and bred—'blue eyes and red hair'—, Barnier is endowed with stereotypical near-Semitic traits, and the other informer could be said to conform to the stereotypes of the gypsy.

It is disturbing that a BD whose aim is partly to denounce the evil of Nazism uses the '*délit de sale gueule*' or '*délis de faciès*' as a means to an end. It must be borne in mind that this reading is an 'adult' reading of a French BD published for a young readership at a time when racism was perhaps not as openly acknowledged as it is today. Nevertheless, the illustrator's (or possibly the script-writer's) decision is unnerving. On the one hand, it shows how taboo the subject of French collaboration was at the time: informers *must* look different. On the other it seems to show an alarming lack of consciousness of racial issues only five years after the end of the Algerian war. However young they were, the readers of *Le Grêlé 7/13* were bound to notice and take stock of these differences. Although it would be wrong to overstress this aspect of *Le Grêlé 7/13*, this visual characterisation represents a *faux-pas* in a journal whose action heroes have always been, from *Vaillant* to *Pif-Gadget*, humanist characters fighting for the good of humanity, helping the oppressed against all kinds of abusive tyrants (Nasdine Hodja, Teddy Ted, Rahan, Docteur Justice…).

In 1973, after the end of the series in the weekly *Pif-Gadget*, an attempt was made to launch *Le Grêlé 7/13* as a quarterly, but only one issue was ever released. Between the creation of the strip and this new publication, the myth of the '*France résistante*' had been shaken thanks, for example, to Marcel Ophuls's 1969 *Le Chagrin et la Pitié* and André Harris and Alain de Sédouy's 1973 *Français si vous saviez*. So had the discourse on Resistance in the new quarterly lost some of its Manichean characteristics or one-sided viewpoint? The answer is no. The single issue simply contains reprints of earlier episodes of *Le Grêlé 7/13* as they appeared in the late 1960s, without any change whatsoever. Accompanying these were a couple of short stories about some courageous feats of the Resistance or actions associated with the historical idea of resistance to oppressors. One of them, *Cent mille hommes en révolte*, relates 'La Grande Jacquerie', the peasants' uprising in l'Oise in May 1358. At stake here is the inscription of the Resistance in the overall History of France. This is a recurrent phenomenon in French Communist discourse and in particular in aesthetic criticism whether it be on painting, cinema, theatre or literature.

More pointedly, the first quarterly issue contains an interview with Roger Lécureux, where the script-writer explains how *Le Grêlé 7/13* came into existence. Lécureux stresses the didactic and pedagogical aspect of a BD:

> N'oublions pas que la plupart de ces lecteurs n'étaient pas encore nés quand se déroulèrent ces événements et que l'épopée de la lutte clandestine restait inconnue d'eux. (*Le Grêlé 7/13*, n° 1, April 1973, 4)

What was lacking in the previous BDs, in particular those that were published in the aftermath of the Liberation, was, naturally enough given the historical context, 'une certaine objectivité que pourra se permettre, trente ans plus tard, notre série "Le Grêlé"'. But he also acknowledges that certain tragic events which took place during the war and when France was occupied were consciously not included. Events such as *le massacre d'Oradour, les Pendus de Tulle*, or the death camps would have been much too distressing to incorporate in the BD, Lécureux says. This may be considered a valid statement as a visually and thematically truthful depiction of the horrors perpetrated by the Nazis could not be considered lightly and would necessitate much contextualisation and explanation with a view to helping a young readership comprehend what happened. Unlike *Pilote* or *(A suivre)*, *Vaillant* and *Pif-Gadget* targeted different age groups, yet, as this study has shown, the issue of objectivity and truthfulness claimed by Lécureux in relation to *Le Grêlé 7/13* remains problematic.

Indeed the frank depiction of violence and collaboration present in the post-war *Fifi gars du maquis*, however dubious the personal trajectory of its creator, were far more truthful than what is depicted in the adventures of Le Grêlé. The aim of *Le Grêlé 7/13* was to teach its readers the French Communist version of the Resistance. It complied with the mythology of a unanimously resisting French people underwritten by the PCF. Just as the *Histoire du PCF* was a textbook for grown-up party activists, *Le Grêlé 7/13* was *l'histoire de France* for their children in a period when the Party was the only major organised political force opposed to the Gaullist regime. While today the PCF looks critically at its Stalinist past, the Party has not yet reexamined its position during World War II to the same extent. At the end of 1999, reviewing the re-issue of Hergé's *Tintin chez les Soviets*, *L'Humanité-Hebdo*'s journalists asked the question: 'Tintin avait-il vu juste?' (Toulat-Brisson et alii 1998). A comparison between the balloons and historical facts leads them to reassess positively Hergé's BD. It will be some time before the Resistance is approached in the same objective way and we see an article entitled 'What *Le Grêlé 7/13* did not show'.

## Bibliography

Birkan, Marcel 1986. '*Vaillant*: Les Débuts tumultueux d'un grand journal de BD', *Le Collectioneur de BD*, 50, 16-22.

Courtois, Stéphane 1983. 'Luttes politiques et élaboration d'une histoire: Le PCF historien du PCF dans la deuxième guerre mondiale', *Communisme*, 4, 5-26.

Filippini, Henri 1978. *Histoire du journal et des éditions Vaillant*, Grenoble: Éditions Jacques Glénat.

Filippini, Henri 1989. *Dictionnaire de la bande dessinée*, Paris: Bordas.

Lavau, Georges 1978. 'L'Historiographie communiste: Une Pratique politique', in Pierre Birnbaum and Jean-Marie Vincent (eds), *Critique des pratiques politiques*, Paris: Éditions Galilée, 121-64.

Lindeperg, Sylvie 1997. *Les Écrans de l'ombre: La Seconde guerre mondiale dans le cinéma français, 1944-1969*, Paris: CNRS Editions.

Parti Communiste Français 1964. *Histoire du Parti Communiste Français (manuel)*, Paris: Éditions Sociales.

Plas, Gilles 1986-87. '*Vaillant*, 2$^e$ partie: 1946-1950', *Le Collectionneur de Bandes Dessinées*, 52, 14-24.

Plas, Gilles 1987. '*Vaillant*', *Le Collectionneur de Bandes Dessinées*, 55, 34-39.

Plas, Gilles 1988a. '*Vaillant*', *Le Collectionneur de Bandes Dessinées*, 56, 40-43.

Plas, Gilles 1988b. '*Vaillant*', *Le Collectionneur de Bandes Dessinées*, 59, 40-46.

Robrieux, Philippe 1981. *Histoire intérieure du Parti Communiste: Vol. 2: 1945-1972*, Paris: Fayard.

Toulat-Brisson, François 1998. 'Hergé ou les dérives de l'esprit scout', *L'Humanité-Hebdo*, 57, 31-35.

Toulat-Brisson, François et alii 1998. 'Tintin a-t-il vu juste?', *L'Humanité-Hebdo*, 57, 28-30.

## *Pilote*: Pedagogy, Puberty and Parents

## Wendy Michallat
## University of Sheffield

*Pilote* swept onto the French bande dessinée market in 1959 with a profile and promotional strategy which, from the outset, set it apart from other bande dessinée weekly publications. Privately funded, unlike the majority of other publications in the *presse de la jeunesse*, which were owned, for the most part, by large publishing houses, *Pilote* compensated for its commercial isolation by allying itself to France's most popular radio station, Radio Luxembourg. The agreement, which guaranteed Radio Luxembourg a high profile in *Pilote* and *Pilote* promotional exposure on the airwaves of Radio Luxembourg, was unprecedented in a bande dessinée market which had made only sporadic use of radio as a marketing vehicle in the past. However the Radio Luxembourg connection was of particular importance in drawing an adolescent readership to *Pilote*. The mass production of the transistor radio on the late Fifties coupled with stirrings of the rock and roll/yé-yé music culture that was to dominate youth entertainment in the early Sixties, had revived radio's popularity in general but had created a *particular* appeal amongst the young.

The magazine also differed from other youth publications in that it aimed to appeal to the adolescent reader in a market which traditionally courted a younger age-group. It founded its appeal to the older reader on extensive textual content the subject matter of which mapped closely onto the core subjects of the school curriculum. It was by design that *Pilote's* textual content should closely mirror the pedagogical subject-matter of the classroom. Its independent status meant that it had necessarily to forgo the alliances with religious youth movements and political parties enjoyed by larger publishing houses, which had traditionally provided a degree of legitimacy for bande dessinée in the eyes of the parents who funded their children's subscriptions. However, by 1959 the influence of youth movements was declining and the emerging adolescent youth culture, which was a factor in precipitating its demise, was perceived as potentially disruptive. With parental influence on sales too important to neglect but without fail-safe legitimising intermediaries, *Pilote* was obliged to scout around for a market that would tap the parental consciousness of adults. In 1959 the most obvious new market was the one spawned by the progressive attitudes towards education.

The educational lobby was one of the most radical reforming movements in post-war France, gaining in influence throughout the Fifties as France's recent requirement to keep apace of new information made schooling for maturing baby-boomers an essential commodity (Rigby 1994, 242). The increase in enthusiasm for education, fuelled by a faith in the social mobility that it promised was accompanied by the extension of the minimum school-leaving age from 14 to 16 by the Berthouin reforms of January 1959.

The interest of this new state-sanctioned enthusiasm for education lies not so much in what it reveals of the social, economic and political conditions that brought it about but in the socio-cultural changes that came of it. One consequence of the new enthusiasm for education was the emergence of an adolescent concerned not only with leisure commodity culture but also with how education might permit him access to it. Unlike commodity-driven youth culture, which by definition excluded adults, education was a dimension of adolescent experience in which the adult, in its role of parent, could participate. Invariably overlooked in analyses of the cultural consequences of the end-of-Fifties baby-boom was the 'parent-boom' spawned by it. In a society championing a prolongation of child dependency through the extension of schooling it was inevitable that parental control and influence should also be extended. Central to the campaigning of education reforms throughout the Fifties was the conviction that parents had a social responsibility to be involved in the active promotion of their child's education.

A magazine such as *Pilote* which set out to educate and inform the child in a society which professed such enthusiasm for education would have inevitably have met with the approval of parents. However, the magazine's concept was less a fortuitous coincidence than a considered, palliative response to the high-profile and long-running post-Liberation debate amongst educationalists about how bande dessinée publications could assimilate the pedagogical imperatives of the new Republic.

In 1953 the educational publication *Enfance* dedicated a collection of essays to discussion of what it termed *le problème de la presse enfantine*. Educationalists had been instrumental in lobbying for the law of 1949 which imposed onerous restrictions on the content of bande dessinée magazines. Whilst certain of the contributions do no more than reiterate the principal provisions of the statute calling, in some cases, for a reinforcement of the law, several adopt a more conciliatory tone. Whereas once there was unanimity about the educational worthlessness of bande dessinée publications *per se*, now a veritable *remise en question* was discernible in articles which sought to locate the poverty of the medium in specific aspects of its expression. For the most part, criticism centred on the non-Frenchness of material which, it was claimed, perpetuated values resembling in miniature those of the French Republic. Predictably for a publication which counted among its contributors the principal architects of the educational reforms of the 1950s the model publication envisaged by many of the commentators was one founded on and best able to promote the values and traditions both of France and of its republican constitution. Publishing monopolies like Edi-Monde (Opéra Mundi pre-war) which founded their success on American-style publications like *Le Journal de Mickey* were charged with driving smaller French publishing houses out of the market thereby preventing the more altruistic and honourable home-grown projects from succeeding:

> L'important tirage de *Mickey* n'est pas l'effet d'un miracle. Il repose sur des bases bien matérielles [...] qui se chiffrent par dizaines de millions dépensés en publicité. On comprend que, devant l'impossibilité d'une gestion saine, maintes personnalités de bonne volonté aient dû renoncer à donner vie aux maquettes mises sur pied. (Bellet 1953, 427)

Foreign-style publications were not the only target of criticism. Catholic and Communist publications, which dominated the market, were chastised for their ideological propaganda. Only bande dessinée deriving its content from French culture, it was claimed, was able to communicate adequately quality humour to a French audience:

> Ainsi, d'ailleurs, le journal d'enfants sera amené à prendre position en faveur d'un idéal, celui qui est dans la tradition de la France républicaine: idéal démocratique de liberté, de tolérance et de fraternité humaine. (Ménard 1953, 460)

The crudeness and unsubtle humour of American strips was compared unfavourably and nostalgically with the intelligence and irony of French *bandes dessinées* like, for example, pre-war favourites 'le Sapeur Camember' and 'la Famille Fenouillard'. French culture was posited as an antidote to the pernicious irrelevance of many bande dessinée narratives that supposedly lured the child into false and distorted perceptions of his environment and his role within it. Against narratives which allegedly peddled pernicious fiction masquerading as reality should be introduced narratives which convinced by their relevance to everyday life. Inevitably, the urge towards verisimilitude in bande dessinée required that narratives be based on situations with which the French child was able to identify, a view that necessitated the prioritisation of 'things French'.[1] It was hoped that an opting for more realistic themes would create rounder central characters who could be seen to engage psychologically, rather than physically, with challenges presented to them in the narratives.

Whilst there was a generalised view that bande dessinée content and narrative should be improved upon there were calls for a greater emphasis on textual material in bande dessinée publications. Whilst this was not an untypical criticism of bande dessinée publications, the observations made by Pierre Fouilhé in particular clearly set out how bande dessinée magazines could adopt a pedagogically constructive format; bande dessinée should be subjugated to text and ideally should be supported by that text to communicate better the educational intention of its authors:

> Désormais, pour vivre, le journal pour enfants devra d'abord compter sur ses histoires en bandes. Et si les productions des organisations éducatives conservent leur public, c'est qu'elles se placent à l'intérieur de ces méthodes, utilisant l'histoire en bandes comme un hameçon qui fait pousser le reste ou mieux en donnant à l'histoire illustrée une structure qui exprimera plus indirectement peut-être mais plus sûrement les intentions pédagogiques de ses auteurs. (Fouilhé 1953, 396)

It was the view of contributors to the *Enfance* publication that parents had a responsibility to supervise their children's reading material. Parents and teachers had to raise their awareness of the problems afflicting the children's press: 'Mais ce qu'il faut se garder de négliger, c'est l'action directe sur l'opinion publique: celle des parents, celle des maîtres, celle des enfants eux-mêmes' (Wallon 1953, 370). They are urged to work together to find 'le juste point' by which was meant a quality publication reflecting the sound values of a French educational system which would form 'des citoyens conscients de leurs

---

[1] One of the provisions of the 1949 bill was that 75% of French bande dessinée publications should be reserved for material of French origin, but the proposal did not make it into the statute book, see Charbonnel 1953, 433.

devoirs et toutes leurs responsabilités civiques et personnelles.' (Labrusse 1953, 456).

The collective enthusiasm for a relevant French-centred, text-based magazine combining educationally relevant material and the tastes of the child would seem to find a response in the *Pilote* formula. Articles on current affairs, French historical personalities, illustrative and text features on scientific and technological innovation coincided closely with the education establishment's blue-print for the ideal young person's magazine. The educationalists' demands for parental and teacher involvement is echoed in the early issues of *Pilote* by the publication of approving letters and by respectful, almost deferential, references to the reader's parent-supervisor intended to demonstrate that the central role of parents and the school in the child's development was accepted and acknowledged. The intention of the magazine to inform was not limited to the *actualités* pages where the news features were bounded with a recurrent, running heading 'comment, pourquoi, où, quand' but in articles (for example, in the first issue, on local and global environment, on the day-to-day lot of the French 'corsaire' and the functioning of the combustion engine). The pedagogical scope of the magazine extended beyond its role as a complement to the curriculum. It assiduously avoided allusion to events, historical and contemporary, like the Algerian war for example, featured in Catholic publications, which would have been a problematic presence in a publication dedicated to promoting a positive, cohesive and culturally unified vision of France for a new age. *Pilote*'s nationalistic message is typical of a publication seeking to gain a pedagogic legitimacy. As Rioux points out in his *Fourth Republic 1944–1958*, it was a traditional Republican ideal that education was seen as second only to bread among the needs of the people and the attempt to perpetuate a Republican idea of nationhood through the State education system was as conscious as it was predictable.

Whilst it is clear that parents and pedagogy are a preoccupation of *Pilote*'s textual material, the extent to which *Pilote* adapted bandes dessinées so as to balance the concerns and ambitions of both the pedagogical lobby and parents against the need to entertain its adolescent audience is central in assessing the extent to which *Pilote*'s initial *bandes dessinées* differentiated themselves from the bande dessinée representations in other magazines which did not have such an obvious rapport with education and the adolescent market of the late 1950s.

A potent motif of modernising France was the motif of speed. On the road, the advent of mass-motoring presaged speed and mobility, in the air, the opening of Orly airport signalled the mass-availability of jet travel. In the home, time-saving devices from washing machines to electronic coffee grinders were evidence of the drive to maximise leisure opportunity. On the global plane, speed of scientific development in space and atomic science became the political currency in the Cold War East-West rivalry. The experience of Hiroshima, that had shown the potential of military power to be in the air, ensured that the speed motif, represented by atomic development, but also by the fighter jet-plane, took on a national dimension. Society's fascination for speed found an illustrative echo in post-war bande dessinée in the form of jet-planes and racing cars. The racing driver strip, 'Michel Vaillant' first appeared in *Tintin* in 1957.

*Tintin*'s 5 November 1959 episode of Michel Vaillant, 'Le Circuit de la Peur', pauses the racing action and situates the relaxing hero in a domestic context in advance of his next race (**Figure 22**). Apparently realistic scenarios that have the hero washing up in the first few frames and calling into a garage to fill up his car with petrol in the last frames only operate as devices to better convey the glamour of the racing-driver by making it more credible. The application of realism to accentuate the glamorous difference of stars is recognised by Edgar Morin in his analysis of the star phenomenon, *Les Stars*, as a practice seen most obviously during what he calls the period of 'la floraison de la star system', the 1950s. It was not the reverence of the ideal projected by the star that had changed but more the nature of the ideal projected. Following what Morin describes as a new urge to realism which found its chief expression in film, stars were obliged to embrace reality but at the same time stand apart from it, as if in triumph over it:

> L'imaginaire bourgeois se rapproche du réel en multipliant les signes de vraisemblance et de crédibilité. Il atténue [...] les structures mélodramatiques pour les remplacer par des intrigues qui s'efforcent d'être plausibles [...]. En France, Brigitte Bardot accomplit parallèlement le même cycle. Après 'Et Dieu créa la femme', elle commence à la fois son accession à l'humanité quotidienne et son ascension vers la spiritualité [...]. Marilyn Monroe, Brigitte Bardot, parties toutes nues, sont devenues femmes totales, multi-dimensionnelles; déesses de l'écran [...] épanouies, heureuses, triomphantes dans le vivre et dans l'amour. (Morin 1972, 32-33)

Michel Vaillant, as even the name suggests, embodies the dual components of the Fifties star inviting identification of the reader whilst at the same time being projected beyond their reality by virtue of the glamour to which he alone has access. In spite of its French content, the use of realism to perpetuate the glamorous myth of the racing-driver effectively perpetuates the bande dessinée formula that found disfavour amongst educationalists. If anything it inscribes it more powerfully.

Similarly *Spirou*'s jet-pilot character Buck Danny did not offer the educational lobby a more palatable bande dessinée hero. 'Prototype FX-13', which appeared in the 22 October edition of *Spirou* in 1959, opens with the hero issuing a physical correction to the businessman crook who had attempted to bribe him. Then, several frames later, Buck is confronted by a pilot disenchanted with his leadership. To silence his critics and reassert his authority Buck leaps in the plane and embarks on an extravagant flying demonstration (**Figures 23 and 24**).

Whilst the physical violence would undoubtedly have been deemed inappropriate by censors, the type of hero represented by Buck Danny would have of itself been vulnerable to criticism. The drama in Buck Danny comes of the requirement for the hero to maintain a heroic identity. The simplicity and predictability of the narrative is a consequence of the fact that it is incumbent upon the narrative to reiterate the reader's presumption of the hero's qualities. His integrity and courage are questioned and his action serves to reaffirm them. Thus emerges a circular impenetrable narrative pattern which simply reproduces the hero formula. Nothing is learnt about Buck Danny other than the predictable and unquestionable qualities of honesty and integrity that one would expect of the traditional bande dessinée hero.

Michel Tanguy, the *Pilote* strip written by Buck Danny's author, Jean-Michel Charlier, presents a radically different pilot-hero. In the initial issues of the magazine, the Tanguy bande dessinée is presented alongside 'reportages' and 'documents' carrying themes that duplicate or anticipate the themes and subject matter fictionalised in the bande dessinée. The first issue of *Pilote* of 29 October 1959 places the 'Michel Tanguy' strip opposite a page entitled 'Un vrai pilote' comprising photographs of the airbase at Meknès, where the first episode takes place, photographs and technical information about the aeroplanes featured in the strip. Alongside the introduction describing Michel Tanguy as the 'prototype', 'symbole' and 'portrait-robot' of pilots currently serving in the French airforce is a photograph of a pilot under which reads: 'ce pilote n'est pas Michel Tanguy, mais l'un des aviateurs dont les aventures ont servi à donner la vie au héros dont nous commençons à vous conter les exploits'. The textual supplement reappears in the fifth issue of 26 November 1959 to coincide with the first airborne activity in the bande dessinée strip. Colour photographs of French jet-fighters appear above a description of their function and history alongside which is a separate feature listing technical specifications and significant physical characteristics. The illustrated aeroplane acrobatics in the bande dessinée find a photographic counterpart in the text. Again, in the seventh issue dated 10 December 1959 the drama of an emergency landing in the bande dessinée is complemented by a text feature on the development of vertical take-off technology which, the article declares, will mean an end to the perilous navigation of runways.

The introduction of a textual backdrop to the bande dessinée and in particular, one designed as a supplement to it, allowed the bande dessinée a much greater freedom in terms of the themes and content it could include. The text familiarised the reader with the subject matter pertaining to the 'real life' experience of the jet-pilot which was then taken up in the strip. Without this preparatory text, certain of the themes would have lost much of their effectiveness as the reader failed to comprehend fully their significance. In its instructive employment of realistic references the 'Tanguy' strip departs radically from the superficial realism of the 'Michel Vaillant' strip and in so doing fundamentally alters the reader's perception of the hero. No longer is the reader's comprehension dependent upon a recognition of a predictable formula but on a comprehension of facts contained in the text. Thus, the hero is reconstructed. He represents the values expressed in the text. The hero no longer perpetuates a traditional heroic stereotype but a range of values and concepts laid out in the supporting text. The reader and the bande dessinée are thus liberated from the traditional hero-formula that had previously facilitated comprehension. What does not change is the fact that the reader is still required to familiarise themselves with a 'model', here in the form of text, in order to comprehend the context of the bande dessinée. Thus bande dessinée still reproduces a formula but, in the case of *Pilote* it is of its own making and not inherited from bande dessinée tradition.

*Pilote*'s flaunting of bande dessinée conventions evidenced a conviction that older readers would respond to a new style which drew the educational and entertainment aspects of the magazine together into a complementary formula. The inclusion of the text as a complement to bande dessinée also addressed the popular criticism that bande dessinée distorted the child's perception of the real. The function of text as a source of content for the bande dessinée underlined bande dessinée's status as fictitious adaptation.

*Pilote*'s first Tanguy bande dessinée adventure, 'L'école des aigles', has Tanguy and 'copain' Laverdure posted to Meknès airforce training base in Morocco to complete the final stages of their pilot training. Laverdure's impromptu acrobatic display on arrival triggers a series of consequences which not only unravel into a narrative that undermines and challenges the preconceptions entertained by the reader about heroic bande dessinée storylines but which also, in doing so, allow an articulation of such deconstruction as the adventure unfolds. The reactions to Laverdure's behaviour mark the point at which two elements are introduced to the narrative. Firstly, the text, in as much as it represents certain values attributable to the pilot, makes its entry by means of the official admonishment received by the pair. Secondly, operating in conjunction with the textual intervention, is a school metaphor.

The location of the action in what is essentially an educational establishment means that whilst elements in the narrative evoke the '*Pilote* ideal' communicated in the text, that ideal is communicated by a reliance on themes and scenarios typical of a school-type environment. Such a conjugation of elements means that the bande dessinée is projected as a lesson and the school-reader, identifying with the hero, is thus directly receptive to the text's didacticism. The process of projection-identification described by Edgar Morin in relation to film can be applied to bande dessinée:

> La participation du spectateur est particulièrement active au cinéma. Toute participation affective est un complexe de projections et d'identifications. Chacun dans la vie, soit spontanément soit sur les suggestions d'indices ou de signes, transfère sur autrui des sentiments et des idées qu'il attribue naïvement à cet autrui. Ces processus de projection sont étroitement associés à des processus qui nous identifient plus au moins fortement, plus au moins spontanément à autrui. Ces phénomènes de projection-identification sont excités par tout spectacle: une action entraîne d'autant plus librement notre participation physique que nous sommes spectateurs, c'est à dire passif physiquement. Nous vivons le spectacle d'une façon quasi mystique en nous intégrant mentalement aux personnages et à l'action (projection) et en les intégrant mentalement à nous (identification). (Morin 1972, 105)

The theory works in this narrative by means of the child/adult ambivalence discernible in the behaviour of both the Tanguy and in particular, the Laverdure character. For example, when the pilots are told that 'le petit vieux', forced to throw himself to the floor to avoid their low flying jet-plane, is in fact the base commander, Laverdure faints. This represents the first appearance of a comic exaggeration cum slapstick humour associated with Laverdure who, given his repeated propensity to provoke chaos wherever he goes, conforms readily to the profile of Morin's idiot-hero, in whom idiocy implies a certain childishness (**Figure 25**):

> L'idiot est l'aventurier, un des deux personnages clés du film occidental. C'est qu'il fixe sur lui des besoins essentiels: il joue le rôle du bouc émissaire, de victime expiatoire, de souffre-douleur, et, dans les cas les plus élaborés et les plus épurés, il n'est pas seulement comique, mais aussi pathétique et fraternel, douloureux, jusqu'à devenir agneau mystique [...] Les héros comiques sont ahuris, naïfs ou idiots. Du moins apparemment, car leur crétinisme ne fait qu'exprimer leur innocence fondamentale. Innocence quasi infantile d'où leur familiarité avec les enfants. (Morin 1972, 172)

A more adult context for the pair is introduced in the form of their arrival at the officers' mess. Yet despite the back-slapping machismo, references to drink and the placing of a bet to see which of them is the more skilled in the performance of aerial acrobatics, these references are tempered by others which do not allow the narrative to stray from the consciousness of its youthful readership. The drink, proposed to celebrate their arrival, is 'jus de fruits bien entendu' and the bet, which Darnier, their Commanding Officer suggests should be for money, is neutralised by Laverdure who suggests that the loser should buy the entire squadron dinner. The necessary acknowledgement of the legal restrictions placed on bande dessinée by the 1949 law does not however stifle a recognition of adolescent enthusiasm for narratives with adult themes (**Figure 26**).

Presentation of risqué themes and the apparent self-censorship that accompanied it can be seen in the opening frames as the pair arrive at the air-base. Laverdure, at the controls, states his intention to impress upon 'les grosses têtes' and 'prétentieux' of the flying school that he and Tanguy merit respect. Initially the identities of the two pilots are not given. Predictably, given bande dessinée's propensity to give the hero centre stage, the reader assumes that the brash, rebellious Laverdure is in fact the strip's hero, Tanguy. When Tanguy's admonishing intervention reveals their identities the reader is obliged to re-interpret the alliance made between the hero and apparent disdain for authority. It is another example of how the *scénariste* is able to tap an adolescent audience's contempt for authority whilst appealing to conservative desires for institutional respect.

'L'école des aigles' episode surprises primarily because the action centres not on the airborne exploits that one might expect to have prominence in a strip about a pilot-hero, but rather on conflicts and challenges that centre on human relations. The arrival of the pilot St Hélier, whose disregard of air traffic control instruction endangers Tanguy's ailing jet, provides, like the arrival of the two pilots in the first part of the adventure, fresh impetus for the narrative. Darnier's conviction that the cowardly St Hélier must not be allowed to progress is not initially accepted by Tanguy who, critical of Darnier's treatment of the recruit, seeks to integrate the stand-offish St Hélier into the team whilst seeking an explanation from Darnier for his actions. This is the principal theme of the first ten instalments thereby introducing a subtle discussion of human flaws. In the process it serves to construct a personality for Tanguy with a psychological dimension untypical of the traditional pilot hero. However, in order to make this lesson in human relations more attractive to a reader deprived of the usual bande dessinée fare of action and adventure, Laverdure's character is assigned the role of introducing a comic dimension, offering a juxtaposition with the more serious themes. When Tanguy returns to the table after a failed attempt to persuade St Hélier to join the squadron for dinner Laverdure mocks him. In response, Tanguy throws a soufflé into Laverdure's face. It is slapstick comedy whose effect is achieved not just by the pictorial illustration of the event but also by constantly maintaining the visual contrast between the uniform features of Tanguy—the serious one—a and Laverdure who, with his elongated features and jutting chin, is a comic caricature (**Figure 27**).

One particularly noteworthy innovation of the Tanguy strip is how it articulates a fidelity to the bande dessinée formula whilst at the same time using that formula to offer a new variation of representation. One of the ways in which this is achieved is through challenging illustrative stereotypes. The pilots erroneously presume that the uniformed, physically imposing, cigarette-smoking pilot perched on the corner of the desk is their commander. Laverdure declares: 'Hé, dis donc, quelle allure hein! Un vrai baroudeur, il me plaît moi!' In fact, they are mistaken. The real commander is in fact a slight, greying man with rolled up sleeves behind the desk who retorts: 'C'est moi, ça vous ennuie peut-être?' (**Figure 28**).

This particular device of mistaken identity is repeated elsewhere in the strip and operates as a lesson to both reader and pilot duo. Typically in bande dessinée physical characteristics are emblematic of the power and authority or moral worth. Here, the denotative aspects of the illustration have reduced potency and the reader is required to re-evaluate the reliability of the image as a communicative device. Thus in such cases the bande dessinée directs the reader away from the encoding encouraged by the passive consumption of stereotypes that educationalists had criticised. The assessment required of the reader is an exercise which bears more relation to the 'real-life' experience which educationalists though bande dessinée scénaristes should make a priority for their narratives.

A theme typical of heroic bande dessinée narratives was that of conflict. It was also one of the themes most consistently criticised by educational lobbyists for its demonstration of non-western culture and crude racist stereotyping. It appeared however that the Tanguy scénariste J.-M. Charlier, a previous target of censors for his account of the Pearl Harbour ambush 'Les Japs attaquent', sought to circumvent this hostility by according the enemy a multi-national anonymity and the campaign a French nationalistic motivation. The pilots are reminded that at stake in their quest for France's missing atomic rocket is not only the prestige of the air-base, but also the security and future of military power in the country **(Figure 29)**.

The association of French national pride and military power are accompanied by an emphatic promulgation of republican values. Darnier communicates his distaste for new recruit St. Hélier in an attack on his aristocratic connections that accuses him of being a pampered, privileged daddy's boy earning favours off the reputation of his dead pilot-hero father. Indeed, in the exchange between the pair it is clear that St. Hélier's aristocratic connections count for nothing in the equitable pilot community. Equally important is the rejection by Darnier of the past as St Helier's means to earn credit in the present **(Figure 30)**.

Darnier's values can see as being synonymous with those of the Republic and which, in their reinsertion, hint at the spirit of national renewal associated with the Liberation and revived by the return to power of De Gaulle that year. Indeed, somewhat ironically, these same values are shared and reinforced by the implications of St Hélier's reference to his father's death in 1940. However, in more specific terms, the allusions to renewal and democratisation of opportunity were the catchwords of the new enthusiasm for education. However illusory the equal opportunity turned out to be, in the 1950s there was a real faith that education would contribute to an eradication of social inequality.

In broad terms the bandes dessinées created for *Pilote* in 1959 sought to innovate. They did so by achieving the quite remarkable feat of appeasing both the educational lobby and a broader, older readership, in their delicate management of the desires of both. The unlikely coincidence of priorities between adolescent and the critics of the bande dessinée was somewhat fortuitous. The facility and inanity of which bande dessinée narratives had been accused by educational lobbyists might have just as easily been a criticism levelled by adolescents who, in their desire to be 'pris au sérieux', also spurned bande dessinée which did not challenge them. They wanted narratives that were entertaining and authentic. The strips in *Pilote* were on the whole more complex because they endeavoured to instruct and entertain a broader audience than that traditionally reached by the medium: and common to all of them was a delicate assembly of elements designed to include one group of readers whilst not excluding another.

## Bibliography

Bellet, Madeleine 1953. 'Problème de la presse enfantine, problème international', *Enfance*, 6, 423-27.

Charbonnel, Paulette 1953. Comment a été votée la loi du 16 juillet 1949', *Enfance*, 6, 433-37.

Fouilhé, Pierre 1953. 'Les héros et ses ombres', *Enfance*, 6, 396-401.

Labrusse, Roger 1953. 'Le point de vue des parents: la presse enfantine, problème délicat, problème soluble', *Enfance*, 6, 454-58.

Ménard, Pierre 1953. 'Le point de vue du syndicat national des instituteurs: le bon journal pour la jeunesse', *Enfance*, 6, 459-61.

Morin, Edgar 1972. *Les Stars*, Paris: Seuil.

Prost, Alain 1981. *L'Enseignement et l'éducation en France, tome IV*, Paris: Nouvelle Librairie de la France.

Rigby, Brian 1994. 'Intellectuals, Education and Culture at the Liberation: the opposition to *la culture scolaire*', *French Cultural Studies*, 5, 241-51.

Rioux, Jean-Pierre 1987. *The Fourth Republic 1944-1958*, trans. by Godfrey Rogers, Cambridge: Cambridge University Press.

Wallon, Henri 1953. 'Préface', *Enfance*, 6, 369-70.

# Jean Giraud / Moebius: *Nouveau Réalisme* and Science Fiction

## Matthew Screech
## Manchester Metropolitan University

Jean Giraud (b. 1938), better known as Moebius, is one of the rare French comic-strip artists to have received worldwide recognition: Federico Fellini (Moebius 1980-85, vol. 4, 2), Stan Lee (Sadoul 1991, 74) and Jacques Lang (quoted in Gir 1986, 5) are amongst the international figures who have praised his work. As for the critics, Alan and Laurel Clark call Giraud 'the most influential French-language comics artist of the last thirty years' (Clark 1991, 108), while Scott McCloud places him among 'the pioneers and revolutionaries' who 'question the fundamental laws that govern their chosen art' (McCloud 1993, 79). Despite such critical acclaim, little has been written about Moebius in English. This article fills a gap by assessing Giraud's originality and his position in relation to contemporary trends; it also establishes his role in giving bandes dessinées an identity distinct from that of American comics. As Giraud's output is huge and inevitably somewhat uneven, the study will concentrate on four of his works: *Cauchemar blanc, Arzach, Le Garage hermétique* and *Edena*.

## *Cauchemar blanc* and *la question du réel*

In 1974, a short strip entitled *Cauchemar blanc* appeared under Moebius's name (Moebius 1980-85, I, 97-108).[1] *Cauchemar blanc*'s contemporary urban setting gave it the appearance of a non-fictional *fait divers*; it was drawn in stark black and white with straight, cold-looking pen-strokes. *Cauchemar blanc* depicts a racist attack in which a gang of white youths in a car try to run a North African off the road, and a fight

---

[1] First published in *L'Echo des Savanes* 8 (1974), 39-50.

breaks out. But that was just a dream from which the ringleader awakes; he then goes out in the car with his cronies, and runs the North African down for real.

Moebius did not evoke the racist's dream with the devices which were conventional in comic strips, namely thought-balloons with wavy, cloud-borders and exaggeratedly improbable decor. Those conventional devices are designed to distinguish the subject's dream from the real world; not using them blurs that distinction in *Cauchemar blanc*, producing disturbing effects. Uninterrupted urban banality provides continuity between the racist's dream and his waking life. His dream occurs in everyday reality. Everyday reality then turns dreamlike, once the racist has awoken: characters grimace nightmarishly, as though making an intense effort; the action is depicted from strange angles; dialogue disappears and the North African knocked of his bike, flies through the air in silence (**Figure 31**). *Cauchemar blanc* shows a racist's violent, irrational fantasies mingling with everyday life.

Moebius was not the first artist to drop the conventional devices for evoking dreams. Hergé had already blurred the dividing line between Tintin's dream and external reality: when an Inca-mummy comes through the bedroom window while Tintin sleeps, readers cannot tell whether or not Tintin is dreaming (Hergé 1948, 32). Bruno Lecigne and Jean-Pierre Tamine mention that in Italian Guido Crepax's strip *Valentina* (1965), the heroine's mental images are barely distinguishable from the world outside her mind (Lecigne and Tamine 1983, 47).

Nevertheless, *Cauchemar blanc* was quite unlike *Les Aventures de Tintin* and *Valentina,* because Moebius used a short *fait divers* to blur the boundary between dream and reality. That narrative structure was apposite, given the nature of *faits divers*: *faits divers,* like *Cauchemar blanc,* exist at the point where mundane reality meets the imaginary and the dreamlike. *Faits divers* are items of news that appear in the media and are then imagined by the public; furthermore, *faits divers* often tell of nightmarish and irrational things happening in everyday life. As Georges Auclair wrote:

> Significatifs, les faits divers ne le sont pas tant de la réalité statistique du crime que des fantasmes que la collectivité forme à son sujet [...] Il suffit parfois de ne pas se laisser impressionner outre mesure par la 'réalité' qu'ils prétendent restituer pour y voir des récits de rêve [...]. [C'est] à une confusion du reél avec l'imaginaire qu'invite le récit d'un fait divers. (Auclair 1970, 122-123, 98 and 160)

*Cauchemar blanc* was the first bande dessinée of many that fits the trend identified by Lecigne and Tamine as *nouveau réalisme.* The term *nouveau réalisme* embraces a wide range of artists, who produced no manifestos and no shared statements of aims. Yet, *nouveaux réalistes* all discovered new uses for pictures of everyday reality; those uses had been previously been unknown in realist bandes dessinées.

In previous realist BDs (eg. Hergé's *Aventures de Tintin*) adventures led, through a rationally linked sequence of developments, to the hero's triumph. Hergean realism made the story plausible: it created the illusion that the hero's triumph was happening in the real world. In *nouveau réaliste* strips, realism no longer created that illusion. Instead, artists used pictures of reality to ask where the real ends and where the imaginary begins; in so doing, they asked what Lecigne and Tamine called 'la question du réel' (Lecigne and Tamine 1983, 11). Many *nouveaux réalistes* asked 'la question du réel' by drawing short, urban *faits divers*, not full-length tales of adventure.

Other aspects of *nouveau réalisme* were also present in *Cauchemar blanc*. Like Moebius, *nouveaux réalistes* saw the city as constantly invaded by irrational fantasies, and as morally bankrupt; revelling in aspects of everyday life which Hergé had tastefully filtered out (sex, violence, swearing, etc), they replaced the virtuous hero's inevitable triumph with a loss of innocence. *Nouveau réaliste faits divers* shattered Hergé's reassuring illusion.

*Nouveaux réalistes* asked 'la question du réel' in various ways. Golo, Frank and Chantal Montellier were particularly similar to Moebius. Golo and Frank's *Sphinx de verre* (1980), like *Cauchemar blanc*, is drawn in cold, black and white pen-strokes. A scruffy man wanders through the Paris metro; then he is almost run over by a train and he suddenly awakes, shivering and sweating. The man is a delirious junkie, who needs a shot of heroin; the sequence in the metro was his waking dream.

Montellier also draws black and white urban nightmares with cold, straight lines. Her *Oscar Brown n'est pas un Espion* (1980), like *Cauchemar blanc*, is a *fait divers* about racism: because of allegations in the media there is conflict between the false reality which everyone believes (Oscar is a black spy) and the truth (he is innocent). Montellier asks 'la question du réel' by using a *fait divers* to suggest that the media falsifies reality.

Other *nouveaux réalistes* broke with Hergean realism, but in different ways from *Cauchemar blanc*. Jean Teulé is one such artist. Teulé's *Banlieue sud* (1984), published as part of his *Copie Rêves*, defies conventional BD realism because his plot does not unfold rationally, and because the graphic style no longer provides the sequences of panels with continuity. Teulé juxtaposes hand-drawings with photographs that are crumpled, over-exposed and bleached. Teulé emphasises *Banlieue sud's fait divers* aspect by opening with a precise date and time, which are written in impersonal-looking typescript: 'Lundi 25 octobre 1980, au sud de Paris' (Teulé 1984, 47). On the next page is a photograph of a dilapidated house in a grim, Parisian suburb. *Banlieue sud* then recounts a typically violent, *nouveau réaliste fait divers*: Clarisse, an old lady, witnesses a gang-rape in the house, and the gang threaten her. But there is uncertainty about what is really happening because, over the course of the story, the rape happens four times, rather like an obsessive, recurring fantasy. The second time, a photograph of the victim is reproduced back-to-front; the third and fourth times, a different photo of her coexists with pictures of matchstick men. Towards the end, in what may be a parody of the conventional hero's triumph, Clarisse beats up one of the rapists, and the house catches fire. On the very last page Clarisse and a child stare at a photograph of the house which gradually becomes creased and crumpled; finally it is unrecognisable.

*Banlieue sud*'s urban décor takes on an allusive, metaphorical dimension. Perhaps the ugly house symbolises life in a run-down suburb. Perhaps the burning is a purifying fire, that will allow Clarisse and the child to make a fresh start. Whatever his photographs mean, we can see how Teulé is using them to play upon interactions between the urban environment and pure fantasy. Was a rape committed? Did Clarisse avenge the victim? Were the rape and the revenge no more than fantasies? If so, whose fantasies? A gang-member's? Clarisse's? Or simply those of the artist?

Silvio Cadelo's *Envie de chien* like Teulé's *Banlieue sud,* uses photographs to ask about relationships between the urban décor and sheer fantasy: a character awakes from a beautiful love-dream, or does he? His apparent return to reality is followed by a photograph of Parisian rooftops, where an invisible character thinks 'un rêve d'après-midi' (Cadelo 1989, 46).

To discover *nouveau réalisme*'s sources we must step outside bandes dessinées, and go back to artistic movements that emerged earlier in the twentieth century, notably Surrealism. From the late 1920s, the Surrealists had sought to free artists from rules and conventions. Surrealists undermined the rational, by emphasising the reality of the subject's mental images, just as the *nouveaux réalistes* were to do. André Breton's second Surrealist manifesto (1930) contains an early echo of bande dessinée *nouveau réalisme* and 'la question du réel':

> Tout porte à croire qu'il existe un certain point de l'esprit d'où la vie et la mort, le réel et l'imaginaire [...] cessent d'être perçus contradictoirement. (Breton 1992, 73-73)

In paintings like *La Durée poignardée* (1939, Art Institute of Chicago), which depicts a steam-locomotive emerging from a fireplace, René Magritte, like Moebius and the other *nouveaux réalistes*, used an everyday setting to confuse the boundary between the real and the imaginary; in so doing, Magritte asked 'la question du réel'.

After World War II, Surrealist influence continued to be felt. Neo-realist painters and sculptors such as Yves Klein and Jean Tinguely, like the *nouveaux réalistes,* sought new meanings for urban trivia; they gave ordinary objects an original, expressive power and used mundane reality to produce unusual effects by operating a 'singularisation du banal' that triggered '[de] nouvelles approches perceptives du réel' (Restany 1978, 39 and 1990, 73). Moebius was, of course, aware of Surrealist painting, but when I interviewed him he told me he was not familiar with neo-realism.[2] Moebius connected with the Surrealist tradition intuitively; he had not consciously looked at other artists for inspiration before asking 'la question du réel' in *Cauchemar blanc.*

*Nouveau réalisme* is peculiar to bandes dessinées, with no direct equivalent in American comics; however, the American Underground provides a distant parallel to *nouveau réalisme.* Even before their European counterparts, Underground artists had turned away from full-length tales of adventure, to focus upon social problems like racism, sexism and urban violence (see Estren 1993). Like *nouveau réalisme,* the Underground frequently gave dreamlike depictions of everyday life. Yet, the Underground did not share *nouveau réalisme*'s predilection for *faits divers* and for 'la question du réel', being primarily influenced by events concerning America: Vietnam, Haight-Ashbury, psychedelia, dropping-out. Moreover, Underground artists such as Robert Crumb drew with grotesque, caricatural exaggeration; their luxuriant visions were far removed from the straight, cold lines of Moebius, Montellier and others.

*Nouveau réaliste* BD artists were different from all those who had gone before: they neither copied reality in the style of Hergé, nor caricatured it, like Crumb. *Cauchemar blanc* was a bold, successful experiment, but after the mid-1970s Moebius turned away from his contemporary society. From now on, he rarely ventured outside science fiction.

---

[2] The interview took place in Paris, December 1998.

## *Arzach:* Science fiction without words

In 1975 Moebius, Philippe Druillet and Jean-Pierre Dionnet founded the BD magazine *Métal hurlant*, which was to provide a new forum for experimentation. Moebius was looking for new directions. In an editorial, he questioned the comic strip's conventional narrative structures such as adventure stories and funny gags, humorously commenting:

> Il n'y a aucune raison pour qu'une histoire soit comme une maison avec une porte pour entrer [...]. On peut très bien imaginer une histoire en forme d'éléphant, de champ de blé, ou de flamme d'allumette souffrée. (Moebius 1980-85, II, 9)[3]

In the mid-1970s science fiction *bandes dessinées* were dominated by American superheroes, and the team at *Métal hurlant* wanted to breathe new life into the genre. Moebius remarked:

> Je crois jusqu'à maintenant que la plupart des bandes de SF n'ont fait que broder sur des thèmes littéraires connus et éprouvés [...] Moi je pense que la SF dans la BD sera sauvée le jour où on aura vraiment des œuvres authentiquement nouvelles et où on aura l'impression d'avoir changé d'atmosphère. (quoted in Couperie and Moliterni 1973, 13)

*Arzach* is such a work (Moebius 1980-85, vol. 2, 17-62).[4] It consists of five episodes in which Arzach flies over a world full of wonders and dangers on a pterodactyl. Like the American SF comic *Flash Gordon*, which Moebius told me he enjoyed, *Arzach* mixes prehistory, mythology, medievalism and futurism. Arzach's world has dinosaurs, a gorgon, rudimentary weapons, sophisticated machinery and more. However, any resemblance between *Arzach* and previous SF comics ends with its setting: *Arzach* has no speech-balloons, no captions and no explanatory text.

Suppressing written words has far-reaching implications for comics. In strips like *Flash Gordon*, words locked time into the unmoving panels because each panel lasted the time needed to say/think the words in the balloons. By contrast, *Arzach*'s silent panels have an air of timelessness, which suggests that the hero's journey is a symbolic quest evoking intemporal, universal truths. The feeling of timeless

---

[3]  First published in the editorial (p.1) to *Métal hurlant* 4 (1975).
[4]  First episode published in *Métal hurlant* 1 (1975), n. pag.

universality is reinforced by the heterogeneous objects surrounding the hero, as Arzach is not tied to one particular place and time. However, if *Arzach* is symbolic, the key to the symbolism is not given, and various interpretations are possible. *Arzach* lacks the specificity written words provide, nothing is explained and all is unresolved. Arzach is mysterious: we do not know who he is, where he is from or where he is going. Moreover, his name is spelt differently in each episode's title.

*Arzach*'s absence of writing focuses attention on the pictures, which are entirely different from those of *Cauchemar blanc*. Using an airbrush, Moebius drew fantasmagorical landscapes and colourful, outlandish architecture. *Arzach*'s panels have a polished, aesthetic quality that makes them look like independent compositions, particularly as some take up an entire page. Panels are not immediately subordinated to the demands of a narrative; yet, they cannot easily be isolated from those coming before and after. Resonances between panels do suggest some kind of a story. Moebius appears to be inverting superhero convention: Herculean heroes like Flash Gordon, Batman and Superman rout evil and save the world, but Arzach is unusually vulnerable. One example: a man drives a vintage car across a desert to a somewhat Mayan-looking building (Moebius 1980-85, II, 37-38). He struggles past attackers, and he enters a room full of futuristic apparatus; on a screen we see Arzach and his pterodactyl, who is apparently dead. The man fiddles with a machine, the pterodactyl is revived, and Arzach flies off **(Figure 32)**. That short sequence reads like an excerpt from a longer story, but readers must imagine what took place before, and what happens next. What was wrong with the pterodactyl? Who are the attackers? What is the relationship between Arzach and the other man? Is the other man Moebius himself, struggling to bring his drawn character to life?

The Moebius who drew *Arzach* can only be compared to two contemporary artists, Philippe Druillet and Richard Corben. Druillet's *Lone Sloane* (1972), like *Arzach*, has pictures of colossal architecture and futuristic machines filling an entire page; however, Druillet's graphic style is more exaggerated, more geometric and more detailed than that of Moebius, and Druillet's panels are supported by written words. American Richard Corben, in works such as *Ci-Dopey* (1975), drew colourful science fantasies in a shiny, airbrushed style that recalls *Arzach* but Corben, like Druillet, told stories using written text. With *Arzach*, Moebius stripped SF comics of their conventional attributes: text, invincible heroes and coherent plots. *Arzach*'s dreamlike aspect, combined with its sense of mystery, its power of suggestion and its symbolism, gave SF comics a new, poetic dimension.

## Dislocating the narrative: *Le Garage hermétique*

*Le Garage hermétique* is set at an undefined point in the future (Moebius 1980-85, III, 47-144).[5] The plot hinges on the technologically innovative 'générateurs expenseurs à effet Grubert' that allow the hero, Major Grubert, to build his own complex, three-levelled universe on an asteroid called Fleur.

*Le Garage hermétique* breaks the rules by which comic strips usually function. In most comics, panels make up a logical sequence of events; each panel develops from the previous one, and prepares for the following one. Artists suggest links between panels, connecting them by cause and effect, using captions and so on. Guided by the artist, readers can discover and/or imagine what happens in the white spaces between panels. *Le Garage hermétique* defies those rules because the links connecting panels are often illogical, and the suggestive power of the white spaces is taken to the limit: readers must work unusually hard to discover/imagine what happens between panels, and thus piece the story together (**Figure 33**). On a first or second reading, *Le Garage hermétique* is a jumble of arbitrary developments and baffling red herrings. On further readings, coherence gradually emerges. A labyrinthine story underlies the apparent nonsense.

Here follows a brief, perhaps over-simplified summary of the plot. On Fleur, an engineer named Barnier damages a machine. Grubert sends out a robot-spy to discover what is happening. Learning that Jerry Cornelius is among his enemies, Grubert investigates himself.[6] Dalxtré searches for Cornelius's brother Eric, and he visits various 'terres aléatoires', one of which resembles the Wild West. Cornelius conquers Fleur's second and third levels, but he unites with Grubert against the superhuman Bakalite, who also seeks control. Barnier befriends Yetchem the archer, who reveals that Grubert has discovered the secret of immortality. Yetchem shoots down an 'aéroplane de la destinée' and Fleur disintegrates into turmoil. Grubert and Cornelius escape to Fleur's first level. Grubert appears before various characters from the story, including the Bakalite, 'le maître de la vie et de la mort', who judges him. The Bakalite reveals that, by damaging the machine, Barnier had inadvertently created anti-time, thereby allowing the Bakalite into Grubert's creation. Grubert runs away, and he suddenly finds himself in the Paris metro.

---

5   First episode published in *Métal hurlant* 6 (1976), 16-17.
6   Cornelius is a time-traveller created by English SF writer Michael Moorcock.

It should be stressed that *Le Garage hermétique*'s plot does not unfold in the linear fashion described above. The narrative is dislocated as panels frequently jump between the various characters (Barnier, Yetchem, Dalxtré, Grubert and more) without explanation. Grubert does not appear until the third episode, he gets lost in his own labyrinthine creation, and he shares the limelight with other characters he never even meets. Following convention for serialised comics, each episode of *Le Garage hermétique* begins with a brief summary of the story so far; however, in *Le Garage hermétique* those summaries often recount trivialities, or even events not previously depicted at all. Readers do not learn about Grubert's 'générateurs' until the summary to episode fifteen (Moebius 1980-85, III, 83). The summary to episode twenty-one is a quotation from Saint Luke (12.2): 'Il n'est rien de caché qui ne doive être découvert rien de secret qui ne doive être connu' (Moebius 1980-85, vol. 3, 99).

*Le Garage hermétique*'s dislocated narrative suspends meaning. Seemingly pointless things happen and their significance is only revealed much later. Barnier damaging the machine appears to have no bearing on the story until the very end. Instability and change dominate: Grubert's appearance alters when he loses his spiked, Prussian helmet to put on a superhero's cape before finally wearing everyday clothes; Barnier turns into a woman. The narrative is dislocated still further by abrupt shifts between science fiction and humour. When Grubert sends out the robot-spy, it appears to argue with itself schizophrenically:

- VOUS! Je... je vous avais pourtant interdit de me suivre.
- Parce que vous interdisez maintenant?
- Vous mériteriez une bonne correction.
- Espèce de brute. (Moebius 1980-85, III, 53)

We then see two human-beings arguing inside the robot's massive head.

Before *Le Garage hermétique*, Underground artists Victor Moscosco and Rick Griffin, whose work Giraud told me he liked, had already produced comics in which panels were not arranged in logical sequences (Moscosco 1968, 6-7; Griffin 1968, 41).[7] The result was different because Griffin and Moscosco drew short series of images, not long, complex SF narratives. Their exaggeratedly psychedelic drawing was much more obviously drug-influenced than that of Moebius. Moreover, *Le Garage hermétique* took narrative dislocation further than

---

[7] I am indebted to Dave Huxley for making copies of Moscosco's and Griffin's work available to me.

the Underground by introducing an as yet unknown fragmentation in the graphic style. In Griffin and Moscosco, as in *Cauchemar blanc* and *Arzach*, the graphic style had a conventional function; it provided unity and continuity. By contrast Grubert's world has no continuity, and disunity reigns on Fleur. Panoramic views of Fleur's futuristic capital, complete with minutely detailed machines, houses and roads, jostle with perfunctory-looking sketches, childishly drawn animals, cowboys and superheroes.

*Le Garage hermétique* questions well-defined conventions of the form by disrupting the narrative's linear flow. The story, which is of considerable length, requires an unprecedented degree of reader-participation to generate meaning. Moebius's approach recalls the *nouveau roman* as exemplified by Alain Robbe-Grillet more than it does any previous comics. Similarities between Moebius and Robbe-Grillet are reinforced by the latter's habit of writing in the present tense: in Robbe-Grillet's novels, as in comics, events happen while the work is being read. Giraud told me he was aware of Robbe-Grillet's experiments with dislocated narrative structures, but that he had not read any *nouveaux romans*. Nonetheless, Ben Stoltzfus's description of Robbe-Grillet's *nouveau roman* fits *Le Garage hermétique*:

> The dislocation of narrative sequence in time-space [...] in terms of a continuous present, is not always easy to follow or anticipate. The reader must contribute actively to the elaboration and metamorphosis of thought and emotion. The fact that everything is happening in the present, which the reader is actively interpreting, gives the narrative an immediacy and impact absent from the traditional past tense story. (Stoltzfus 1964, 12)

Even after several readings *Le Garage hermétique*, like Robbe-Grillet's novels, remains enigmatic. But despite their similarities, Robbe-Grillet and Moebius produced dislocated narratives by different means. Robbe-Grillet, of course, wrote prose texts. Moebius combined words with a sequence of panels. He placed considerable onus on the reader to imagine events between panels, thereby making various interpretations possible.

Perhaps *Le Garage hermétique* is just a superbly drawn 'shaggy dog story'. On another level, it reworks the ancient theme of the man who would be God, and who is punished for his ambition. Grubert raised himself to the level of the godhead by creating his own universe. The narrative is dislocated with good reason: human presumption throws creation into disorder and blocks clear communication, as with the story of the Tower of Babel. Following biblical tradition Grubert is judged, and he must go back to being a normal human. *Le Garage hermétique* is also a cautionary tale for the technological twentieth century: Grubert built a world using fantastic technology, but scientific knowledge is not an agent of his salvation, and he cannot control what he made; his works turn against him, causing confusion. Moebius himself called Grubert 'une projection symbolique de moi-même' (Sadoul 1991, 182), a point which Jacques Goimard, quoted in Moebius's *Oeuvres complètes*, expands:

> Le vrai créateur de Fleur, l'inventeur de cet univers imaginaire, ce n'est pas Grubert, c'est Moebius. [...] Quand cet univers se révolte et exige d'accéder à l'existence, l'auteur est pris entre deux feux: d'un côté, le désir passionné de faire exister son rêve; de l'autre, la conscience de ne pas pouvoir lui donner la vie autrement qu'à coups de crayon. Voilà pourquoi il a cherché... à multiplier les surprises, à nourrir son récit d'enchaînements aléatoires qui, espère-t-il, lui feront perdre le contrôle des événements. Voilà pourquoi, vaincu, il comparaît devant tous ses personnages... Dès lors il ne lui reste qu'à fuir, à se réfugier dans la réalité la plus banale—le métro de Paris. (Moebius 1980-85, vol. 3, 149).

*Le Garage hermétique* did much to stimulate interest in Moebius outside Europe. Moebius drew other volumes about characters from *Le Garage hermétique*, including two with Americans Eric Shanower (*The Elsewhere Prince*) and Jerry Bingham (*Onyx Overlord*).

## *Edena* and After

During the 1980s, Moebius became interested in Buddhism (Sadoul 1991, 196). Moebius's as yet unfinished *Edena* series (1985-) was influenced both by his personal mysticism and by the dietician Guy-Claude Burger, whom he read with enthusiasm (Sadoul 1991, 79). In his book *Instinctothérapie*, Burger advised eating only food untouched by industrial processing: 'seulement d'aliments crus, sans autre règle que l'instinct du plaisir' (Burger 1990, qtd. from back cover). Given Moebius's preoccupations, it is perhaps surprising that *Edena* began as an advertisement for Citroën cars. At the end of the first volume, a pyramid goes up into the air and then it turns into the Citroën logo, a double chevron. Nonetheless, *Edena* soon became a story in its own right.

Stel and Atan, *Edena*'s two main characters, are conditioned by a future society that has lost all contact with nature and where food is synthetic. They are androgynous and they think that the natural world is disgusting **(Figure 34)**. Following a space-accident, Stel and Atan are marooned on a planet of great natural beauty where they eat a raw apple for the first time, and their sexuality is aroused; that episode is a clear reference to Adam and Eve, and to instinctotherapy. Burger wrote:

> La nutrition concerne l'ensemble de l'organisme. Pourquoi pas la fonction sexuelle? [...] En supprimant l'intoxication culinaire, on observe des changements dans toutes les fonctions psychiques et instinctives. (Burger 1990, 129 and 422)

After eating the apple, Stel and Atan change and develop: they struggle to lose their conditioning and to reinvent themselves; they try to comprehend what they have never seen or known before. Stel and Atan experience complex, conflicting reactions (fear, enthusiasm, denial) as they come to realise that they are a man and a woman.

*Edena*'s emphasis on character-development is very unusual in science fiction comics. In the 1980s and 1990s, the majority of SF comics (particularly in America) followed the conventions of the genre as defined by Umberto Eco: stories were reiterated in which heroes triumphed; reiterating that narrative structure ruled out character development, immobilising the hero 'in an emblematic and fixed nature which renders him easily recognizable' (Eco 1979, 110). Moebius's interest in characterisation is far more common in nineteenth-century novels than in SF comics. *Edena* recalls *La Faute de l'Abbé Mouret* by Emile Zola (1875), a similarity particularly unexpected as Giraud told me 'je n'ai jamais lu une ligne de Zola'. Nonetheless Zola's novel, like *Edena*, explores conflicting states of mind that accompany release from conditioning and sexual awakening in Edenic surroundings. Like Zola, Moebius turned the biblical story upside-down:

> The act of love (corresponding to the eating of the apple) performed by his new Eve and Adam beneath a tree which is less the 'arbre du mal' than the Tree of Life, is surely not meant to be regarded by the reader as a transgression. Serge and Albine are complying with the natural law. (Hemmings 1966, 107)

Despite those similarities, Zola and Moebius used very different narrative techniques. Zola wrote psychological analyses of Serge and Albine, describing their idyll in detail. Moebius represented Stel and Atan's thoughts with balloons, drawing pictures of their surroundings. His graphic style is mostly simple and calm, while colours are soft and gentle.

Moebius criticised what he called 'la surenchère dans le bombardement d'informations, donc le blocage du rêve du lecteur' (Sadoul 1991, 122). Moebius was drawing pure, clear, harmonious lines, and he was very interested in developing a:

> dessin purement objectif [...] totalement dénué de traces de l'ego. [...] Le seul véritable dessin sans ego est le dessin sacré [...] qui va de pair avec une démarche spirituelle approfondie. (Sadoul 1991, 196)

Moebius's pronouncements suggest Zen influence. Artist and Zen practitioner Frederick Franck, who used drawing as a meditation technique, also associated his art with absence of over-stimulation and with self-transcendence:

> A 'non-creative' environment is one that constantly bombards us [...] with noise, with agitation and visual stimuli. [...] [Seeing and drawing] establishes an island of silence, an oasis of undivided attention. [...] I forget this Me, am liberated from it and dive into the reality of what confronts me. (Franck 1973, xii and 6)

## Conclusion

Jean Giraud / Moebius is an influential artist whose work constantly evolves, its eclecticism finding unity in the creator's tireless drive to experiment. Giraud has given bandes dessinées an identity distinct from that of American comics. *Cauchemar blanc* was a violent *fait divers* whose cold, harsh lines introduced 'la question du réel' to bandes dessinées. Moebius's shift to science fiction comics in the mid-1970s challenged that genre's most basic assumptions. Arzach, Grubert, Stel and Atan are the opposite of US superheroes, as they are all fallible and vulnerable. Furthermore, *Arzach* had no written text. *Le Garage hermétique* was not a series of panels arranged in a logical sequence. *Edena* brought in a new complexity of characterisation, drawing upon Moebius's personal preoccupations of religion and instinctotherapy.

What, broadly speaking, is Giraud's position in relation to contemporary trends? Since his career began in the early 1960s, 'post-modernism' has become a fashionable term, although its precise definition is still contested. According to Andreas Huyssen, contemporary post-modernism:

operates in a field of tension between tradition and innovation, conservation and renewal, mass culture and high art, in which the second terms are no longer automatically privileged over the first. (Huyssen 1992, 66)

Although Giraud did not set out to be part of a post-modern dialectic, Huyssen's description fits him. Giraud's comic strips are marked by a strong interest in ideas. His innovative science fiction stories encourage metaphysical speculation, and in so doing they conserve and renew ideas coming from religious traditions. *Le Garage hermétique* renews the story of the Tower of Babel, Stel and Atan are a latter-day Adam and Eve, and *Edena*'s artwork suggests Zen influence.

Like a number of other major postwar talents (two further examples are SF novelist Stanislaw Lem and musician Frank Zappa), Jean Giraud falls between mass culture and high art.[8] Giraud, a fan of Lem and of Zappa, told me that 'jeter une passerelle entre ces deux cultures a toujours été [s]on ambition'. Giraud's chosen form, the comic strip, is not associated with 'high art'. Giraud aims directly at the mass market, his work has the raw immediacy typical of comics and it requires no education in taste. Yet, Giraud's comics consistently point to 'high art', by which I mean painting, sculpture, poetry and novels. *Cauchemar blanc* asks 'la question du réel' in the manner of Surrealism. It also operates a 'singularisation du banal' comparable to neo-realist sculpture and painting; *Arzach* has the suggestive power and the mysterious symbolism of poetry; *Le Garage hermétique* exchanges old forms for new by disrupting the narrative's linear flow; it involves readers in generating meaning in a manner similar to Robbe-Grillet's *nouveau roman*; *Edena* recalls a Zola novel.

The name Moebius suits Giraud remarkably well. His body of work fuses contrasting, even opposing ideas, registers and styles with the ease of the Möbius strip; a circle that joins one side of a piece of paper to its opposite. As Giraud said, the Möbius strip risks becoming 'le cercle dont on est prisonnier à jamais' (Moebius 1984, 30). Hence, his need to push back the limits of the form and to seek new horizons.

---

[8] Mark Rose, for example, cites Lem as an SF writer who makes 'the very concept of "high" versus "popular" culture seem beside the point' (Rose 1976, 7). Ben Watson says that Zappa is for 'anyone who thinks that […] the high/low cultural divide is something that needs dismantling' (Watson 1994, 553).

## Bibliography

Auclair, Georges 1970. *La Mana quotidien: Structures et fonctions de la chronique des faits divers*, Paris: Anthropos.

Bingham, Jerry and Moebius [Giraud, Jean] 1992. *Onyx Overlord*, New York: Epic.

Breton, André 1992. *Manifestes du Surréalisme*, Paris: Gallimard. [First published 1930.]

Burger, Guy-Claude 1990. *L'Instinctothérape*, Paris: Rocher.

Cadelo, Silvio 1989. *Envie de chien*, Tournai: Casterman.

Clark, Alan, and Laurel Clark 1991. *Comics: An Illustrated History*, London: Greenwood.

Corben, Richard 1975. *Ci-Dopey*. Self-contained work that appeared in *Métal Hurlant*, 1, n. pag.

Couperie, Pierre, and Claude Moliterni 1973. 'La SF en France', *Phénix*, 26, 2-15.

Druillet, Philippe 1972. *Les Six voyages de Lone Sloane*, Paris: Dargaud.

Eco, Umberto 1979. *The Role of the Reader*, Bloomington: Indiana University Press.

Estren, Mark 1993. *A History of Underground Comics*, Berkeley: Ronin.

Filippini, Henri 1989. *Dictionnaire de la bande dessineé*, Paris: Bordas.

Franck, Frederic 1973. *The Zen of Seeing*, London: Wildwood House.

Frank and Golo 1980. *Sphinx de verre*. Self-contained work that appeared in *Charlie Mensuel*, 137, 79-93.

Gir [Giraud, Jean] 1986. *L'Univers de Gir*, Paris: Dargaud.

Griffin, Rick 1968. *Oxo 69*. Self-contained work that appeared in *Zap Comics*, 2, 4.

Hemmings, Frederick William John 1966. *Emile Zola*, Oxford: Oxford University Press [first published 1953].

Hergé 1948. *Les Sept boules de cristal*, Tournai: Casterman.

Huyssen, Andreas 1992. 'Mapping the Post-Modern', in Charles Jencks, ed., *The Post-Modern Reader*, London: Academy Editions, 40-72.

Lecigne, Bruno and Tamine, Jean-Pierre 1983. *Fac-Similé*, Paris: Futuropolis.

McCloud, Scott 1993. *Understanding Comics*, New York: Harper Perennial.

Moebius [Giraud, Jean] 1980-85. *Œuvres complètes*, 6 vols., Paris: Humanoïdes associés.

Moebius [Giraud, Jean] 1987. *Les Jardins d'Edina*, Tournai : Casterman.

Moebius [Giraud, Jean] and Shanower, Eric 1990. *The Elsewhere Prince*, New York: Epic.

Montellier, Chantal 1980. *Oscar Brown n'est pas un espion*. Self-contained work that appeared in *Métal Hurlant*, 56, 36-45.

Moscosco, Victor 1968. *Untitled*. Self-contained work that appeared in *Zap Comics*, 2, 6-7.

Restany, Pierre 1978. *Le Nouveau Réalisme*, Paris: Union Générale des Editions.

Restany, Pierre 1990. *Trente Ans de Nouveau Réalisme*, Paris: La Différence.

Rose, Mark 1976. *Science Fiction: A Collection of Critical Essays*, Englewood Cliffs, NJ: Prentice Hall.

Sadoul, Numa 1991. *Moebius: Entretiens avec Numa Sadoul*, Tournai: Casterman.

Stoltzfus, Ben 1964. *Alain Robbe-Grillet and the New French Novel*, Carbondale: Southern Illinois University Press.

Teulé, Jean 1984. *Banlieue sud*. Self-contained work that appeared in *Copy Rêves*, Grenoble: Glénat, 47-89.

Watson, Ben 1994. *Frank Zappa: The Negative Dialectics of Poodle Play*, London: Quartet Books.

Zola, Emile 1875. *La Faute de l'Abbé Mouret*, Paris, Charpentier.

# Figuration and configuration: mapping imaginary worlds in BD[1]

Teresa Bridgeman
University of Bristol

## Introduction

One of the reasons why BD is often dismissed as a less stimulating form of reading than linguistic texts is its *there*ness: the apparent lack of constructive and imaginative activity required of its readers as a result of the presence of both text and images. This article considers the implications of *there*ness (the graphically explicit, the techniques of representation of different elements of the narrative toolbox, the visual limits of text and image) for the way in which readers construct imaginary worlds in their heads.[2] In particular, it examines the relationships which can be set up between fictional 'fact' and modalised subjective experience as conceptually separate narrative elements. Its focus is thus on the means by which readers recognise and track centres of perception and experience, establishing *who* is experiencing or perceiving *what*, and thereby assigning different epistemological and ontological status to various elements of the text. My approach is largely cognitive, viewing the reading of a text as the mental construction of one or more 'worlds' by the reader. In this view, the subjective experiences of fictional protagonists, their dreams, memories and desires, can be constructed as 'subworlds' in the notional larger world of the fiction,

---

[1] The discussion of many of the world-building issues raised in this article has been enriched by debates with Nina Bastin on the configurations of Queneau's fictional worlds.

[2] This is, of course, only one way of approaching the constructive aspects of BD. See, in particular, McCloud (1994), who suggests that an Iserian gap-filling process is at the heart of reading comics, both with regard to empathy with the adumbrated iconic figures which inhabit cartoon, and with regard to the imaginative construction of narrative elements in the gaps between the frames.

experienced by all the protagonists (this larger world will be described as the textual-actual-world, see below for definitions). In this, I draw in particular on the work of the cognitive linguists Werth, and Emmott.

As will be seen, Werth (1995, 1999) offers a view of communication founded on world-building, in which a world is a cognitively constructed arena in which interactions occur. He suggests that when we process texts, we construct spatialised worlds in our heads. Thus, readers allocate different aspects of texts to different worlds (private thoughts are not public knowledge, and therefore occupy a subworld). Emmott, in her work on what she calls frames (1994, 1997), looks more specifically at how readers must also constantly monitor and update their worlds, and need to be able to identify shifts between worlds if they are to process the text successfully.

The BD albums discussed, by Crepax, Franc, Tardi, Juillard and Mathieu, are useful in that they share a preoccupation with subjective experiences of the fictional world yet they also provide a very wide range of text types. There is a relatively high proportion of first-person narratives among them compared with the occurrence of this mode of narration in BD as a whole. Crepax, in his *Valentina* narratives (the two albums discussed here were originally published in strip form in Italian in 1968 and 1973), creates world and subworld narratives through the fragmented psychodelics of 1960s hippy culture. Franc's work explores simultaneity of experience through different formal experiments in a universe of the everyday and the non-event (nevertheless liberally scattered with references to a wide range of intertexts in different media). Tardi's hyperrealist 'retro' texts offer an unusually high proportion of sustained written first-person narrative combined with a profound physical encounter with the images of his fictional worlds (here *Brouillard au pont de Tolbiac* (1992) is the main text under discussion). Juillard offers, in *Le Cahier bleu* (1994), an exercise which includes, among other elements, the play between subjective and objective representation in the 'classic' realist style. Last, in the *Julius Corentin Acquefacques* series, begun in 1991, Mathieu exploits the perceptual material configuration of the text in pursuing the conceptual configuration of experience of time and space.

This discussion does not provide a catalogue of techniques of modalisation. These are to be found in Peeters (1991) and McCloud (1994), who provide excellent discussions of how emotions and thoughts can be represented in words and images.[3] Instead, it concentrates on how, in practice, the combination of such techniques can enable the

---

[3] See also Kress and Van Leeuwen (1996) for a discussion of modality in images in general.

reader to decide to which world s/he should assign different elements and sequences in the text, and to construct various relationships between worlds. It will also look at how the physicality of the layout of the text can produce a particular type of ambivalence in the reader's configuration of world relationships. This will show how great a capacity we have to build worlds which are constructed according to protocols which differ from those we apply when processing our own experience of the world. But it will also show how BD can exploit similarities with the way that we process our own world, in order to operate a highly constructed manipulation of our meaning-making activities as readers.

**World-building and the cognitive approach, some key concepts**

It is useful here to provide a brief summary of my own adaptation of Werth's model of worlds (1999). Werth's account of world-relationships is largely founded on the embedded Chinese box model (see **Figure 35**). His model is a general one, including non-narrative and non-fictional texts, whereas the elements outlined here are more specific to narrative fiction. I have also borrowed one term from Ryan (1992), whose work in IT modelling is also founded on a principle of world-building.

DISCOURSE WORLD: the context for the 'communication event' of the text, constituted by 'participants' (here being author(s) and readers), and those parts of their environment which are relevant to the act of communication.

TEXT WORLD: the world constructed from the text itself, including the narrative world (if there is one), the textual-actual-world, and various subworlds. The text world may also include aspects of the discourse world, through reference to them.

NARRATIVE WORLD: Werth calls this the narrative envelope, suppressing its importance in fiction as a potentially discrete area of common ground between narrator and narratee (although he does distinguish between character-accessible subworlds, and participant-accessible subworlds). As all who are familiar with Genette (1972) are aware, the narrative world may be presented as either external or internal to the textual-actual-world, and this has significant implications for the way in which the reader builds it into his/her world model.

TEXTUAL-ACTUAL-WORLD: this is the world which the characters inhabit and which they consider to be the discourse world.

SUBWORLDS: Werth describes three kinds of subworld: deictic, attitudinal and epistemic. The first group are 'departures from the basic deictic "signature" of the conceptual world, e.g. "flashbacks", direct speech, "windows" on to other scenes'. The second comprise 'notions entertained by the protagonists, as opposed to actions undertaken by the protagonists in the discourse'. Epistemic subworlds are produced by 'modalised propositions expressed either by participants or characters' (Werth 1999, 216).

It should be stressed that I have presented these worlds in an extremely simplified form. In the complex models of processing Werth sets up, multiplications and overlaps of different worlds in a given stretch of text are the norm.

**Iconic organisation of worlds**

One of Werth's basic contentions is that we use spatialised metaphors and configurations to build imaginary worlds from non-iconic texts. What will be of interest in this article, is to see what happens when the spatialised configurations of theorists meet the different spatialised configurations of BD, and their particular mix of word and image.
    Werth proposes that spatial relationships govern our mental perception and construction not only of narrative worlds, but also of abstract concepts and relationships (1999, 7-16). But, as we are all aware, the use of diagrammatic representations of world relationships is common practice in narratology, and in many respects these borrow or share the visual protocols of the cartoon. With the increase of IT, and the commensurate increase in iconic methods of mapping information, this relationship may produce interesting developments in the near future (see, for example Chris Ware's work in his computer-generated *Acme Novelty Library* series, begun in 1993).

**Some world-relationship mappings**

The two patterns which are most common in theoretical work on narratological voice are those of the Chinese box and the concertina pattern of layers, which are often used together (see Lanser 1981, 144-45). Werth uses the Chinese box in his depiction of the communication situation. But other non-narratological world models also produce a 'world' and its satellites structure, in which the 'world' is the primary world of experience (the real world), and its satellites are 'peripheral' worlds, with degrees of remoteness from the centre (Ryan 1992, 543-44, for example).

The structure of the cartoon allows versions of both the Chinese box and the central world with satellites to be integrated in the representation of world relationships. Indeed, what might be described as the default mode of representation offers a particular combination of elements. In this default mode, the dominant frame tends to be that of experience of the textual-actual-world. Within this are embedded the subworlds of thought and speech of the characters, following the conceptual Chinese box pattern. The narrative world is portrayed in a different way from the encompassing world of the narratologists' model. At a basic level, the narrative world is, of course, as much a drawn world as a told world. But it is with respect to words that 'bande dessinée' allocates a demarcated narrative world in which storytelling occurs, and this manifestation is represented as a peripheral world. It is often separated from the main textual-actual-world in a box, and only just intrudes on the experiential environment of the frame, usually occupying a narrow strip on the upper or lower margin. Unlike the world of narration in linguistic texts, this world is not represented as a context in which the invisible puppeteer pulls the strings of the characters in the textual-actual-world, or in which the performing teller passes comment on events. Unless a human agent is explicitly introduced, for example the storyteller figure in Tardi's *Secret de la salamandre* (1981, 3), the contents of the narrative box tend to be perceived as a supplement to the image, and not the generative source of the fictional world. Even in first-person narrative, where the narrative agent tells his/her own story, there is no obligation for 'x-as-narrator-now' to be depicted—we may see only 'x-as-protagonist-then'.

**Worlds of words and pictures**

There is considerable flexibility in BD in the choice of words or images as the vehicle for different world elements. A thought can be represented iconically or through words. Narration is both iconic and linguistic. Thus, although certain elements lend themselves to words (temporal relations, abstract ideas), while others lend themselves to images (spatial relations, emotions), there is not necessarily a division between words and images in the portrayal of different worlds. Nevertheless, as the examples below will show, when more than one world is being presented over a stretch of text, the use of each medium as a vehicle for a different world can be a useful strategy. More often, though, we construct worlds through a constantly changing and flexible set of combinations of word and image, where roles shift between 'ancrage' and 'relais', to use

Barthes's terms (1982, 32), and where it is the combined visual and verbal signals of an experiencing centre of consciousness which dictate our interpretations.

## Updating and monitoring

The above configurations of the relationships between worlds are largely holistic, representing an aspect of meaning-making which does not take account of the sequence and ongoing processing required in building and maintaining worlds in narrative texts.

When reading, we are constantly updating and sometimes modifying textual constructs (this is the process which Emmott 1994 and 1997, explores). Our creation and memory of character constructs need to be maintained, as does our view of states of affairs. In this process, we also have to track the fundamental constituent elements of any given scene in a written narrative, monitoring who is where and who knows what in relation to both current circumstances and previous events. This sort of tracking is rarely at the forefront of the attention of the reader, but it is nevertheless necessary to the successful processing of texts.

Some types of monitoring which are necessary for linguistic texts (written or spoken, printed or radio) are not necessary for BD, or film. For example, the continued presence of a protagonist mentioned at the beginning of a scene ('priming' them as present, see Emmott 1994, 160), which needs to be held in memory as background knowledge for the linguistic text, can be manifest in successive shots or frames in film and BD, although we must still be able to identify this figure as the 'same' protagonist.

Where worlds are concerned, though, BD shares the capacity of other narrative media to switch between worlds for more sustained stretches of the narrative. This entails a similar tracking process by the reader. So, in addition to the above examples of worlds within a single cartoon frame, which offer the textual-actual-world as the default environment for the strip, it is also possible to operate a shift in focus, which allows either a subworld, a narrative world, or a representation of the discourse world to occupy the main frame. Thus, a subworld can expand, not just for one frame, but to fill a sequence of frames (in extended flashback for example), the narrative world can be portrayed visually, through an image of the narrator, or the textual-actual-world can apparently contract to reveal elements of the discourse world around it. This last case occurs in Mathieu's *L'Origine* (1991, 46), which shows the author setting light to his own work as a way of ending the story. In all these cases, the change in the world which occupies the main frame operates a visible physical shift in the projected arena of experience of the sort which is achieved by choices of camera focus and angle in film.

**Points of world switch**[4]

When such shifts in focus occur over a sequence of frames, strips or pages, the BD, like both written narrative and film narrative, has a number of standard devices to signal the shift between world levels. Obviously, the point of entry to a different world needs clear flagging if the reader is to construct the text world in a coherent fashion. Crepax provides us with both crude and more subtle examples of this technique. In **Figure 36**, memory flashback is reinforced through a range of means. These include the modification of the frame pattern from straight to scalloped edges to indicate thought, the abrupt shift from adult protagonist to child, which on the grounds of probability is likely to signal identity, and the rather obvious inclusion of place and date in the corner of the first frame. It should be said in mitigation of this crudity that the indication of the specifics of time and place is always a problem when operating within a style which calls for a minimum of boxed narratorial comment, such as that of Crepax (see Peeters 1991, 90).

The creation of emotional tension through rapid and irregular switches between textual-actual-world and a protagonist subworld is to be seen in another sequence from the same work (1983, 24), in which the employment of a semi-permeable dotted line around the subworld frames of Valentina's thoughts allows an illusion of direct access to her mental images.

Entry into embedded worlds may also occur through the traditional device of framed nested narratives. This device can often signal a 'retro' atmosphere in the text, certainly in the case of Tardi, who, through his actualisation of a strange and anonymous narrator seated in a book-filled study in *Le Secret de la salamandre* (1981, 3) from the historical *Adèle Blanc-Sec* series, evokes a period of literature, as well as a world, which is firmly set in the past.[5] A variation of this pattern is found in Juillard's *Le Cahier Bleu*, which at the beginning of Chapter 2 follows a version the Disney technique of the opening story-

---

[4]  The term 'world-switch' is used by Bastin (2000), as a useful reformulation of Emmott's 'frame-switch'.

[5]  It is interesting that Tardi (1979) inserts the same decrepit and archaic narrator to give a frame narrative linking the series of his early works collected under the Pepperland imprint. In this instance, the narrator is explicitly equated with Tardi as author, and the result is a powerful anachronic disjunction between the retro image of the author-figure and his account of the context of Tardi's own writing and publication in the 1970s.

book narrative world, which is soon replaced by images of the textual-actual-world (**Figure 37**).

There are a range of ways of continuing the signals of the world-status of a given sequence: whether through indicators in the written boxed narration, through the adoption of a particular colour palette, through graphic contrasts in iconicity, and, of course, through the nature of the contrasting contents of such a world. However, once the new world has been entered, continued signals of its particular status are not necessary. We assume that, like primed characters in Emmott's model, the world continues to be that set up at the entry point, unless evidence to the contrary is provided, such as signals of the return to a previously constructed world. There is thus no convention that a subworld is required to appear any different from the textual-actual-world.

**Where point of view is not represented by point of view**

Continued signals of world-status are not only unnecessary, some modalisation techniques if continuously employed to indicate textual-actual-world or subworld status positively hamper the processing of the text. One such device is the manipulation of visual perspective which is the source of the umbrella metaphor under which we tend to classify a wide range of types of modalisation: point of view. As film makers have found, consistent and continuous representation from one particular 'ocularisation' point is not a felicitous technique (see Branigan 1992, 142-46).[6] Although consistent subjective ocularisation can be used for short sequences of special effects, focalisation as subjective experience is better conveyed through a variety of means, while a variety of ocularisation points are used.

Subjective ocularisation can, of course, be employed as an empathy device (see **Figure 38**). Here, it is used in combination with other devices which suggest that we 'are with' Louise (see Deleuze on the 'être-avec' of the camera [1983, 106] and Chatman on 'interest focus' in film [1990,157-59]). In this case, the opening sequence, which allows us access to the private space of her bathroom is as instrumental as the point-of-view frame in establishing empathy. But empathy is not the automatic result of subjective ocularisation. Our access, for example, to Armand's viewing point (**Figure 39**), while it gives a fair idea of the nature of his interest in Louise, does not necessarily bring about empathy

---

[6]   Jost (1989, 22-23) uses this term to denote the visual point of perception, in order to distinguish this purely physical position from the more general representation of a protagonist's thoughts and feelings which are included in Genette's term of 'focalisation'.

(especially for female readers). Indeed, when interpreted in combination with signals of the invasion of her personal space, made explicit by the function of the doorframe as the territorial threshhold and the body language of both figures, empathy is unlikely.

## Running more than one world at once

The graphic layout of BD not only allows more than one world to be present in a single frame, it also allows sequences in more than one world to be presented as simultaneous. The degree to which the reader's processing of such sequences can occur simultaneously depends on the complexity and predictability of the information involved. Here, the reader's initial cognitive apprehension of the co-presence of worlds may be 'instantaneous' but the process of interpretation and extrapolation is likely to be sequenced.

The division may often be achieved through separation into a word sequence and an image sequence. Such a passage occurs in Tardi's *Brouillard au pont de Tolbiac* (1992). This album situates Nestor Burma's intense physical experience of the thirteenth 'arrondissement', as the detective wanders its streets in search of clues to past events, at the heart of the reader's response to the text. As an enhancement to this experience of place, much of the text brings words and images together to trace out the topography of the 'quartier'.

The separation of word and image worlds occurs in relation to a letter of confession found by Burma (**Figure 40**). A full world-switch appears to occur, as the opening and key scene in the letter, a murder, is represented in both written text and image. However, in the next frame, which is the beginning of a new 'planche', or full-page format, the image sequence reverts to the textual-actual-world, and the subworld information is contained only in the written text, marked by italic lettering. In the course of this sequence of frames, Burma is shown reading the letter, and then walking along a series of streets and steps. Only the last frame on the page brings together the worlds of word and image once again, to show a second murder, to which the writer confesses in a postscript. The first frame of the next page closes both sequences. It shows Burma on a bridge, and the written text supplies the end of the letter, and the narrator's remark 'Ainsi se terminait la lettre de LACORRE. Je me trouvai sur le pont National, essayant de percer l'obscurité du côté d'Ivry'.

At the level of processing, once the reader has established that the image sequence shows Burma walking the streets, attention is shifted to the written text. This presents no particular processing problems, and the relationship between the different aspects of the text is not hard to justify. The effect is not to produce a logical impasse, but instead to shift the grounding patterns of the BD away from a focus on event-sequences and towards an emphasis on durative experience. Thus, although the reader's attention is concentrated on the plot-advancing elements of the written text in this sequence, the absence of any images associated with these past events other than the depictions of the two murders (the second of which is decidedly undramatic), and the alternative image sequence of Burma wandering the streets, serve to 'downgrade' this sequence, reinforcing instead the detective's uneasy and aleatoric experience of the thirteenth 'arrondissement' as a more important aspect of the text than the revelation of past events (see Bridgeman 1998 on this pattern in the original Malet story).

A question remains concerning the assignment of the contents of Lacorre's letter to a narrative box, rather than a series of thought bubbles as Burma walks along. Had this been represented in a thought bubble, a clear hierarchy would have been set up, in which the letter is a sub-subworld in the subworld of Burma's memory and a greater effect of integration would have been achieved. Instead, the letter is preserved as an independent text sequence in its own right. The effect of this is to produce two simultaneous subworlds, whose relationship to each other is not explicit. Although we may infer that Burma is remembering the letter as he walks along, we are not given access to his thoughts at all, only to the text which *may* be in his mind as he walks along.

This technique allows, at the most basic level, an efficiency gain for Tardi, through the overlap of two consecutive sequences. But it would have been equally efficient to illustrate Lacorre's narrative, and cut the sequence of Burma's wanderings. As has been suggested, this allows the emphasis to be shifted from 'what happened?' to 'what is it like for Burma?'. It also reinforces his passivity—he is not the agent for the relay of the contents of the letter to the reader, and he would apparently appear not to have been a conscious agent in getting himself to the Pont National.

This technique of the spatial overlap of two temporally successive scenes, and the ambivalence of the use of the narrative box in the process will be encountered again in the discussion of a passage from *Le Cahier bleu* (see below, **Figure 47**). A more overt version of the spatio-temporal separation of the worlds of word and image is to be found in the opening sequence of Loustal and Paringaux's *Barney et la note bleue* (1982), as has been remarked by Peeters (1991, 91-92). In the latter case, again, neither image world nor word world can be constructed as a subworld of the other; two separate spaces and centres of experience are represented through the different media. However, what is significant for the purposes of this article in the example from

Tardi, is that, in BD, it is perfectly possible to run separate worlds simultaneously in this way without breaking the protocols of realism in this medium.

In the Tardi case, while different worlds can occupy the space of the narrative box, or of the image frame, a rigorous separation is nevertheless maintained between these spaces in the graphic layout. In Juillard's *Le Cahier bleu*, by contrast, we not only see that worlds and subworlds can be transferred between these spaces, we also see a form of superimposition of one world on the other. This can operate in more than one way. For example, as Louise begins to read the 'cahier' of the title, her mediation of its text is not particularly evident (see above, **Figure 37**), as we read 'over her shoulder'. However, at the end of this section of narrative, she is more clearly the mediator, as she turns the words of the text over in her mind while sitting and showering (**Figure 41**).

In other cases, rather than a straight word/image split, graphic representation (either through lettering styles, or styles of drawing) can differentiate between the world-status of different elements of text (see McCloud 1994, chapter 2, for a discussion of the possibilities and significance of the full iconic range). Towards the end of Mathieu's *L'Origine* a complex set of embedded worlds are represented, but there is no iconic contrast between the putative world layers other than a little less detail on the 'innermost' frames. However, iconic differentiation is to be found at the beginning of the following album, *La Qu...* (**Figure 42**). Here, Acquefacques and his neighbour fall through dream space towards a photographic representation of the author performing the act of destruction with which the previous album, *L'Origine*, ended (notice not only the cover design of the first album lying on the table, but also the visual trick of the seemingly 'complete' photographs from which the photographic image of the artist figure is drawn). While this is initially presented as the intrusion of the discourse world into the cartoon world, the relationship is then reversed as the two characters then fall *into* the writer's coffee. Their journey does not end here, as they continue into the 'noir' of the coffee, and back into cartoon representation. The degree of iconicity is essential here in identifying and enjoying these shifting world relationships.

The successful processing of simultaneous worlds does not necessarily demand any of these contrasts. As Franc demonstrates in his manipulations of the strip, both horizontal and vertical, all that is required to track different worlds is the predictability from one frame to the next of the graphic location of their different elements. **Figure 43** shows the presentation of what would appear to be simultaneous subworld narratives within a panoramic textual-actual-world, exploiting the non-linearity of the graphic layout of BD. Although grounding may create a hierarchy of significance between these narratives, their *temporal* ordering at the level of reading is ultimately dictated by the reader's choice of reading strategies (each narrative straight across, or each strip in a particular order) (see Peeters 1984, 25-26). The non-separation through framing of separate narrative segments in Franc's work evokes a pre-standardisation era of BD production (for example, the work of Herriman, exemplified by his *Krazy Kat* series in the early years of this century, or even Saint Ogan's *Prosper et Toutoune*, 1935), before the album norm of the sequenced series of frames developed as the dominant format. A similar process, but in a horizontal format is to be found in other works by Franc, such as *Souvenirs d'un menteur* (1979) and *Le Café de la plage* (1989).

## Half-way worlds

To a certain extent, the previous example can be said to create worlds which are half way between the conceptually separate textual-actual-world and subworld. It thereby exposes that, however intuitively appropriate such a simple categorisation might be, there may well be a number of uncomfortable conceptual spaces which do not properly fall into either of these categories once we move away from a form of narrative in which the time-space centre occupied at any moment in the narrative exists in a fixed relation to past and future moments, and to other spaces.[7]

Here, it is the possibility in BD of an explicit visual mapping of the relationship between such conceptual spaces which exposes the fluid relationship which can exist between a 'world' and a subworld. While the reader is processing a given narrative image in **Figure 43**, the other narrative elements may be seen as peripheral subworlds, but this is immediately reversible once attention turns to another narrative in the same frame. Moreover, the possibility of the panoramic view, in which all elements can be processed, first as potentially accessible details in a whole, and then as individual centres of experience, but where exactly the same word-image combination is the source of both readings, shows that the work of construction of meaningful relationships between world elements must be the reader's, and that shifts in the significance of a given element in relation to others is as easily operated in the spatialised

---

[7] Werth is aware of the problematic classification created by what he describes as the 'Meanwhile back at the ranch' variety of switches in location within the same time frame, proposing that some should be classified as alternative text worlds within the same time frame, while others can be classified as subworlds in relation to a principal situation (1999, 224-25).

medium of BD as it is in the temporally sequential medium of written narratives, once a reading protocol has been established.

The undecidability of the world-status of sequences of the narrative can, however, be posed as a greater issue for readers, and it is possible to signal 'in-between' worlds which are neither wholly 'actual' nor wholly 'sub'. Crepax, in *Valentina et Baba Yaga* (1985), does precisely this, using two different devices to 'frame' this third plane of experience. Crepax's fragmented and often hallucinogenic worlds contain a number of events which occur in the spirit plane of the supernatural. In one sequence Valentina experiences a vampire attack which she ascribes to her own subworld of dream, and in such a scenario, she would be the initiating agent responsible for this world. Crepax, however, presents the sequence in such a way as to suggest a different status for this sequence, by using a frame border with rounded corners, half-way between the right-angled box of the 'actual' world, and the scalloped border of her subworld (see **Figure 36** for an example of the scalloped pattern). This is established as an intermediate world which can apparently affect the contents of both the textual-actual-world and Valentina's subworld.

A more complex play on world-status is achieved by Crepax through the reappearance of the intermediate frame shape, which now signals 'other world', in a two textual-actual-world screens: Valentina's television and a screen forming part of an installation at an artist's studio party. All images on these screens are therefore marked by association as having potentially unstable world-status. The screens are part of two intercalated narrative sequences. The first screen becomes the means by which the evil Baba Yaga influences Valentina and her henchmen gain access to her appartment (imitating the image on a security system screen). The second is the object of a range of 'mise en abyme' comments by the guests at the artists' installation. These confirm and extend the problematic relationship between 'reality' and 'non-reality':

> A mon avis on ne peut pas juger laquelle des deux est le modèle [...] si c'est celle à l'extérieur de l'écran TV ou celle de l'intérieur [at this point, the narrative switches to the Valentina sequence, and the 'hors-cadre' narratorial voice comments, 'C'est une partie de l'action qui se prépare, mais elle provient de l'extérieur'].
> - Elles pourraient se trouver **hors-cadre!...**' [bold in the original]
> - Hm... je ne vois pas comment les insérer beh, j'y vais!
> - Les installations en circuit fermé servent à surveiller normalement. (Crepax 1985: 41).

These overt metafictional remarks prepare the reader for the invasion of Valentina's personal space by Baba Yaga's minions whose faces have appeared so menacingly on her television screen. We can see in this sequence a modern version of the use of the mirror as a privileged threshold between the mortal and spirit worlds prevalent in nineteenth-century fantastic narratives

**Playing the space game: *there*ness**

The comic strip has been a highly self-aware form from its earliest manifestations. Getting in and out of the artificial limits of the frame has been a ingrained habit of comic protagonists, as has the re-concretisation of the speech bubble (a favourite gag in Geluck's *Le Chat* albums). A recent series of explorations of the physicality of the album form in relation to the construction of fictional ontologies has been produced by Mathieu in the *Julius Corentin Acquefacques, prisonnier des rêves* albums (see above, **Figure 42**).

To a certain extent, the series subtitle 'prisonnier des rêves' could be said to provide a sufficient let-out clause for any strange happening in each narrative, as dream-logic requires no defence for its infringement of naturalist criteria for ontological relationships. But this exploration by Mathieu provides an extreme example of how we convert physical space to story space, and how this, in turn, can face the conundrum of its own *there*ness.

One aspect of Mathieu's work involves the problematics of the construction of past and future time-space sequences in relation to a perpetually shifting *present*, which, moreover, can be subdivided into different types of present, occupying three deictic centres: the 'now' of reading, the 'now' of the narration, and the 'now' of the textual-actual-world, all of which are in a state of change in relation to their own earlier 'nows', and none of which have any fixed relationship with each other (see Reichenbach 1966, 288-90 for an early formulation of the speaker—event—point of reference relationship, outlining the principle of the shifting temporal reference point).

In *Le Processus* (1993), Mathieu sets up the familiar trope of the time-traveller, who has access to his own past, including confrontation with his past self (which, of course, for the past self, is confrontation with a future self). What is interesting here, is not the time-travel conundrum, but the way in which the temporal sequence of the frames of the cartoon, presented graphically on the page, becomes a physical matrix for Acquefacques's return to an earlier frame of his own experience (**Figure 44**). Here, the reading of the frames' juxtaposition in space as an iconic representation of sequence in time in the BD album is transformed in Acquefacque's world into the direct mode of physical ingress to a previous time-space 'now'. The protagonist walks back along and across his own timeline, standing on the 'roof' of the frames of the text which have gained three-dimensional status (**Figure 45**). What, in Werth's model, would be the sub-world of the past, only accessible through the memories of protagonists, instead becomes a world which is presented as equivalent in its '*there*ness' to a notional textual-actual-world 'now'.

All this is, of course, represented three-dimensional space, remaining on the flat surface of the page. However, Mathieu takes the physicality of the spatialised representation of inter-world relationships one step further, as Acquefacques appears to fall down a spiral which has been physically cut from one page, representing a vortex. The nature of the vortex is unknown, but the following possibilities are afforded to Acquefacques by the archivist: 'épicentre du rêve? foyer de la création? antre de l'absolu? coeur du temps? spirale de la grande explication? trou blanc? avatar tri-dimensionnel? simple gag? ou tout cela à la fois?' (1993, 33). His fall ends in a different and unidentified world on the following page.

Mention has already been made of the contrasting degrees of iconicity which can occur in Mathieu's work, and this has a significant role to play in this album. In the earlier parts of the narration, and in its closing pages, the 'now' of the narration, and the intruding 'now' of the future self in the past are represented with an identical degree of iconicity, suggesting exact equivalence between the two (see above, **Figure 44**). But once Acquefacques has fallen down the vortex, and out of his own world into a photographically represented strange sand-filled other world, he comes across sketch versions of the pages we have just read. Here, fully conscious of the 'risques inhérents aux paradoxes temporels' (1993, 42), he avoids tumbling into the sketch version, but instead finds a fully inked page which is identical to **Figure 44**, representing the beginning of the narrative sequence which has led to this point. He climbs into this. We thus have a situation in which Acquefacques could not gain direct access to his past 'from the inside' by walking the suddenly concrete and three dimensional borders between the frames of the narrative so far. His actions in scrambling away from the sketched page of his past experience are motivated by an instinctive sense of the wrongness of the mismatch in the degree of iconicity of his own body and his potential environment, not to mention the fact that he has already experienced this moment from the other side as unsuccessful. It appears that reentry to his own past and world can only occur 'from the outside', in circumstances where both his dimensionality and iconicity are matched to those of the page. And thus, as the title of the final part suggests, 'La boucle se boucle' (1993, 45).

The final page of the album shows the sequence of the opening pages, but these are no longer represented in standard strips across and down the page. Instead they are represented in an inwardly moving spiral for which the vanishing point cannot be defined. This creates the impression of an endless loop, like a Moebius strip, which can be ridden forever by Acquefaques. Unlike the vortex, which led him to a different page and a different world level, the optical illusion of infinite regress traps the continuing narrative at the centre of the page (the concept of the 'volume à une face' will be explored in the subsequent album, *L'Epaisseur du miroir: Le début de la fin/La fin du début* (1995, planches 10-11).

## Illusions

When more substantially naturalist texts play with patterns something different happens. Unlike overtly metafictional texts, their protocols serve to maintain the illusion of world relationships which simulate those of our own experience. The hierarchy of the authority of worlds and subworlds is far more strictly observed; for the subworld fantasy of a protagonist to expand and materially affect the textual-actual-world would not follow these principles. They may, however, still employ a variety of graphic possibilities in the representation of worlds; the simultaneity of a textual-actual-world and a subworld in one frame, for example.

In many ways, Juillard's *Le Cahier Bleu* is a pattern book of subtle techniques to represent different worlds, and to distinguish between them, exploiting a full range of word/image combinations and lettering and colour variations, combined with different graphic layouts. The plot of the album hinges on the gap between subworld knowledge or representation of events, and a notional sequence of true textual-actual-world events, so it is important for readers to be able to establish the authority of and responsibility for the various worlds of the text. Constructed as a progressive 'unveiling' of the full facts of a sequence of events through the device of different points of view and a number of embedded narratives, the album employs a series of misdirections.

## *THERE*NESS

The presentation of the first chapter ('Louise') following the default convention of 'objective' narrative, but with empathy for Louise (see above, **Figure 38** and discussion) gives no indication that we are being provided with anything other than all the relevant features of the textual-actual-world. However, the arrival in her letterbox of the 'cahier bleu' of the title undoes the fullness of the authority engendered by the apparent '*there*ness' of this first chapter by revealing additional world information, re-classifying and downgrading it to an epistemologically limited subworld. The contents of the 'cahier', recorded by Victor, comprise the second chapter of the album.

A different aspect of *there*ness is exploited in this second chapter, in that the original text of the 'cahier' has been altered by the third player in the love-triangle plot of the album, Armand, without the knowledge of its fictional reader, Louise. It is is no more a 'full' revelation than the first chapter, as Armand's friendship with Victor and their co-presence in the opening sequence of both chapters one and two have been erased from it. The reader is presented with the doctored version of the text three times, twice in the textual contents of the iconic representation of the book, and once in the narrative box (see above, **Figure 37**). It is hardly surprising then, that when we encounter the opening page again (**Figure 46**), embedded in the visual narrative at the point where Victor begins his diary, we read it only in its iconic form, as the representation of a speech-act, and do not bother to read the contents for a fourth time. This is, of course, a well-laid trap, for in this, undoctored version, the presence of Armand (or Bobo, as he is called by Victor) is recorded on the page of the cahier.

These two exploitations of *there*ness raise the complicated issue of the relative authority of words and images in our processing of BD. The authority which is set up in chapter one depends on the protocol that no subjective limitations are placed on the world information provided by the text (see above, **Figure 38**, again). Our confidence that we are not being presented with a limited view of events hinges on the lack of a first-person narrator, and the apparent objectivity of the image, reinforced by the lack of access to Louise's private thoughts. Thus, although there is a degree of *emotional* modalisation, there is no epistemic modalisation signalled in the format employed. The apparent objectivity of the visual text is exploited and then undermined.

In chapter two, it appears that the written word is a more reliable source of authority than the preceding images, but this authority is also undermined. If we, like Louise, read the 'cahier' in its doctored version as a faithful record of Victor's experiences, we will find ourselves, once again, caught in the trap of assuming the part to represent the whole. We are set up to assume that the relationship between the textual-actual-world text in the narrative boxes and the images present in the main frame is one of 'ancrage' and 'relais', where both areas of the text combine to represent the 'same' subworld—that of Victor's experience. But the mismatch between the initial versions of the written text and that in **Figure 46** suggests that the latter cannot inhabit the subworld constituted by the former. It must, instead, be part of another world, either that of Victor's production of the 'cahier' or some putative prenarrative world of events.

If this frame represents a different world from the narrative boxes, this creates a question-mark over the relative status of all written narrative and images in this section. Whose images are these? Are they an illustration of the written narrative? Do they have independent status from the narrative, in which case they would be textual-actual-world images, running simultaneously with a subworld narrative? Again, a question of *there*ness becomes a question of *where*ness. The suspicion concerning epistemic authority already brought to the forefront by the first half should continue here.

**Unfairness**

I end with an example of the manipulation by Juillard in the final chapter of the album of some of the world-patterns which have been described above, in particular, the simple transfer of subworld text to the narrative box, and the condensing of the time-line by running more than one world at once. The effect of this manipulation is to exclude Louise from Victor's world at the end of the text through the choice of the graphic layout of worlds.

The fabula can be constructed as follows: Hélèna, comes forward as a witness, proving Victor innocent of the murder of Armand. As a result, Victor is released from a cell where he has been held on suspicion of Armand's murder. Louise, who apparently knows of his release, is late in coming to meet him, instead, when he emerges, Hélèna is there, and Louise arrives in time to see them leave together.

The graphic layout offers a slightly different configuration (**Figure 47**), which exploits three conventions: the representation as simultaneous of elements from more than one experiential world; the dual world-status of a single element of narrative; and the effect of rapid world-switches between frames. This allows a non-realist relationship to be set up between the separate worlds of the official's predictive words to Hélèna and the textual-actual-world image of Victor's release. The former, when situated in the context of their enunciation, have the status of a non-actual future subworld whereas the latter, which initially may appear to be the subworld illustration of the official's words, also functions as the initiating frames of the textual-actual-world sequence in which Hélèna meets him and Louise fails to do so.

This overlap between world sequences is the result, as I have suggested of the doubling of the world-functions of certain elements. Thus the spoken narrative of the release switches from frame to frame between the speech bubble of the official's words to the narrative box accompaniment to the visual sequence of Victor's exit from his cell (as we saw in the example of the letter in **Figure 40**). And the visual narrative of Victor's release is transformed from subsidiary 'ancrage' of a subworld text to the main plot-advancing sequence.

The single word, 'rapidement', which occupies the narrative box of the final frame of p.59 also has dual referents. It designates the textual-actual-world process of Victor's liberation, but, of course, it also designates the artefactual acceleration produced by the simultaneous presentation of two sequential narrative segments.

Once the sequence between Hélèna and the official ceases to be woven in with Victor's release, it is replaced by an apparently more straightforward alternation of the release narrative with that of Louise hurrying to meet Victor. But Louise has little hope of success as all the textual structures are stacked against her. Victor is already, textually, on his way out before Louise leaves her appartment building. And Hélèna, by contrast to Louise, has mysteriously had time to go home and change her clothes before arriving in time to carry Victor off to eat.

## Conclusions

The above discussion has demonstrated that any assumption that iconic representation entails a simple presence or absence of fictional entities in a stable world is ill-founded.

BD has as sophisticated reading and world-building protocols as any other form, some of which are peculiar to its own codes of representation. Its systems of modality and world-relationships are no more standardised and fixed than are those in the most flexible and ambiguous passage from *Madame Bovary*. Indeed, the degree zero of 'naturalism' in BD contains an extremely rich set of variations in representational techniques. What is, of course, striking, is how easily we process such complex combinations compared, say, with the diagrams produced by Werth.

It is clear that, in BD, the conventionally transparent can be re-'figured' as opaque, just as the flexibility of layout can be exploited to produce ambiguities. It will also be obvious from the above examples that the patterns and nuances of world building in the albums discussed have not been exhausted by this discussion. Assumptions concerning the relative authority of text and images, the portrayal of attitudinal worlds, and the production of empathy have all been touched on, here, but not developed. Further consideration also remains to be made of the relative functions of different centres of experience in the interpretation of BD.

## Bibliography

Barthes, R. 1982. 'Rhétorique de l'image' in *L'Obvie et l'obtus: Essais critiques III*, Paris: Seuil, 25-42.

Bastin, N. 2000. 'World Games: Constructing and Configuring the Worlds of Queneau's Novels', unpublished Ph.D thesis, Bristol.

Branigan, E. 1992. *Narrative Comprehension and Film*, London: Routledge.

Bridgeman, T. 1998. 'Paris-Polar in the Fog: power of place and generic space in Malet's *Brouillard au pont de Tolbiac*', *Australian Journal of French Studies*, 35, 58-74.

Chatman, S. 1990. *Coming to Terms: The Rhetoric of Narrative in Fiction and Film*, Ithaca: Cornell University Press.

Crepax, G. 1983. 'Les Souterrains' in *Valentina*, tome 1, Paris: Echo des Savanes and Albin Michel, 19-67.

Crepax, G. 1985. *Valentina et Baba Yaga*, Paris: Futuropolis.

Deleuze, G. 1983. *Cinéma I. L'Image-mouvement*, Paris: Minuit.

Emmott, C. 1994. 'Frames of reference: contextual monitoring and the interpretation of narrative discourse', in M. Coulthard, ed., *Advances in Written Text Analysis*, London: Routledge, 157-66.

Emmott, C. 1997. *Narrative Comprehension: A Discourse Perspective*, Oxford: Oxford University Press.

Franc, R. 1979. 'Le Chant du castrat le soir au fond des bois', in *Souvenirs d'un menteur*, Paris: Dargaud, 7-10.

Franc, R. 1984. 'Le Roi du monde', in *Le Marchand d'opium*, Paris: Dargaud, 26-9.

Genette, G. 1972. 'Discours du récit: essai de méthode', in *Figures III*, Paris: Seuil, 65-273.

Green, K. (ed.) 1995. *New Essays in Deixis: Discourse, Narrative and Literature*, Amsterdam: Rodopi.

Jost, F. 1989. *L'Oeil-Caméra: Entre film et roman*, 2nd, revised edition, Lyon: Presses Universitaires de Lyon.

Juillard, A. 1994. *Le Cahier bleu*, Bruxelles: Casterman.

Kress, G. and T. van Leeuwen 1996. *Reading Images: The Grammar of Visual Design*, London: Routledge.

Lanser, S.S. 1981. *The Narrative Act: Point of View in Prose Fiction*, Princeton: Princeton University Press.

Loustal, J. and P. Paringaux. 1982. *Barney et la note bleue*, Bruxelles: Casterman.

McCloud, S. 1994. *Understanding Comics The Invisible Art*, New York: Kitchen Sink for Harper Perennial.

Mathieu, M.-A. 1991a. *Julius Corentin Acquefacques, prisonnier des rêves: L'Origine*, Paris: Delcourt.

Mathieu, M.-A. 1991b. *Julius Corentin Acquefacques, prisonnier des rêves: La Qu...*, Paris: Delcourt.

Mathieu, M.-A. 1993. *Julius Corentin Acquefacques, prisonnier des rêves: Le Processus*, Paris: Delcourt.

Mathieu, M.-A. 1995. *Julius Corentin Acquefacques, prisonnier des rêves: Le Début de la fin/La fin du début*, Paris: Delcourt.

Peeters, B. 1984. 'Une exploration interrompue', *Cahiers de la bande dessinée*, 57, 24-26.

Peeters, B. 1991. *Case, planche, récit: comment lire une bande dessinée*, Tournai: Casterman.

Reichenbach, H. 1966. *Elements of Symbolic Logic*, New York and London: Free Press and Collier-Macmillan. [First edition 1947.]

Ryan, M.-L. 1991. *Possible Worlds, Artificial Intelligence and Narrative Theory*, Bloomington: Indiana University Press.

Ryan, M.-L. 1992. 'Possible Worlds in Recent Literary Theory', *Style*, 26.4, 528-53.

Saint-Ogan, A. 1935. *Prosper et Toutoune*, Paris: Hachette.

Tardi, J. 1979. *[Mouh Mouh] Un Cheval en hiver ... La Torpedo rouge sang ... [...]*, Brussels: Pepperland.

Tardi, J. 1981. *Les Aventures extraordinaires d'Adèle Blanc-Sec: Le Secret de la salamandre*, Brussels: Casterman.

Tardi, J. 1992. *Brouillard au pont de Tolbiac*, d'après le roman de Léo Malet, Brussels: Casterman.

Werth, P. 1995. 'How to Build a World (in a lot less than six days, and using only what's in your head)', in Green (ed.), 49-80.

Werth, P. 1999. *Text Worlds: Representing Conceptual Space in Discourse*, London: Longman.

# Narratives of Adolescence, Ethnicity and Masculinity in the Work of Baru

## Ann Miller
## University of Leicester

This chapter discusses the themes of ethnicity and masculinity in the work of the bande dessinée artist Baru and investigates his narrative techniques, in particular his use of the medium to manipulate narrative time and voice. Baru, whose real name is Hervé Barulea, was born in 1947 in the small town of Thil in Lorraine. His father, an Italian immigrant, was a steel worker. Baru's 1980s albums focus on adolescent rites of passage in the working class immigrant community in Lorraine, and are narrated in the first person by a character usually called Hervé Barulea. The documentary precision of the décors offers an ethnographic study of the everyday life of the first and second generation Italian community. The characters, in contrast, are portrayed in an expressionist style that allows Baru to depict the uncertainties and terrors of the Oedipal dramas enacted by the adolescent narrator and his friends. Baru has been compared to the Italian Hugo Pratt and the Argentinian Muñoz, the masters of expressionist BD, and he acknowledges their influence on his work (Baru 1996). In the work of both Pratt and Muñoz, however, the graphic style of the backgrounds accords with that of the characters, whereas Baru's work offers an emotional and moral portrayal of characters against a background that is rendered with meticulous realism. In the 1990s albums, the stability of the local setting and the consistent perspective of the first person narrative voice both disappear. The loss of the traditional forms of working class community and masculinity through the demise of the steel industry in Northern France gives rise to a dislocated narrative which draws on a number of intertextual sources and generic conventions, including the road movie, allowing for the exploration of a range of alternative masculinities.

The albums that Baru produced in the 1980s for Dargaud, the three volumes of *Quéquette Blues* (between 1984 and 1986) and *La*

*Piscine de Micheville* (1985), have masculinity as their central theme. They follow the progress of the narrator, Hervé, along an Oedipal trajectory as his sexual identity is gradually constructed and affirmed through male bonding rituals and through encounters with the feminine and with representatives of male authority. Both take place under the sign of the paternal signifier, the factory chimney in the case of the first album and the blast furnace in the case of the second. In *Quéquette Blues*, Hervé is waiting for his friend Robert to emerge from the house of a married woman so that he in turn can accomplish his *dépucelage*. The chimney symbolises an obvious castratory threat to Hervé, which is likely to be materialised by the return of the husband from night shift. At the same time, it evokes the kind of masculinity that the boys expect to attain as adults: as they look at it against the night sky, one of them says: 'Ça a de la gueule, non?', an admiration scarcely diminished by the mocking comments of the others about industrial accidents and diseases. As he waits, Hervé tries to take his mind off the impending ordeal by thinking back to his younger self: a series of flashbacks is dominated by two motifs that recur elsewhere in Baru's work. The first is the figure of the teacher, always viewed from a terrifyingly low angle, which emphasises the castrating power of the bespectacled (and, in *La Piscine*, squinting) gaze. The other motif is the mirror: Hervé sees his own image reflected back as a sexualised, hard, dangerous rock singer, with an impressive quiff, although his father forces him to flatten it down. The mirror motif also occurs in *La Piscine*, but here it is the rain that causes the quiff to collapse. *Quéquette Blues* ends without any need for Hervé to affront the female element: Robert has taken so long that the men are returning from night shift and it is too late. To Hervé's relief, he can go back into the male sphere, the bistro: 'On va pouvoir souffler encore', he says.

The front cover of *La Piscine* (**Figure 48**) dramatises the anxieties involved in living up to the symbol of patriarchal power, the blast furnace that looms in the background. The red trunks suggest continuity between the male organ and the phallic signifier, but the character wearing the trunks is seen by Hervé stuffing a handkerchief down them, revealing the insecurity of masculine sexual identity, especially when under the scrutiny of the female gaze. In an almost symmetrical frame further on, we see the terror inspired in Hervé himself by the vision of sexual difference as the body of a female swimmer suddenly appears at his eye level. The swimming pool of the title is owned by the steel works: it offers various models of masculinity, including the *maîtres-nageurs*, renowned for their mythical sexual exploits with women who remain inaccessible to Hervé. Later in the album an attempt to look at a naked woman ends in humiliation. Hervé visits the *bains-douche* that also belong to the factory. The paternal presence is doubly in evidence during this visit: the blast furnace is in the background, and the man who sells the tickets, having been pensioned off from the factory for ill-health, knows his father. Hervé looks over into the next cubicle where a woman is taking a shower. When she looks back at him his fear that his father will discover his transgression leads Hervé to flee out of the cubicle and down the steps: a panic-stricken *dégringolade* in the shadow of the paternal signifier.

Hervé's sexual ambitions are further thwarted in the penultimate episode by another figure whose authority derives from the factory: the doctor. Hervé has been taken to the surgery by his mother when, not daring to admit that he has a hangover, he tells her that he is suffering from nervous fatigue. The doctor sends him off to the factory summer camp, where access to girls is denied, and he has to comfort himself with memories of childhood, when summer camp allowed a fantasy of fusion with the maternal body of the *monitrice*.

The final episode focuses on the first generation of immigrants, as Hervé takes us on a sociological tour of ethnically differentiated masculine rituals. He satirises the communist mayor's discourse of international fraternity by explaining that there were only two occasions when different ethnic groups would speak to each other: once when all the non-Italians joined in with a Luxemburger to gloat over the fact that Fausto Coppi had been beaten in the *Tour de France* by Charly Gaul, and the second time when... and here the reader expects something of the same order. Instead there is an unexpected gesture of solidarity: a Pole is lighting the cigarette of a Ukrainian, an image brought into sharp focus by its double framing through bars. In the next frame the wider picture is revealed: the factory gates are locked. This was a strike, this was the time when rivalries gave way to joint action. The tone has changed: this is 'pas rigolo', as the narrator says, and the story comes to an abrupt end. On the final page we are suddenly projected forward into the present: 'Aujourd'hui l'usine a été rasée'. There is no narrative closure: we never find out the outcome of the strike but it is irrelevant now. We are doubly disconcerted: the trajectory is cut short and there is no Oedipal resolution for the narrator. The blast furnace, the phallic signifier, is simply razed to the ground, and where it was there is a void. The kind of masculinity figured by that signifier is no longer on offer.

We are also disoriented by what seems to be a sudden change in the positioning of the narrator, or rather a realisation that we have been misled regarding the relationship between time of enunciation and time of the events recounted. The album had at no point offered the elegiac tone and sense of loss associated with nostalgia. It was narrated predominantly in the present, and did not take up the enunciatory stance of the flashback, apart from the brief evocation of the child clinging to the summer camp *monitrice*. The final chapter is narrated in the past tense, but the verbal and visual point of view is that of the adolescent Hervé: the repeated use of a slightly low-angled perspective emphasises this. Suddenly the reader is catapulted into the present, and is forced to realise just how distant the time of narration is, and therefore has been all along, from the time of the events recounted. That realisation induces a radical sense of loss.

This album may be contrasted with the work of Max Cabanes, in *Colin-Maillard*, published in 1989, where loss is built into the narration from the very beginning. The album opens on the loss of the mother, and from the outset there is a clear separation between the very literary narrating voice of the adult, and the child that he was. Nostalgia is also built in through the evocation of powerful sense impressions: images, smells, sensations. The distance of the present of narration from events recounted is also suggested by the emblematic status of frames that end episodes, signifying images forever hallowed by memory. Cabanes's narrative is in some ways similar to that of Baru in that it involves rites of passage, encounters with the feminine and with male authority figures; it differs from Baru's account, however, in that it is set in the 1950s and evokes a mainly rural society in the south of France. This is the kind of nostalgia familiar from 1980s cinema: a yearning for the idealised innocence of rural pre-industrial society from the standpoint of urban industrial society. But what Baru recounts is his 1960s adolescence in a northern industrial setting, and on the final page we abruptly realise that the narrating position is from the perspective of the complete dislocation of post-industrial society. It is, then, industrial society that suddenly, even if retrospectively, seems to have offered community and security. We are left with nothing but the abrupt, shocking failure of the paternal signifier. That failure gives rise to the narrative of Baru's 1995 album *L'Autoroute du Soleil*, which opens on the destruction of the blast furnace, and which will be discussed further on in this chapter.

Baru's other 1980s albums were produced for the now defunct publisher Futuropolis. In the first of them, *La Communion de Mino*, published in 1985, the setting remains unchanged from the Dargaud albums: the Italian immigrant milieu in Northern France. The narrative perspective changes, though: the narrator is not identified with the author, and the episodes are narrated in the past tense by Mino, not as a thirteen-year old *premier communiant* but as an adult. Baru uses a number of techniques to build in an ironic distance between the narrator and his extended family. The question of the identity of second-generation immigrants is raised immediately as the narrator demarcates himself from his parents:

> Bonjour, je m'appelle Cosimo Graziani, mais tout le monde m'appelle 'Mino'. Je suis né en France et je suis français ... Mon père et ma mère, eux, sont venus d'Italie—chacun de leur côté, et ils se sont rencontrés ici.

Mino himself is never depicted, other than in the communion photographs. His detached stance is conveyed through the frequent use of high-angled drawings, particularly at the end of episodes, suggesting the superior knowledge of hindsight. The only episode which does not contain one of these omniscient frames is that in which Mino evokes his terror of the *institutrice*, who is drawn from a child's eye viewpoint: it would seem that even in recollection his fear of her has not been overcome. The impression of a retrospective vision is further reinforced by the fact that the vignettes are not presented as sequences of actions decomposed and recomposed to convey movement, as in classic BD, but as significant moments, often with no particular temporal ordering. Where there is a sequence, the ellipses represented by the inter-frame blanks are massive: Mino's uncle works all hours, ascends in the hierarchy, buys a car. Three frames have taken him from youth to middle age.

The ironical stance of the narrator is further emphasised through Baru's exploitation of the medium to create a visual equivalent of the *style indirect libre*. This occurs, for example, where Mino recounts his aunt's desperate desire to make money:

> Merde! Elle avait pas quitté Gubbio—elle avait 12 ans—seulement pour pas y crever de faim ... fallait un 'plus'!!

In the accompanying images the high-angled omniscient view is juxtaposed with the subjective optical viewpoint of the aunt. The control of the narrator is asserted, even as his perspective gives way to the affective vision focalised through the aunt (**Figure 49**).

The demystifying project of the album in relation to mythologies of family and immigration is evidenced by the undermining of the testimonial status of the document which has given rise to the narrative: the communion photograph. Although the subjects are posing, Baru makes no attempt to give his drawing the appearance or ontological weight of a photographic reproduction of a real event. It is therefore not imbued with the poignant sense that what once existed exists no more, Barthes's 'ça-a-été' (Barthes 1980); pathos is avoided and the eye of the satirist is pitiless.

*Vive la classe*, published by Futuropolis in 1987, returns to the present tense narration of the adolescent Hervé, but it moves onto ground not covered in the Dargaud albums of adolescence. It is concerned with the articulation of citizenship and with rites of passage to masculinity, as all the boys in Hervé's class prepare to leave for military service in 1968. Their soon-to-be attained status as men, sanctioned by the mayor and the priest, allows for the rabid and drunken pursuit of girls, including Marie, their elected mascot.

For Hervé, the prospect of imminent departure promises an escape from his devouring mother. In this album it is she who seems to possess the phallic power in the house: juxtaposed with a phallic-looking stove, ressembling a domestic version of the blast furnace, she stands over him and tells him that he must get his *bac* if he is not to end up in a factory like his father, whom we never see. But she has another, more fearsome, incarnation: as Hervé dreams of Marie, a speech balloon traverses the inter-frame blank, suggesting that its source is from outside the world of the dream. When we turn the page the space of the dream invades the space of the fiction, as Hervé is caught between dreaming and waking, and Marie's sex converges with the mother's castrating mouth, quite literally a *vagina dentata*. The phallic mother has turned into the monstrous archaic mother. As Barbara Creed says, 'the former ultimately represents a comforting phantasy of sexual sameness, and the latter a terrifing phantasy of sexual difference' (Creed 1993, 158).

The Republic too may be a devouring mother. The initiation into masculinity and citizenship may be presided over by representatives of patriarchal authority, but it is through the figure of a mother that the equation between citizenship and death is made. Rivalry over Marie is silenced by an image of a horse pulling an ornate carriage, an ornament on the table of an old Italian woman whose son had been killed in the Algerian war: the Republic may demand the death of its citizens. Ethnic identity now asserts itself against national identity, as Hervé and his friend decide that if they are called upon to fight in a war they will escape to Italy, and shout 'Viva la classa!!' before disappearing into the bistro.

Baru's albums of the 1990s move out of the home-town setting and away from the adolescent narrator. *L'Autoroute du Soleil* (1995) opens by introducing Karim Kemal, a Beur, in the working-class quarter of a town in Lorraine, but the title and the cover picture indicate that he will soon be on the move. A third-person *récitatif* reports the racist discourses which circulate as gossip about Karim, both mythologising him as irresistible to women and pathologising him as an AIDS-carrying drug dealer. The other main protagonist, Alexandre, a second-generation Italian, is fascinated by Karim's masculine competence. The album moves immediately to what was not shown in *La Piscine*: the destruction of the blast furnace, which signals in a spectacular way the demise of traditional types of working class masculinity (**Figure 50**). Unmanned, the father of Alexandre weeps. Narratives of migration are evoked, and then abruptly terminated: Baru offers a brief flashback to the journey that had brought these workers, the generation of Alexandre and Karim's fathers, from Italy, the Ukraine, Poland and Algeria, to employment in the steel industry in Lorraine, but with the closing of the steel works, 'ils n'étaient plus rien'.

With the ending of that narrative, another one begins for Karim and Alexandre, but it is a post-industrial narrative that borrows from the conventions of the road movie, a genre that becomes prominent when 'hegemonic concepts of masculinity seem to have become unhinged' (Aitkin and Lukinbeal 1997, 366) and that constructs a new type of masculine identity disassociated from local roots and romanticising mobility. There will be no more of the sites in which the rituals of masculinity were played out in the 1980s albums. The factory has gone, and the *Salle des Fêtes* of the firm, *La Lorraine des Aciers*, is now used by the fascist *Elan National Français* to hold meetings. The discourse of working class solidarity, in spite of inter-ethnic rivalries, from the end of *La Piscine,* has given way to the incitement to racial violence in the speeches of Faurissier, the local leader. The road-movie narrative is set in motion by the need of Karim and Alexandre to flee when Faurissier discovers that Karim has been sleeping with his wife and sets his thugs on him.

The replacement of a first person narrator by a heterodiegetic approach to narration allows for the multiplication of points of view, both verbal and visual, even if Alexandre's hero-worshipping gaze dominates our perception of Karim. Once all the elements that will trigger the road-movie plot are in place, they are briefly summarised in a series of images taken out of their temporal and spatial context and brought together on the same page. A self-reflexive *récitatif* announces the story as a fiction: 'Bien, voilà! Toutes les pièces importantes du puzzle sont en place... ' The final image on the page, Faurissier's hand opening the door of the bedroom in which his wife is with Karim, not only represents a key plot moment, it also symbolises, through the opening of the door, the mechanism of the narration itself. If this self-referential discourse foregrounds the artificiality of fictional conventions, the drawing style also disrupts the illusion of reality through its very excess: the detailed, almost photographic rigour of every feature of interior and exterior architecture and landscape in *L'Autoroute* approaches hyperrealism. Whereas the décors of the 1980s albums could be read as a transcription of the real, a recreation of

Hervé's milieu, the referent of *L'Autoroute* would seem instead to be an already-mythologised version of France, from Provençal village to neo-Renaissance bourgeois town house.

The ideological project of the road movie is described in the advertising slogan for Dennis Hopper's 1969 film *Easy Rider*: 'A man went looking for America and couldn't find it anywhere'. Karim and Alexandre's journey will inevitably involve the exploration of a French identity, and its various reconfigurations in terms of nationality, ethnicity and gender. The notion of a French national culture is problematised by the Americanisation of the cities and spaces through which Karim and Alexandre travel, many of them relating to an anonymous mass culture: the hyperreal graphic style raises the service stations, diners and motels to the same iconic status as the image of Provençal rooftops or provincial station hotel.

The album's investment in Karim as a figure of masculinist fantasy is reinforced by his explicit adoption of the persona of James Dean through the clothes that Dean wore in Nicolas Ray's 1955 film *Rebel without a Cause*. The portrayal of an Americanised 1990s France is thus partly overlaid by the iconography of 1950s America, including its cars. The characterisation of Karim as a 1950s hero leads to a regressive gender politics: a number of female characters have the sole function of guaranteeing Karim's heterosexual prowess. Any homosexual subtext to the relationship between Karim and Alexandre remains unacknowledged, as Karim takes on the role of Alexandre's heterosexual mentor.

The sense that gender roles are firmly situated in the 1950s is reinforced by a section of the album that draws upon a different set of popular cultural references, this time from within bande dessinée. Towards the end of the album Karim and Alexandre find refuge in a château which bears a powerful resemblance to Hergé's Moulinsart. The owner is René Loiseau, whose name evokes the Frères Loiseau, characters from Tintin albums. The fictional universe of the Tintin albums has already been conjured up when Karim disguises Alexandre: a sharp haircut and a bottle of peroxide turn him into a Tintin lookalike with added street credibility. Before Karim and Alexandre's arrival at the château, René's masculinity is in the kind of crisis into which Haddock was thrown whenever la Castafiore appeared (Hergé 1963). Here she is in permanent residence, in the form of the monstrous and castrating wife, who had taken advantage of René's naïveté to give her own family financial control of the business. Karim's masculine expertise enables René to regain some phallic power: he repairs René's valuable 1950s Facel Vega, which the wife had not appropriated, believing it to be permanently broken-down. This restoration of René's manhood leads him to call Karim 'fils', suggesting the possibility of an idealised all-male community: unlike Moulinsart this community would be inclusive in terms of its ethnic make-up, but, as in Moulinsart, the feminine element would be entirely expelled.

It is the overcoming of ethnic divisions that provides the utopian moments in the album. Ethnic conflict is, of course, dramatically depicted, not only through Faurissier's persecution of Karim, but also through the depiction of the Z.U.P. in Lyon as a war zone, where Beurs, subject to constant harassment, engage in organised resistance. Karim's own experiences with the police are recounted, and provide the pretext for prolonging the narrative: he refuses to go to the police to establish his and Alexandre's innocence when they have been framed by drug dealers. There are, however, key scenes where a fantasised solidarity and community suddenly reassert themselves: the lorry drivers defend Karim and Alexandre against Faurissier and his thugs in spite of Faurissier's attempts to mobilise the discourse of the Arab as sexual predator and abuser of young girls. Whereas in *Easy Rider* Utopia was attained by a retreat into the marginality of alternative lifestyles, that option is rejected in *L'Autoroute*: the life style of drug culture is depicted as criminal and violent, and the commune in the Provençal village has been vacated by all but one middle-aged hippy. It is the regeneration of working class culture achieved by bringing the ethnic margins to the centre that is offered as a way forward.

The positioning of a Beur character at the centre of a narrative which draws on 1950s genre conventions seems, then, to offer a redrawing of ethnic boundaries whilst keeping gender boundaries rigidly in place. The excessive and violent masculinity of fascism is defeated when Faurissier finally destroys himself with his own phallic weapon, but there is a certain ambiguity about Faurissier, whose psychotic obsession with Karim seems to be coded as homo-erotic. Each time that he catches up with him he is unable or unwilling to pull the trigger, and the pursuit is transformed into a repeated *coitus interruptus*. It may be as much for his sexual deviance as for his excessive masculinity that he is eventually punished.

It is above all women, though, that the two buddies blame for all their troubles as they set off for home, now reconciled with the law, and the final image offers the exhilaration of a car, and the road. In a genre which arises out of the breakdown of the Oedipal narrative and the destabilisation of male subjectivity, the protagonist's identity is, according to Corrigan, 'displaced onto the mechanical vehicle as that vehicle becomes transformed into a human or spiritual reality' (Corrigan 1991, 145). *L'Autoroute* is faithful to its generic roots in providing what is ultimately a male escapist fantasy, predicated on the absence of women.

Baru's next album *Sur la route encore* (1997), another road odyssey, would seem to offer a change of perspective and even an Oedipal resolution, in that it is partly narrated by a woman: chapters alternate between the viewpoints of André and Edith, whom we discover in the final chapter to be André's wife. Edith's role in the album is primarily, however, a plot device: the police trail her because they believe that she will lead them to Claude, an old acquaintance who had turned to crime to finance his left-wing journal. Moreover the middle-aged André may be married but he has clearly not attained stability. Unlike the adult narrator of *La Communion de Mino*, whose perspective was that of distance and hindsight, André is at the mercy of events which bear down upon him. Baru renews his narrative techniques here in a radical way by restricting the first three chapters narrated by André to his optical point of view, with the exception of a few establishing shots. The narrator's hand can be seen, or his feet, but nothing else that would logically be outside his field of vision. He does not appear in the frame until the final chapter, where we are able to see that he has a striking resemblance to Baru himself.

André and Edith meet up, by arrangement, on the Ile de Groix at the end of the album, but we learn little of their relationship or why they had temporarily separated. The album focusses instead on recollections of André's adolescence as he travels through Northern France (where his presence at a concert encourages his two fortyish friends in the band to abandon 'la soupe disco' for some rock'n'roll) and relives in his imagination his ignominious failure to make the desired impact on girls at a dance. His politically militant twenties are evoked by the plot involving Claude, and the album ends as he and Edith stand under a lighthouse, speculating, with some lack of conviction, as to the likely success of Claude's projects to revive the newspaper on his release from prison. André is at the very end of France, an island off the coast of Britanny, his belief in political activism has turned to scepticism, and the lighthouse seems to represent not a stable signifier of masculinity achieved, but a sense that this is the end of the road.

*Bonne Année*, published in 1998 by Casterman, returns to adolescence and to the *banlieue*, only to offer a dystopian futuristic scenario. It is the year 2015. The extreme right has been in power since 1998 and all *banlieues* have been walled off from the town centres by barricades and police patrols. Any enactment of the rituals of adolescence takes place in a context where there is no future: drugs are made freely available to aid the autodestruction of the population of the *cités*, where contraceptives are banned to promote the spread of AIDS.

The inclusion of a character dressed as Franquin's BD character Spirou emphasises the bleakness of the portrayal of a totalitarian state rather than undermining it. While the subversion of the boy scout morality of one hero of classic BD in *L'Autoroute* offers undoubted pleasures to the reader (a trouserless Tintin emerges into the road movie text and observes its conventions by indulging in sex and rock'n'roll, if not drugs) the mood in *Bonne Année* is altogether more sombre. The text into which Spirou has stumbled is made up only of repressive discourses: Spirou is brutally sodomised by the border police. This happens out of the frame but his screams appear in a speech balloon.

The album may end on a moment of optimism when one of the border guards, Kovack, tired of racist taunts from his colleagues, releases two young people who had been arrested for illegally entering the city centre, but the overall tonality is chilling. The path to masculinity through the rites of passage of Baru's own youth is now definitively blocked: encounters with the feminine will lead to infection and death, and conflicts with male authority can only take the form of an unequal struggle against the forces of fascism. Even the post-industrial scenario from *L'Autoroute* of a multi-ethnic working class community which combats the menace from the extreme right is rejected in this album: that fight has been lost.

The closing off of the future may have led to the closing off of his own past as a creative source for Baru. His other album of the 90s, *Le Chemin de l'Amérique* (1990), was co-written with Jean-Marc Thévenet. It pursues Baru's obsessive themes of adolescence, masculinity and ethnicity through a historical subject. He chronicles the life of an Algerian boxer, Saïd Boudiaf. There are no *récitatifs* until the very end of the album: conflicting discourses on the Algerian war are juxtaposed with letters from Boudiaf's brother, an FLN militant, occupying the inter-frame space and thereby suggesting that the rise-to-fame story is invaded by a grander narrative of anti-colonial struggle. The fiction of Boudiaf's life collides with history when he disappears in Paris, along with hundreds of his compatriots, on the night of 17th October 1961.

If the autobiographical vein has dried up for Baru and the road movie hero is stranded in middle age, it would seem that more directly political subject matter offers a way forward for his continued exploration of masculinity and ethnicity.

## Bibliography

Atkin, Stuart, and C.L. Lukinbeal 1997. 'Disassociated Masculinities and Meographies of the Road' in Steven Cohan and Ina Rae Hark, eds, *The Road Movie Book*, London: Routledge, 349-370.

Barthes, Roland 1980. *La Chambre claire*, Paris: Seuil.

Baru 1984-86. *Quéquette Blues*, Paris: Dargaud. [Re-published by Albin Michel in 1991, under title *Roulez Jeunesse*].

Baru 1985a. *La Communion de Mino*, Paris: Futuropolis.

Baru 1985b. *La Piscine de Micheville*, Paris: Dargaud. [Re- published by Albin Michel in 1993].

Baru 1987. *Vive la classe!*, Paris: Futuropolis.

Baru 1995. *L'Autoroute du Soleil*, Tournai: Casterman.

Baru 1996. 'Sur la route de Baru', *Rêve-en-Bulles*, 12, 22-24 [interview with Pierre Polomé].

Baru 1997. *Sur la route encore*, Tournai: Casterman.

Baru 1998. *Bonne année*, Tournai: Casterman.

Baru and Thévenet, Jean-Marc 1990. *Le Chemin de l'Amérique*, Paris: Albin Michel. [Re- published by Casterman in 1998.]

Cabanes, Max 1989. *Colin-Maillard*, Tournai: Casterman.

Corrigan, Timothy 1991. *A Cinema without Walls*, New Brunswick: Rutgers University Press.

Creed, Barbara 1993. *The Monstrous-Feminine*, London: Routledge.

Hergé 1963. *Les Bijoux de la Castafiore*, Tournai: Casterman.

# Femmes en Images et Images de Femmes:
## L'Héroïne de *La Femme Piège* d'Enki Bilal

### Dominique Le Duc
### University of Brighton

Pour lutter contre l'invasion des comic books américains qui étalent érotisme et violence,[1] le courant moralisateur qui traverse la France d'après-guerre conduit à la promulgation en France de la loi du 16 juillet 1949 sur la protection des publications destinées à la jeunesse.[2] Soutenue par les instances catholiques et communistes de l'époque, cette loi impose également des contraintes thématiques, graphiques et narratives à la bande dessinée franco-belge (et est en partie responsable de l'absence presque totale des personnages feminins). Cette législation entraîne également les éditeurs, anxieux de se voir interdire toute production, à adopter une autocensure (mesures qui trouveront écho outre-mer, avec l'adoption aux Etats-Unis en 1954 de la *Comics Code Authority* après la parution du livre moralisateur *Seduction of the Innocent* du Docteur Fredric Wertham). Les femmes-papier seront dès lors systématiquement livrées aux ciseaux des censeurs comme le souligne le scandale d'une

---

[1] Forbes et Kelly (1995, 74) notent à ce propos sur la présence en France des produits culturels américains: 'Along with Disney, came the less morally hygienic adventures of assorted superheroes and crimebusters Buck Rodgers, Dick Tracy, Tarzan, Flash Gordon, Superman, Batman and others. The lurid excitement and sensuality which thrilled young French readers was a cause of alarm for many of their elders, who saw both moral and political danger in them.'

[2] M. Pierre (1949): extrait de la loi 1949 sur les publications pour la jeunesse: Article 2 de la loi du 16 juillet 1949. 'Les publications visées à l'article premier ne doivent comporter aucune illustration, aucune chronique, aucune rubrique, aucune insertion présentant sous un jour favorable le banditisme, le mensonge, le vol, la paresse, la lâcheté, la haine, la débauche ou tous actes qualifiés crimes ou délits ou de nature à démoraliser l'enfance ou la jeunesse, ou à inspirer ou entretenir des préjugés ethniques' (Cette dernière mention fut ajoutée par la loi du 29 novembre 1954).

minuscule couverture lue par un personnage de l'hebdomadaire *Tintin*.[3] Les personnages féminins prennent alors des allures hautement stéréotypées de viragos où se voient reléguées à des rôles secondaires (on notera l'absence des partenaires de la joyeuse bande de Gaulois autour des tables du banquet final dans les aventures d'Astérix; voir Le Point 1975).

A partir des années soixante, avec la découverte de l'érotisme, la BD, produite comme les autres médias en grande majorité par des hommes, va passer à l'âge adulte sous l'influence contestataire de 1968 et s'accompagner d'un lectorat principalement masculin. L'érotisation des femmes-papier, toujours sous les feux de la censure, naît sous les traits de *Barbarella*, héroïne française qui va révolutionner l'univers de la BD (suite au succès international de son auteur, Jane Fonda lui prêtera ses traits dans le film de Roger Vadim; voir Horn 1977, 21). Dès lors, la production croissante de publications pour adultes (e.g. *Pilote*) et l'évolution, grâce aux mouvements féministes, des stéréotypes attachés au rôle de la femme dans la société, conduit la BD à promouvoir de nouvelles images de femmes.

Dans les années soixante-dix, tandis que Moebius innove dans *Arzach* (1976) une technique narrative révolutionnaire, *Charlie Mensuel* remplace les charmes discutables de *Bianca Castafiore* par ceux plus séduisants de la jeune japonaise informaticienne *Yoko Tsuno* (Leloup 1970) ou encore ceux de l'hôtesse de l'air *Natacha* (Walthéry 1970). Le renouveau de BD de qualité pour adultes entraîne des rôles plus aboutis pour les femmes en image, comme celui de l'aventurière *Isa* (Bourgeon 1979) ou de *Adèle Blanc-Sec* (Tardi 1976).

Les années quatre-vingt vont confirmer cette progression encore timide d'héroïnes par une consécration graphique et narrative des femmes-papier dans des rôles d'héroïnes principales, comme la pulpeuse *Pelisse* (Loisel et Le Tendre 1982).[4] Une dérogation à la loi de 1949 au début des années quatre-vingt, qui reconnaît la nécessité de considérer le nombre croissant de publications pour adultes de façon distincte des publications enfantines, conduit au relâchement de la censure. Les femmes trouvent désormais droit de cité dans la bande dessinée et les auteurs peuvent explorer des territoires défendus jusqu'ici dont

---

3      Peeters (1993, 83-85) décrit l'anecdote de *La Marque Jaune* de Edgar P. Jacobs (1954). Il souligne également comment l'insipidité des figures féminines s'explique par la pudibonderie de l'époque.

4      La première publication de *La Quête de l'Oiseau du Temps* voit le jour dans le premier numéro de *Imagine* en 1978, mais comme le magazine disparut rapidement, la série s'interrompit aussi. *Charlie Mensuel* publia les aventures de *Pelisse* et *Bragon* de nouveau en 1982. Cette série acquit d'emblée le statut de classique du 9ème art lors de sa publication chez Dargaud.

l'érotisme, thème que l'on retrouve dans les oeuvres du maître italien de l'art érotique, Milo Manara.[5]

\*\*\*

*La Femme Piège* (1986), deuxième volet de la *Trilogie Nikopol* d'Enki Bilal, fait partie de la 'bande dessinée contemporaine d'auteur' (Loustal, Pratt, Tardi...). Cet album témoigne d'ambitions narratives basées sur un récit aux structures complexes, et graphiques avec une puissance d'évocation de l'image. Quelques mois après la publication de cette œuvre, la reconnaissance du style nouveau de ce jeune auteur, à la fois scénariste et dessinateur, était consacrée par le Festival d'Angoulême, fief du neuvième art.[6]

De même, la place du personnage féminin au premier plan de la couverture, primauté relevée dans le titre même, justifie l'exploration de la représentation graphique et textuelle de cette femme-papier et du portrait-type de l'héroïne, selon les deux systèmes signifiants étroitement imbriqués (iconique et linguistique) de ce média. La sensualité de cette bande repose sur l'utilisation d'une technique à hauts risques aux 'couleurs directes' par l'auteur qui lui permettent d'approcher la lumière et la matière de façon plus physique.[7] Bilal développe une forme d'art nouvelle où les couleurs sont évocatrices. L'effet monochrome de la froideur des tons gris ternes, parfois parsemés de quelques taches de couleurs vives, contribue à souligner un mystère inhérent dans cette bande. Contrairement aux méthodes traditionnelles, il s'agit ici pour l'auteur qui cherche une symbiose des traits et des couleurs, à saisir la spontanéité de son élan créatif et dessiner et peindre en même temps. Tandis que les méthodes classiques du coloriste vont rendre compte de la réalité, les couleurs directes permettent de s'en détacher tout en accentuant une atmosphère fantastique. Les planches présentent une dominante de teintes sombres et froides, où le dessin souligne un monde cruel et sans poésie.

S'ils servent d'exutoire aux fantasmes de leur auteur, comme moyen d'exorciser sa peur de la violence, les lieux troublants, violents et inquiétants dépeints dans l'univers de science-fiction de *La Femme*

---

5     Moliterni et al. 1996, 122.
6     Gaumer et al 1994, 68: 'Considéré à juste titre comme l'un des meilleurs auteurs réalistes contemporains, Enki Bilal se détache très vite des influences de ses aînés (Moebius, Mézières) et acquiert très vite sa propre dextérité graphique, complété par un sens inné de la mise en couleurs.'
7     Groensteen 1996, 31.

*Piège* donnent au décor une valeur essentielle.[8] Ils confrontent aussi le lecteur à la sécheresse d'un monde déroutant et déprimant où, dans une lumière crépusculaire, Bilal statufie les habitants de ces villes en ruines, à l'image des personnages multiformes de 'l'architecte spatial' Philippe Druillet, évoluant dans des citadelles d'un autre âge. Bilal utilise une forme de narration littéraire, celle d'un journal intime, plus proche du roman que de la BD en général. Les textes assez longs recréent le journal imaginaire de l'héroïne Jill Bioskop et complètent visuellement les vignettes sans briser l'harmonie de ces véritables tableaux—assurant la complémentarité sémantique avec quelques rares phylactères. Les cases, parfois sans texte, laissent le champ libre à l'imagination du lecteur.[9]

Les décors apocalyptiques ne cessent en effet d'avoir une influence sur l'héroïne, sans famille et sans enfant et dotée de traits physiques exceptionnels. Prisonnière d'un monde oppressant, elle est en proie à des visions hallucinées, représentées par de grands à-plats de rouges et de verts denses. Le rouge sang sur sa main est le signe iconique de ses fantasmes sanglants, qu'elle tente de repousser par un 'cri monstrueux mais libérateur' dans la case-tableau de la page 41 (**Figure 51**; les couleurs froides gris pâles de cette scène extérieure sont symboliques de la peur et de l'anxiété). Produit par une main d'homme, ce personnage féminin est marqué par l'ambiguïté d'un portrait doté d'attributs à la fois valorisants (qui seront remis en question lors d'une lecture plus attentive). La non-conformité graphique dans l'originalité de ses traits physiques, sa fonction de journaliste et son rôle dans le récit comme narrateur principal s'accompagnent en même temps d'attributs dévalorisants. En effet, stigmatisée d'images accablantes, sa représentation vélléitaire de femme-objet fait écho aux images récurrentes dans la BD pour adulte, l'un des lieux privilégiés de l'expression érotique.

La représentation graphique et textuelle de l'héroïne va permettre de souligner l'ambiguïté de cette femme-papier, figure érotique tour à tour femme fatale sans scrupule, victime ou jeune femme dans les bras de son héros, lors d'un retour à une réalité plus séduisante dans la phase finale du récit.

La représentation graphique de l'héroïne surprend le lecteur dès le premier coup d'oeil (p.14; **Figure 52**). L'originalité de sa peau

---

8    L'émission radiophonique 'Roue Libre: invité Enki Bilal' sur France-Inter (mars 1997), rapportait que l'artiste 'vivait exactement le contraire de ce qu'il dessinait' faisant écho à Charaudeau: 'Parler du mal, c'est toujours essayer de l'exorciser à travers le fantasmatique propre à chacun de nous' (1983, 117).

9    Notons que si le texte est présent dans 90% des planches, l'image tient une place extrêmement privilégiée, faisant de cette bande une oeuvre à dominance picturale.

blanche et de ses cheveux bleus la classe à part. Bilal déroge aux conventions classiques de la couleur mais, comme le souligne Druillet, dans un monde futuriste, tout est possible (Groensteen 1996, 38). Les albums de Bilal accorde une place privilégiée aux dessins du corps humain. Symbole de pureté, la blancheur de son corps est marquée jusqu'aux ongles par le 'bleu-Bilal'. La beauté de ces artifices (ses lèvres, ongles et bouts de seins sont bleus également) porte une signification particulière car ils soulignent le pouvoir de séduction de l'héroïne, contribuant à lui donner une image valorisante. L'auteur établit une relation avec ses personnages et sans doute ce personnage féminin a-t-il séduit son créateur. Présente dans quatre-vingt-cinq vignettes l'héroïne confirme sa place de personnage féminin principal dans cette bande.

Quant aux autres personnages féminins, présents dans une vingtaine de vignettes seulement, l'intertextualité entre ces figurantes (p.51) avec les personnages baroques du peintre allemand, Otto Dix, est frappante. Dans le monde sidéral et futuriste de cette bande, les personnages monstrueux à la laideur parfois repoussante, aux visages pétrifiés et cauchemardesques qui entourent l'héroïne contribuent à rehausser sa beauté.

Le trait graphique noir et uni du dessin de Bilal donne un ton 'réaliste' à l'héroïne avec une force du détail qui semble lui prêter vie. La représentation érotique de l'héroïne est aussi soulignée par le graphisme, soit à travers des traits spécifiques, comme ses lèvres charnelles, ses grands yeux marqués de noir, soit par ses formes voluptueuses. La beauté de l'héroïne fait écho aux critères de beauté attachés à notre culture occidentale, qui définit un modèle esthétique, érotique et fétichiste de la beauté du corps.

La représentation textuelle de l'héroïne s'appuie sur son rôle de narrateur principal, où elle s'exprime à l'aide d'un journal intime, présenté sous forme de bandeaux. L'auteur explore une nouvelle technique narrative, réservée jusque-là à la littérature traditionnelle et le texte n'est plus dans les bulles, mais sous l'image, le récitatif témoignant du sensoriel et du souvenir. Malgré ce rôle valorisant, l'héroïne n'est pas l'instigatrice des évènements qui composent le récit. Ce sont plutôt ses amants multiples, existants ou potentiels qui mènent l'action, s'imposant avec des rôles traditionnels de protecteurs ou de libérateurs.

Son amant Jeff Wynyatt la sort d'un 'coma profond', son amoureux John la délivre de la mort, le dieu égyptien Horus la libère de l'emprise de son amant Ivan Vabek et le héro Nikopol, doté de ce don d'ubiquité constitutif du héros de BD, lui offre l'évasion. Sa fonction de journaliste (statut qui correspond aux changements socio-économiques de ces dernières années, qui ont permis à la femme d'accéder à des sphères professionnelles jusque-là inaccessibles aux génerations précédentes), est exprimée davantage par son journal intime que par l'action. En effet, sa crédibilité professionnelle est remise en question dans le texte comme, lors de l'une de ses enquêtes journalistiques, elle se prononce: 'de toute façon les histoires de fusées, ça m'a toujours fait chier... et Europa 1, finalement, je m'en fous' (p.41).

C'est aussi le texte qui permet de souligner la personnalité complexe de l'héroïne et la richesse syntaxique et lexicale de son journal monologal varie d'un registre poétique à un registre très familier. Poète à son heure, lorsqu'elle décrit la mort de son amant, elle offre un portrait fragile et délicat d'elle-même: telle cette métaphore 'j'efface mes larmes bleues'. Démon, elle peut aussi se montrer provocante: 'c'est dans l'espoir de me resauter un jour que tu fais tout ça, Jeff?'. Sa représentation textuelle par des personnages masculins souligne aussi son pouvoir de séduction ('la fille aux cheveux bleus') et son incapacité à contrôler sa vie ('petite conne').

La représentation textuelle et graphique de l'héroïne se double d'une représentation érotique dans cette bande, qui fait écho aux stéréotypes classiques de la fiction populaire. La juxtaposition explicite dès la deuxième page (p.8; **Figure 53**), des mots 'Herotica' et 'women' sur une enseigne qui se détache au premier plan de la case supérieure corrobore le lien, qu'il nous reste à découvrir, entre érotisme et femme, dès la phase initiale du récit.

Sous le pinceau masculin fantasmatique de son créateur, l'héroïne s'épanouit dans un univers où dominent le sexe et la violence, et où elle est typiquement représentée comme femme fatale ou victime. Ainsi, la représentation graphique de l'héroïne portent les signes explicites du discours érotique. Sa beauté sublime et peu commune est la création tout à fait originale et dans le ton du 'bilalisme' évoqué plus haut. Représentée fréquemment sous un angle érotique grâce à un cadrage subtil, elle se laisse surprendre dans son intimité, dévoilant les charmes d'un corps très séduisant: sur quarante-huit cases, dix montrent l'héroïne entièrement nue et neuf cases, demi-nue. Les scènes d'intérieur exhibent ainsi ses formes féminines voluptueuses au regard du lecteur... ses longues jambes galbées ou encore la rondeur de ses seins sont mises en valeur par des pièces vestimentaires suggestives, porte-jarretelles et lingerie fine, signes d'un lien privilégié avec le sexe féminin (Tisseron 1987, 61).

Dans les histoires de science fiction ('*Barbarella*'), le corps de l'héroïne est typiquement exhibé beaucoup plus souvent que celui des personnages masculins qui sont entièrement habillés et parfois même, comme son amoureux John l'alphératzien, masqué. Ainsi, même lorsque rien ne vient le suggérer, la représentation textuelle de l'héroïne se double parfois d'une interprétation érotique visuelle. Bien que rien ne vienne l'indiquer dans le bandeau de la case (p. 13; **Figure 54**), l'héroïne est représentée de dos, en tee-shirt et fesses nues devant le miroir de sa salle-de-bains. C'est un lieu récurrent et symbolique dans cette bande, dotée d'une référence aquatique connotative d'un érotisme et prétexte à l'exploitation de la nudité de l'héroïne. Le lien érotique entre le dessin et le texte est typiquement souvent absent du récit et l'érotisme est présent dans cette case pour remplir une fonction 'distrayante', celle du plaisir du lecteur: la vision dérobée de scènes érotiques fait partie intégrante de la BD, marque évidente des albums pour adultes.

La fonction fétichiste de l'héroïne est réalisée dans sa représentation de femme fatale. Ainsi, tel un signe extérieur du processus interne à la transformation de l'héroïne en femme fatale, son apparence vestimentaire dans certaines cases prend une signification particulière. Sa tenue (classique) de femme fatale, robe courte noire très décolletée devant et dos, bas, jarretelles et talons hauts fait appel aux fantasmes masculins.[10] Cette transformation s'opère également dans le texte qui renforce sa représentation de femme-objet: 'je change rarement de coiffure, ce soir j'en ai envie'. La dynamique visuelle de la case de la page 49 est fortement sexualisée (**Figure 55**). Le cadre s'est agrandi pour épouser la position très suggestive de l'héroïne: étendue les jambes écartées sur un lit s'offrant à un homme, les seins nus que dévoile sa robe et son porte-jarretelles, qui vient compléter son apanage de femme fatale, pas si fatale.

Tour à tour victime de ses propres fantasmes sanglants et témoin horrifié d'un carnage réel cette fois, elle soulève la sympathie du lecteur, 'ce qui se passe cette nuit est en effet effroyable'. Il y a ici un message moral évident qui remet en question l'horreur de ce monde et le condamne. Cette case, qui montre le carnage de son partenaire, dont la tête éclate sous la pression de l'aigle Horus, marque un changement dans la structure profonde du récit et cette violence, soulignée aussi par les couleurs chaudes de la case, est choquante pour le lecteur. Les signes graphiques de cette violence, mêlée à la nudité (partielle ici) de l'héroïne, correspondent à un discours typiquement masculin et ancre la fonction de voyeurisme dans le rôle du lecteur de manière implicite.[11]

---

10   Notons comme exemple l'apparence aguichante du costume porte par Wonder Woman: 'Le discours implicite d'un costume est loin d'être un simple ensemble arbitraire de conventions' (Reynolds 1992, 29).
11   S. Tisseron rend compte de la façon dont la BD est encore 'si souvent rangée du côté de la transgression'; le plaisir que procure la lecture d'une BD vient, selon lui, bien souvent de ce que 'le sexe et la violence n'y sont pas cachés, d'où un genre avant tout masculin.' Tisseron compare ainsi le déroulement narratif de la BD à un 'strip-tease,

Cette fonction se double, dans une case de la page 20 (**Figure 56**), du voyeurisme du personnage masculin, dont les bottes de cuir enserrent presque le corps nu de l'héroïne, à qui il 'inflige' un 'supplice' avec de 'l'eau glacée'. Ce code textuel oriente le lecteur vers une interprétation spécifique et vient renforcer les détails graphiques, qui deviennent évocateurs à leur tour. Les bottes lourdes, les pans du long manteau noir, la position en plongée de Wynyatt s'opposent à la nudité et la vulnérabilité de l'héroïne et dont le visage porte les signes visibles de la souffrance.

\*\*\*

En conclusion, la représentation intimiste de l'héroïne impose au lecteur de confronter seul, tout au long du récit, la nudité de cette femme-papier, confirmant la place privilégiée de l'érotisation des images de femme dans cette bande, exploitée au profit de la violence, phénomène typique dans la fiction populaire. Malgré l'originalité textuelle et graphique de cette bande, qui s'accompagne d'une utilisation distincte des couleurs, il est difficile ici de distinguer une évolution notable de la représentation de la femme depuis la première bande adulte érotique (*Barbarella*). Bilal montre une volonté de satisfaire ses lecteurs en exploitant, une fois encore, le potentiel érotique de l'héroïne dans une thématique de violence, de sexe et d'érotisme, de voyeurisme et de fétichisme.

La représentation de l'héroïne comme femme-objet renforce les images stéréotypées rétrogrades et accablantes pour les femmes dans ce média, où dans un monde presque exclusivement masculin, les femmes ne contrôlent pas leurs propres images. A son tour, l'ambiguïté de l'auteur réside en même temps dans sa volonté de se démarquer de ces clichés. Mais, loin de créer une nouvelle image de la femme, il fait une représentation ambiguë qui valorise initialement cette femme-papier mais qui s'écaille au fil du récit au cours d'une lecture plus attentive, mettant à jour l'ambiguïté de l'héroïne. D'une part, la beauté du dessin réaliste et non-conformiste de l'héroïne, la forme novatrice de la narration (son journal) et son statut de journaliste consacrent cette femme-papier au rang d'héroïne. D'autre part, l'acceptation des conventions liées au média lui-même, chargé d'une fonction (érotique) distrayante par son créateur, pèsent lourdement sur le portrait complexe de l'héroïne, qui vient rejoindre la collection analogue d'images stéréotypées de femme passives et n'existant que comme objet du désir masculin.

mimé par l'écoulement des vignettes et les lignes blanches qui les séparent, l'équivalent des lignes noires du porte-jarretelles' (1987, 61).

A l'arrivée du nouveau millénaire, après s'être affranchie de tous les tabous et avoir exploré les expériences narratives et graphiques les plus diverses, souhaitons que la bande dessinée, enrichie par une présence plus importante d'auteurs féminins,[12] continue de véhiculer des images de femmes plus proches de celles de la réalité et que *La Femme Piège* reste le symbole, pour les générations futures, de l'époque révolue des larmes bleues...

## Bibliography

Baetens, Jan, and Pascal Lefèvre 1993. *Pour une lecture moderne de la bande dessinée,* Bruxelles: Sherpa/CBBD.

Bilal, Enki 1990. *La Femme Piège,* Nouvelle éd, Genève: Humanoïdes Associées.

Bilal, Enki 1999. *L'Etat des Stocks milleneufcentquatrevingtdixneuf,* Genève: Les Humanoïdes Associés.

Charaudeau, Patrick 1983. *Langage et discours,* Paris: Hachette.

Forbes, Jill, and Mike Kelly 1995. *An Introduction to French Cultural Studies,* Oxford: Oxford University Press.

Gaumer, Patrick, and Claude Moliterni 1994. *Dictionnaire Mondial de la Bande Dessinée,* Paris: Larousse.

Groensteen, Thierry 1996. *La Bande dessinée,* Toulouse: Les Essentiels Milan.

Horn, Maurice 1977. *Women in the Comics,* New York: Chelsea House Publishers.

Joly, Martine 1993. *Introduction à l'analyse de l'image,* Paris: Nathan.

---

[12] Citons Claire Brétécher, la plus connue parmi les quelques auteurs féminins, dont le parcours est décrit par Forbes (1995, 251): 'She co-founded the magazine *L'Echo des Savanes* in 1972 with Gotlib and Mandryka as a breakaway from *Pilote*. The following year she began her long running weekly page in *Le Nouvel Observateur* under the general title 'Les Frustrés'. Aimed at, and depicting, the post-1968 educated middle classes, it dissects the hypocrisy and self-deception of intellectuals or would-be intellectuals on the slippery surface between overweening complacency and existential Angst.'

Lainé, Pascal 1974. *La Femme et ses images*, Paris: Stock.

Massart, Pierre, Jean-Louis Nicks, and Jean-Louis Tilleuil 1984. *La bande dessinée à l'Université et ailleurs: études sémiotiques et bibliographiques*, Louvain-la-Neuve: Presses universitaires de Louvain.

Moliterni, Claude et al. 1996. *Les Aventures de la BD*, Paris: Gallimard.

Pierre, Michel 1976. *La Bande dessinée*, Paris: Larousse.

Pilloy, Annie 1994. *Les Compagnes des héros de BD: des femmes et des bulles*, Paris: L'Harmattan.

Le Point 1975. 'Astérix manque de femmes', 151, 11 août 1975, 46.

Propp, Vladimir 1965. *Morphologie du conte*, Paris: Seuil.

Peeters, Benoît 1993. *La Bande dessinée*, Paris: Flammarion.

Reynolds, Richard 1992. *Super Heroes: A Modern Mythology*, London: B.T. Batsford Ltd.

Tisseron, Serge 1987. *Psychanalyse de la bande dessinée*, Paris: Presses Universitaires de France.

# Les Bidochon assujettis académiques

## Libbie McQuillan
## University of Glasgow

The hugely popular and resolutely funny Robert and Raymonde Bidochon, stars not only of the BD but also of stage and screen, are traditionally described by critics as caricatures of the *Français moyen*, the *Français très moyen*, as the phrase frequently goes.[1] Although it would be a difficult statistic to prove, most readers' reaction to the series is to claim to know their very own Bidochon family. Indeed, their widespread popularity has merited them an entry in the 1999 *Petit Robert de noms propres*.

Unlike most artists of his generation, Christian Binet (the series' author—born in Tulle in 1947) never worked for Goscinny's *Pilote* magazine (1959-1989). From 1969 to 1977, Binet worked for various magazines directed by the Catholic Fleurus and Bayard Press: *Record*, *Formule 1*, *Djin*. Marcel Gotlib noticed Binet's work in a minor adult journal *Mormoil*, and asked him to collaborate on his newly founded *Fluide glacial* (1975-present). Binet's collaboration at *Mormoil* had been brief, the space of seven issues, when he made an almost direct leap from a very particular sector of the children's press to adult BD.[2] Binet's first offering for *Fluide glacial* was Kador the Kantian philosophising dog in 1977.

---

[1] The theatrical script is available in Binet 1990. The film *Les Bidochon* was produced in 1997, directed by Serge Korber.

[2] *Mormoil*'s own existence was equally brief from 1974-1975, publishing only these seven issues. Binet had previously published *Poupon la peste* with Fleurus, which recounted the antics of a troublesome and somewhat violent baby. The *Poupon la peste* series was not published in album format by Bayard or Fleurus as the Catholic publishing houses had no tradition of doing so. The albums, of which there are two volumes, were first published by *Fluide glacial*'s AUDIE label in 1979 and 1980.

By 1977, *Fluide glacial* had become a monthly magazine and was thriving even without advertising revenue.[3] Despite Binet's personal lack of notoriety (he had not as yet published an album), Gotlib selected him for his team. During the 1960s and 1970s, a repeated cycle emerged in the BD world, that of an author coming to national attention thanks to another author/sponsor. Indeed, Gotlib was Goscinny's protégé par excellence.[4] This was no doubt because certain structures and publishing supports were in place in Paris, which guaranteed national notoriety if an author was published in these particular publications. Both Paris and *Pilote* had centralised post-war BD production. This cultural centralisation of Paris was all-important in the rise of the *9ème art* in the 1970s. It was as a direct result of the complicity of the younger members of the *Pilote* group led to the breakaway and creation of adult journals such as *L'Echo des Savanes* (1972), *Métal hurlant* (1974) and *Fluide glacial* (1975).

Almost all histories of the BD point to the *Echo* as the first truly adult French BD journal. The *Echo* was the inheritor of the spirit of the illustrated (twice-banned) satirical journal *Hara-Kiri* (1960). Despite drawing inspiration from the American underground comix movement (its narcissistic, self-referential and autobiographic tendencies for example), *L'Echo des Savanes* had more thematically in common with its French satirical predecessors than the work circulated by the American Underground Press Syndicate. *L'Echo des Savanes* was like the *Astérix* phenomenon in the late sixties and the new more adult *Pilote* that emerged 1968-1973 in that it was above all the satirical nature of its contents that BD became more adult. It was thus by borrowing from BD's turn of the century journalistic satirical roots that BD took its first steps towards adulthood in the 1970s.

The *Echo* itself was in turn to give birth to direct stylistic descendants.[5] *Fluide* was such a successor and proposed a similar type of sexual and scatological humour. This time, however, the emphasis was on specific and recurring series rather than on self-expression, self-

---

[3] *Fluide* like the *Echo* was originally tri-monthly. As with *Hara-Kiri*, *Fluide* did not originally benefit from any advertising revenue primarily because of the transgressive nature of its contents.

[4] Marcel Gotlib deliberately worked in the same manner as Goscinny, hand-picking his authors, as did Jean-Pierre Dionnet for *Metal hurlant*.

[5] Adult-satirical humour as exemplified by the *Echo* has popularly endured in France Other BD magazines in the same vein were much later established, such as *Psikopat* in 1982 and *Bo Doï* in 1992, testifying to adult-satirical humour's continued popularity. The 'newspaper' *Charlie-hebdo* carries on a more political strand of the tradition as do the *Guignols de l'info* daily on Canal +. In its BD form, Gotlib's *Fluide glacial* is its principal and longest running representative.

promotion and one shot *planches*. In this sense *Fluide* marked a return, at least in structure if not in content, to more traditional BD. This is perhaps not so surprising given the way in which adult BD first emerged in France. The new adult BD directly parodied the traditions and subverted the style, content and constraints of traditional BDs from which it evolved.

When the Bidochons emerged in the 1980s, BD had already been accepted as an adult art form and BD could be, almost unproblematically, expected to contain more adult humour. The Bidochons as a series presented itself as a BD series proper with recurring characters, vestimentary codes and repeated comic idiosyncrasies. The series thus conformed to many of the canonical expectations of a traditional BD. This acceptance, combined with the fact the series came packaged with certain traditional BD elements, helped to increase the series' popularity and accessibility with the general public.[6]

At first glance it would seem that the cultural specificity of such a popular series are unquestionable. However, the series borrows from wider European comic literary traditions. This paper argues that the very obvious 'Frenchness' of the series is, in itself, a joke and not the primary motivation of the series. Moreover, on closer inspection, the inclusion of more traditional BD elements does not stop the series from subverting some of the less obvious codes of the *école franco-belge*, nor stop the black and white caricature emerging, at times, as subtle characterisation.

The Bidochon series is an ambivalent mix of borrowing and invention, combined with culturally specific and non-specific elements. In particular, the comically exaggerated 'Frenchness' of the series, the series' very own caricature of cultural specificity, would not prevent a carefully crafted translation of the series into another language. This chapter will therefore develop these problematics and examine the development of the Bidochons, as a series *per se*.

Clearly there are many aspects of the Bidochons' life and personalities that are, undeniably, a caricature of some sort of French rustic peasants. Straightforwardly, the Bidochons are a caricature of a *campagnard* aunt and uncle or of a particularly disagreeable neighbour. There is, however, more to the laughter of the Bidochon series than this initial reaction. Indeed, it is not so much Robert and Raymonde who are caricatured as specifically French, but, as it will emerge, it is rather the French institutions and their bureaucrats who exercise power over the Bidochons' life that are the real target of Binet's social satire.

---

[6] The Bidochons is one of France's most successful selling series. In 1999, *Les Bidochon toniques* sold 180, 000 copies (Pialut 2000, 65).

Arguably, the tradition of caricature proper is to attack the powerful and the political. In comparison Robert and Raymonde can, on one level, be reduced to essentially bawdy comic figures. Beyond the obvious linguistic and graphic caricature of the 'Frenchness' of Robert Eugène Louis Bidochon and Raymonde Jeanne Martine Galopin-Bidochon, and the buffoonery of their Punch-and-Judy-type antics, lies a much more sensitive portrait of two seemingly insignificant characters. An unhappily married couple, of modest means and ambitions, struggle with a society that has given them little chance in life. Much of the series' humour comes from the slippage between the Bidochons representing the remnants of a more rustic France, and the Bidochons living in a global consumer society. Living a timeless past in the ostensible present, the Bidochons are de-racinated in an urban environment.[7]

A clear distinction can be made between two types of Bidochons albums. Firstly, the albums which concentrate on the banality of their daily private existence (which can be conveniently labelled the 'home' albums). Secondly, and in contra-distinction, the albums, which involve the Bidochons coping badly with, mass phenomena such as television, the French social security system or package holidays (which can be predictably called the 'away' albums).[8] The distinction is being made not only to facilitate the analysis of Binet's corpus of work but also because there is a shift in the nature of the comedy when 'playing at home' or when 'playing away'.

Initially, this may sound like an attempt to trivialise the subject matter. However, a great many comic BD series rely on this sort of repeated paradigm of distinction. Notably, the *Astérix* series is either set in the Gaulish village or abroad. More generally, the home and away distinction can be thought of as belonging to a wider literary tradition, such as the 'home' and 'away' division in Rabelais's Gargantua series,

---

[7] Although it is unclear where the Bidochons actually live exactly, they are undeniably a remnant of a more rustic and rural France. For example, when in *Roman d'amour* they meet for the first time in the Gare St Lazare, Paris, Raymonde carries a joint of ham and Robert a watering can for identification. Unfortunately, however, most of the other travellers in the station are also carrying watering cans, causing comic confusion. Binet is perhaps suggesting, via this joke, that such nostalgia for the countryside is a not exclusively symptomatic of the Bidochons.

[8] There are eight away albums: *En vacances, En habitation à loyer modéré, Maison sucrée maison, En voyage organisé, Assujettis sociaux, Les Fous sont lâchés, Usagers de la route, Téléspectateurs*, and nine home albums, *Roman d'amour, Ragots intimes, Vent du soir, Matin midi et soir suivi par matin, midi et soir, La Vie de mariage, Des Instants inoubliables, Bidochon mère (môman), Les Bidochon toniques, Les Bidochon utilisent le forfait.*

or Voltaire's parody of the picaresque novel *Candide*, which exaggeratedly swings between Eldorado and one's own back garden. The comparison of the elements of this dichotomy helps to generate some conclusions about the nature of the series' ambivalent laughter.

It is worth noting in passing that Binet has claimed that almost every Bidochon adventure has an autobiographical source:

> Il y a toujours un peu d'exagération, c'est une caricature, de l'humour, donc à un certain moment, je pousse plus loin, mais tous les points de départ sont authentiques. Même pour leur Roman d'amour c'est l'histoire de ma mère; elle s'est remariée par une agence matrimoniale avec tout ce que ça peut comporter.[9]

The comedy situations are therefore allegedly based on real, if somewhat exaggerated, experiences but are significantly narrated through two stock, buffoon type, figures in order to increase laughter. Perhaps this explains, in part, why readers so often claim to recognise the Bidochons as people they know but never as themselves.

In twenty years Binet has published twenty-one albums featuring the Bidochons.[10] It may seem somewhat surprising therefore that the series, which on average publishes an album annually, and which can be described best as a social critique, does not follow the various social concerns of the 1980s and 1990s. Conventionally, journalistic satire deals with topical issues, ridiculing different fads and fashions. Binet's comment on modern consumerism emerges, however, from the contradictions and conflicts arising between the private world of the Bidochons and the real world that surrounds them.

The Bidochons are, of course, unavoidably involved with the modern world: they meet via a dating agency, they buy new electronic gadgets that predictably never work, and they once managed to go jogging. However, these are not the main thematic concerns of the series despite generating plentiful humorous anecdotes. The humour in the home albums comes from the Bidochons' naive misinterpretations: they often literally follow the advice in newspapers and on television.

---

[9] Binet, cited in Frémion 1984, 16. Some of Binet's other works have an overt autobiographical basis; for example *L'Institution* is based on his memories spent at Catholic run summer camps and a short visual story in *Histoires ordinaires* (Binet 1979, 5-10), is based on his brother's death in a road accident. Reliance on an author's biography, interpreting his/her original intentions in order to read a text is, of course, theoretically suspect. However, in terms of the BD researcher's starting place there is very often little critical work to which to refer.

[10] There are seventeen albums focused on the couple and four focused on their dog Kador.

Lacking any powers of discernment they believe everything they hear and see. On discovering that their horoscope predicts a happy day for them, their feuding ends and plans for dinner are made but are subsequently cancelled when they realise the paper chanced upon is yesterday's news (Binet 1989, 8). Or again, after watching a television documentary, Robert insists:

> Il faut mettre un préservatif si on veut pas attraper leur sida [...]. Pourquoi tout le monde pourrait l'avoir et puis pas nous !!! (Binet 1989, 16)

Although the reader laughs at their literal stupidity, it is more the absurdity of society that is in question. By documenting their ordinary mundane existence and their inability to evolve, Binet is in truth attacking the society that keeps the Bidochons down rather than the Bidochons themselves.

Binet himself comments of his heroes:

> Leur monde se réduit à leur salle à manger. Ils n'ont pas la capacité de se nourrir d'assimiler la vie qui s'épanouit autour d'eux. Ils sont pris dans un carcan. Ils n'ont pas conscience de ce qu'ils subissent et donc ne peuvent pas se défendre. Robert, agressif, gueule à tout bout de champ. Il cherche à s'imposer pour compenser son mal-vivre. (Binet, cited in Tiberi 1991, 113)

Robert and Raymonde have, therefore been fighting with each other for the last twenty years. If Binet were overly concerned with documenting the evolution of modern French society in the 1980s the Bidochons would most certainly be divorced by now. Binet's work is indeed social commentary, but, significantly, there is very little which differentiates the thematic concerns of the albums produced over the last twenty years.

Originally, the Bidochons were the stupid and somewhat cruel owners of the would-be Kantian philosophising dog. Robert and Raymonde were then only the *mise-en-valeur* characters of Kador. However, the Bidochons quickly evolved form this secondary position to become the stars of their own series.[11] Most notably, the nature of Raymonde regressed from being a female version of Robert, aggressive and outspoken, to a frustrated, disillusioned, submissive housewife, who had almost seemed to give up expecting anything good from life after

---

[11]    'Au départ les Bidochon sont des personnages secondaires, les faire-valoir de Kador envers qui ils sont plutôt méchants. Ma vision des êtres ayant évolués, les Bidochon se sont humanisés. Dans mes premières histoires mes personnages étaient très caricaturaux [...] Actuellement on se rend compte que les Bidochon sont des victimes de la société. Au départ vu leur condition leur vie était vouée à l'échec à la médiocrité'. (Binet cited in Tiberi 1991, 112).

making the mistake of marrying Robert.[12] Binet backtracked to invent for them a biography in *Roman d'amour* (1980c) where it is revealed they met via a computing dating agency and finally adopt Kador as a result of Robert's impotence.

This act of rewriting is in itself significant. Firstly, the album provides a coherent background for the rest of the series, and indeed launches the narratives as a traditional BD series with recurring heroes, rather than episodic *planches* with incidental characters. Robert and Raymonde retell their story, inventing ten years of shared history. They face forward on a black background addressing the reader. The Bidochons are almost never featured without a background environment. They are both product of, and subordinated by, their environment. However, in this album much fun is had by not drawing any background or by situating them in a background which has no connection whatsoever with the story. Binet plays with the convention of BD background, by informing the reader through written text and an arrow what we should assume the non-existent background looks like.

By subverting such BD convention, Binet calls into question the illusions of reality and movement that the reading processes of a BD produce. Similarly, this is the only album in which the unspoken convention of not addressing the reader, which is employed in order to encourage the illusions of movement and reality, is subverted. This album provides the basis for the Bidochon play. However, theatrical elements already exist within the text, as Binet offers the reader a BD version of the theatrical suspension of disbelief. Whilst calling into question the illusory and escapist elements of the BD as a medium, he offers us a fictitious comic story, but one that is of social relevance.

From their honeymoon, spent rather unhappily (for Raymonde) at Robert's parents' house, they progress to their first holiday, in a holiday village, and finally win an exotic package trip to Russia, thanks to a 'Patzani Ravioli' competition. Moving from their first flat in an ex-brothel to a housing scheme, they finally install themselves in the house they order to be built (but which is mistakenly built backwards by the team of Algerian immigrant workmen who read the instruction booklet

---

[12] The Bidochons first appear in *Histoires ordinaires* (Binet 1979, 15-20), featured in a collection of independent stories of about four to five *planches* in length. They were curiously named Marthe and Richard. Binet extended this 'sketch' about the structural inconveniences of living in HLM into an album (Binet 1982). Significantly, Marthe is more aggressive than the subsequent Raymonde. Binet gives no reason for this change of name, but the new alliteration is certainly more comic, announcing a comic duo and also follows in a whole tradition of literary alliterative heroes, such as the medieval Erec and Enide. Perhaps Raymonde also loses something of her independence, by having a more phonetically similar name.

from right to left). By the end of these first four albums the Bidochons establish their place in society and the rhythm of their life, and *Les Bidochon* as a series has defined the nature of its humour and areas of social attack.

Significantly, as the series progresses, the comedy duo develops the added dimension of also being portrayed as a couple, and they begin to escape their caricature. If we were to relieve Robert of his beret and his braces, which he refuses to remove even in bed, and Raymonde of her kitchen apron, there is very little of them graphically which remains typically French. They are, after all, the only French people in the series dressed in a traditional manner, excepting Robert's parents, which thereby signals them as the rustic fools and traditional buffoon characters. Such anachronistic and caricatured dress is an ironic comment on the BD convention of the hero appearing timelessly, year after year, in the same clothing. The comment is made obvious by the fact the Bidochon family are the only participants dressed as such in a contemporary setting.

Ignoring their repeated diet of herring and potatoes or a slice of ham, such food is principally a sign of both a modest income and modest ambition, there is again very little that remains characteristically French. They certainly remain *moyen* but are no longer necessarily French. What remains is a combination of their own comic idiosyncrasies and a fundamental unhappiness caused by their social status. In fact, any unhappily married couple could argue endlessly as our heroes do. Raymonde's continual complaints of Robert's lack of romance, Robert's complaints that the odour of his wife puts him off his food or that the food is cold, are perhaps not the most immediate hallmarks of a caricatured French couple.

Instead, such a set up is the basis of any domestic comedy; although dissatisfied and disagreeing between themselves they never seek to find an exterior reason for their unhappiness. Robert's domination of Raymonde is based on his inability to lord it over anybody else, including the dog. Their social circle is limited to two or three friends who rarely deign to visit, and their world revolves around the hire-purchased sofa and television, the kitchen and food, and habitually, on the first Saturday evening of every month, the bedroom.

Repetitious *cases* structuring, repeating panels of similar dimensions and shapes with *plans américans*, minimalist background and depth of field usually express this sort of banal repetition of their actions. The visual movement within the *planches* is most often contained within the panels and not suggested by the relationship between the panels. Frequently, sketches of Robert are superimposed on each other: when Robert is angry his head is sketched several times within a single frame. This is not only graphically funny, but also confines several movements to one panel which conventionally should only represent one fractional instant. Such a strategy is an ironic comment on the traditional dynamism of a *mise-en-page*, which suggests movement via the panels' interdependency rather than their self-sufficiency.

Similarly, linguistically, the joke is often contained to one panel rather than shared over several panels. Thus a speaker often has two or three connected speech bubbles within the same panel. The panels therefore tend to resemble the single panels of a cartoon rather than forming a continuous strip. This privileging of the single panel could be considered more as a traditional satirical technique than as a BD technique.

On a linguistic level it is worth noting the very French rhythm Binet creates with his *lettrage* within the word balloons. Whereas the dynamism of a *récit* is conventionally left to the *mise-en-page*, because most of the comedy comes from their conversational exchanges, Binet ensures a *lettrage* that is in itself dynamic. For example Robert comments over the space of two inter-linked balloons contained within the same panel:

> Je fais ça pour
> t'embêter, mais mets-toi
> un peu à ma place! Si tu
> crois que c'est facile
> de se lever dans les
> mauvaises haleines
> dès le matin !!
>
> déjà que
> je suis
> d'un na-
> turel patraque. (Binet 1989, 8)

In its original format, the entire lettering is capitalised. The words are spaced in such a way to bring maximal attention to the lexical choice itself and to the irony of Robert's exclamation that he is of a rather delicate nature. The space within the panel is not constraining, yet such a double balloon layout is chosen to increase the comedy. Although Binet's word spacing and choice often seems particularly French, it would not be inconceivable to achieve similar effects with translations.

The humour exemplified in the 'home' albums is crass, bawdy and scatological; a great deal of humour is derived from Robert breaking wind in bed. Not only is this the sort of humour the reader expects from

*Fluide glacial* (indeed such humour is the self-styled vocation of the magazine as its subtitle suggests: 'Amusement, humour, dérision, hilarité et toutes ces sortes de choses'), but also the insistence on this sort of humour probably explains its continued success amongst a certain readership. Such scatological humour, as exemplified with *Les Bidochon*, *Fluide* and the *Echo*, is also part of a much wider European tradition of popular bawdy laughter. A comparison could be made between the crasser scatological elements of the Bidochons, and Bakhtin's theories of the democracy created through the liberating use of the bawdy and of swearing in terms of the popular carnivalesque feast.[13]

The laughter at Robert Bidochon's bodily functions comes from a degree of superiority that we adopt as readers. Unlike Monsieur Bidochon, the reader would never defecate in the sea and then tell a young boy where to find fish (Binet 1981, 6-17). The purely scatological serves to deride Robert as all too human. Such incidents are also, characteristically, *Fluide glacial*-type shock tactics rather than a comment on being on a French holiday. Importantly, there is perhaps a link between such derision and the derision in classical comedy at physical infirmities, or indeed the traditional description of caricature as being an exaggeration of people's deformities.[14] Although both reader and author sympathise with the social status of the Bidochons, Binet still holds them up to the reader for physical ridicule, and the reader laughs hypocritically.

However, the laughter is not purely and simply bawdy; the reason the Bidochons cannot have children is a result of the curious fact that M. Bidochon testicles never dropped. This is not straightforwardly funny, even though the images of Robert's reaction to the news as he desperately jumps up and down to let gravity take effect are. Raymonde's childlessness is also the source of almost all her angst and her feeling of failure in life. This disappointment is portrayed with sympathy and kindness rather than derision. Large oblong, vertically elongated, panels, becoming progressively thinner, interrupt the usual rhythm of Binet's horizontal cases. Robert and Raymonde seem to move into the distance, becoming smaller and smaller, by moving to the centre

---

[13] Such considerations, however, perhaps explain the wider and persistent popularity of the series, with a diverse range of readers despite its, at times, outrageous content (Bakhtin, 1968).

[14] 'Among painters and sculptors caricature signifies a method of making portraits, in which they aim at the greatest resemblance of the person portrayed, while at the same time, for fun and sometimes for mockery, they disproportionately increase and emphasise some defects of the features they copy, so that the portrait as a whole appears to be the sitter himself, whilst its components are changed'. Filipo Baldinucci 1681, *Dictionnary of Artistic Terms*, cited in Gombrich 1977, 290.

of the rectangles. At this moment, their drama becomes more poignant for the reader.

This kind of ambivalence complicates the nature of the series' laughter, and of course in terms of *Fluide* seems out of joint. At such moments, the caricature of Robert and Raymonde thus tends towards characterisation. Such a sympathetic reaction on the part of the reader is not only achieved through structural spatial arrangements but also through the complicity built up between readers and characters in such a long running series. It is striking that, despite the seemingly static nature of the couple's lives, that Binet can, at will, subvert the nature of the series in an instant. At this moment the Bidochons are no longer the traditionally fixed BD caricatures but are pitiful characters deserving of our sympathy.

The laughter then in the 'home' albums is, in many senses, very traditional, and European, precisely because it is essentially domestic comedy. The comedy is always very predictable, we know that a gift offered will cause a fight, we know a night out at a party will end in disaster. This predictability is again a paradigm belonging to all comedy. This familiarity, however, also creates complicity, and we therefore sympathise with the Bidochons as victims of their own mediocrity even though we never expect them to better themselves.

In comparison, the 'away' albums in which the Bidochons escape their daily drudgery are generally less about the Bidochons than the mass phenomena in which they participate. On holiday the Bidochons automatically bond with others of the same social grouping, they move in a herd without questioning their movements and are constantly assured by others that they are having a good time. Robert and Raymonde therefore re-become incidental characters; their reactions are entirely dependent on the rest of the group.

The institutions that surround them are in a sense more French than they are: the VVF (in the canteen there are pigeonholes to store your bottle of cheap wine, missing bottles frequently causing arguments), the tax inspector's office (where Robert feigns a generalised cancer in order to avoid paying an unmerited fine), the French penchant for 'les tables rondes' on television (where Robert appears as a 'spécialiste sur le tas'). The structures and phenomena are recognisably French. These phenomena mark Les Bidochon as French in a very obvious way. French bureaucracy is perhaps Binet's favourite area of attack and the bureaucrats the true focus of his caricature of French society.

In *Les Fous sont lâchés* tax inspectors are described as originating from the sewers and consisting entirely of mud. A letter is sent to Raymonde inviting her to collect her widow's pension; the government computer has registered Robert as dead. The idea that a computer organises and determines one's life is taken to a logical but absurd conclusion. The streets become apocalyptically inundated with official paper and Raymonde follows the President's instructions calling on all citizens to digest internally as many forms as they can to participate in clearing up the mess.[15] This sort of nonsensical exaggeration is not present in the home albums, but the hyperbole here serves to caricature French administration.

Significantly, the away albums form the basis of the filmic version of the Bidochons and the home albums the theatrical version. Their domestic antics become a *comédie de mœurs* and their ventures in to the outside world become a cinematic sociological portrait. Such a division of the home and away material perhaps reveal more about general expectations of the content of French cinema and theatre than the BD themselves.

Without the humour of their iconic representation the film tends towards drama. The film is faithful to Binet's text (almost word for word) but has an overall serious tone lacking in the BD. It is of course impossible to translate the medium specificities of iconic BD into film, however, since more than the graphics are lost in the transition. The film reproduces a scene from *Les Fous sont lâchés* where Robert tries to obtain a 'pre-appointment form' in a hospital for Raymonde. Unfortunately, he unwittingly asks the boss rather than the boss's secretary, to which the boss replies, 'c'est pourtant visible que je suis le chef' (Binet 1987, 8-10). In the BD as Robert persists on having the form, the boss's sign marked 'chef' becomes bigger and bigger until it is the size of the entire planet. The literal meaning of the phrase becomes visualised. In the BD hospital Raymonde sits unblinkingly beside comedy cobwebbed skeletons. The iconic specificity is therefore all-important in creating the laughter. In the away albums the pair cease their domestic squabbles. They are united against the common enemy of the outsider. In the film, the pair emerges as downtrodden yet happy to be together, which is not entirely in keeping with the spirit of the series.[16]

---

[15] Much of the humour in *Les Fous sont lâchés* caricaturing the nightmare-ish aspects of French bureaucracy is perhaps borrowed from Terry Gilliam's 1985 film *Brazil*. In particular, presenting the bureaucrats as mud that emerges from sewers echoes the constant use in the film of plumbing and heating ducts somehow being connected with twenty-four hour State surveillance.

[16] Curiously, in the film, Robert works as a door to door salesman selling encyclopaedias, which seems entirely at odds with the life led by the BD Robert.

Perhaps one reason the Bidochons are so popular is precisely because the immediate reaction is to think of them as specifically French. The beret and braces reinforce certain myths about being French. The *Astérix* series' popularity with the French is based on the reinforcement of the popular myth amongst the French that they are descended from the Gauls. The Bidochons, in comparison, are always the Other. They are our neighbours; the portrait is so unflattering it could never be ourselves.

The comedy techniques are based on a much wider European comic tradition than purely French, but the structures that surround them in the away albums are unmistakably French. This perhaps helps to give an overall impression of 'Frenchness' to the series. However, the Bidochons are, arguably, not that culturally specific. Binet has cast the Bidochons as both Algerian immigrants and as Louis XIV and spouse in two *planches* unpublished as a series (Tiberi 1991, 43, 122-25). Louis XIV Bidochon's one concern is planting his vegetable plot at Versailles whereas M. Ben Bidochon refuses to answer the telephone to the President of the Republic because he is in the toilet. Despite nationality, time and social status, the gags and the Punch and Judy antics remain the same.

One reason the readership of *Fluide* probably love the series so much is precisely because it refuses to recognise any sort of multiculturalism in modern France. In a sense, both Binet and *Fluide* are like Robert and resolutely refuse to be politically correct. Black and white then does not only reflect the mediocrity and monotony of the Bidochons' life, but reminds us that the Bidochons are in a sense fixed in the 1950s, in a non-modern, non-multicoloured and non-multiethnic society.

Although the Bidochons' appeal is much wider than the magazine itself, the series was, in part, created to compliment the nature of the magazine's laughter. *Fluide glacial*'s continued success in the industry is, on one level, perplexing. *Fluide* is the longest running BD magazine in France and has outlived every other BD magazine support. Indeed, the initial impulse to scandalise petit-bourgeois sensibilities in the early 1970s is still the motivation that drives *Fluide glacial* today.

*Fluide* was taken over in the early 1990s by the publishing giant Flammarion and is still incredibly successful, with a monthly readership of ninety thousand and an annual turnover (in 2000) of fifty seven million francs of which seventeen million francs is clear profit (Pialut 2000, 62). Although the nature of its derisive and transgressive laughter, is arguably a counter-current in the 'sophisticated' and 'artistic' world of 1990s adult BD, and therefore remains a 1970s timepiece, *Fluide* is still very much appreciated and enjoyed. Its existence as a monthly journal seems equally anachronistic in the now album-dominated industry.[17] However, the satire of *Fluide* has still more in common with its BD predecessors and its journalistic links, than with the 1990s BD market. Like our heroes Robert and Raymonde, *Fluide* is somehow relegated to the past, but it is an existence that is both popular and profitable.

Binet created a winning series that defined his brand image. This brand image was aesthetically recognisable as belonging to the genre of adult-satirical humour, which had defined its parameters in the 1970s. Like the hard backed album itself, which came to be a trademark of all French BD, or an easily recognisable French branding and packaging of the comics form, the Bidochons became highly visible as Binet's trademark. The Bidochons inevitably became the object of spin-off merchandising and plastic products. On one level, Binet's transposition of *Les Bidochon* into play and film format was not only proof positive of the series popularity, but also, quite simply, yet another BD by-product.

Binet's work contained culturally specific subversions of Franco-Belgian BD codes, whilst adding his own unique formal inventions by reinterpreting these codes. Ultimately, the new cultural heritage for French BD that emerged in the 1970s stylistically and jokingly referred to its roots, which had emerged earlier in the century in both France and Belgium. In as much that the laughter of *Les Bidochon* is a hybrid mixture of literary based comedy and journalistic satire; Binet's work reflects BD's hybrid origins emerging from turn of the century observational comedy and the illustrated press. These origins, in turn, partly explain the popular success of the series with a wide adult readership.

We could perhaps compare the false appearance of 'Frenchness' of the Bidochons to the status of the BD as an art in France. Certain myths are superficially evoked in the Bidochons to make them appear French, yet comic borrowings come from a much wider cultural heritage. In the same way as BD's ultimate State institutionalisation was arguably motivated primarily by politics, and the BD became chiefly a vehicle for a more general promotion of French culture abroad rather than a vehicle for the promotion of the comics form, so too *Les Bidochon* is a vehicle for a more general laughter and comedy rather than specifically French comedy.

It is perhaps for such reasons then that the Bidochons remain relatively unknown outside their native country. It is not that the humour is specifically French or untranslatable, but rather France has advertised

---

[17] *Fluide* is, however, one of the first BD journals to go on line. Entitled @Fluide, access to the site cost in 2000 one hundred and twenty francs per year and had a thousand subscribers, see Pialut 2000, 66.

its BD production as a serious art-form abroad and perhaps the unflattering portrait of the *Français moyen* that so many critics characterise the Bidochons as being is not one the French would like to boast about too much about away from home.

## Bibliography

Bakhtin, Mikhail 1968. *Rabelais and his World*, trans. by Hélène Iswolsky, Cambridge, MA: M.I.T. Press.

Binet, Christian 1979. *Histoires ordinaires*, Paris: AUDIE.

Binet, Christian 1979. *Poupon la peste*, Paris: AUDIE.

Binet, Christian 1980a. *Bédés juveniles*, Paris: Bédérama.

Binet, Christian 1980b. *Poupon la peste 2,* Paris: AUDIE.

Binet, Christian 1980c. *Les Bidochon roman d'amour tome 1*, Paris: AUDIE.

Binet, Christian 1981. *Les Bidochon en vacances tome 2*, Paris: AUDIE.

Binet, Christian 1982. *Les Bidochon en habitation à loyer modéré tome 3*, Paris: AUDIE.

Binet, Christian 1983a. *Les Bidochon, maison sucrée maison tome 4*, Paris: AUDIE.

Binet, Christian 1983b. *Les Bidochon, ragots intimes tome 5*, Paris: AUDIE.

Binet, Christian 1984. *Les Bidochon en voyage organisé tome 6*, Paris: AUDIE.

Binet, Christian 1985. *Les Bidochon assujettis sociaux tome 7*, Paris: AUDIE.

Binet, Christian 1986. *Les Bidochon vent du soir tome 8*, Paris: AUDIE.

Binet, Christian 1987. *Les Bidochon les fous sont lâchés tome 9*, Paris: AUDIE.

Binet, Christian 1988. *Les Bidochon usagers de la route tome 10*, Paris: AUDIE.

Binet, Christian 1989. *Les Bidochon, matin midi et soir suivi par matin, midi et soir tome 11*, Paris: AUDIE.

Binet, Christian 1990. *Les Bidochon se donnent en spectacle*, Paris: J'ai lu BD.

Binet, Christian 1991. *Les Bidochon téléspectateurs tome 12*, Paris: AUDIE.

Binet, Christian 1993. *Les Bidochon la vie de mariage tome 13*, Paris: AUDIE.

Binet, Christian 1995. *Les Bidochon des instants inoubliables tome 14*, Paris: AUDIE.

Binet, Christian 1997. *Bidochon mère (môman) tome 15*, Paris: AUDIE.

Binet, Christian 1999. *Les Bidochon toniques, tome 16*, Paris: AUDIE.

Binet, Christian 2000. *Les Bidochon utilisent le forfait, tome 17*, Paris: AUDIE.

Frémion, Yves 1984. *Binet: Dossier*, Paris: Ed. Sedli.

Gombrich Ernst. 1977. *Art and Illusion: A Study in the Psychology of Pictorial Representation*, London: Phaidon.

Lecigne, Bruno 1981. *Avanies et mascarade: l'évolution de la bande dessinée en France dans les années 70*, Paris: Futuropolis.

Pialut Fabrice 2000. 'Les Sept défis de la bande dessinée', *Livros Hebdo*, 363, 61-68.

Tiberi, Jean 1991. *Jean Tiberi présente Binet: Portraits de famille, Tome 1, 1945-1991*, Paris: SELD.

## Some Observations on BD in the US

### Roger Sabin
### Central St. Martin's College, University of London

There is a scene in a 1995 Hollywood adventure movie that says a lot about the relationship of American comics readers to European comics—or at least purports to. The movie is the box-office hit *Crimson Tide*, a thriller about a mutiny on a nuclear submarine, and the scene comes early on and involves the aftermath of a scuffle between two crew members—one the olive-skinned Rivetti and the other the Aryan-looking blond-haired Bennefield. In the following extract, an officer (Denzel Washington—note, a black officer) picks up the pieces:

> Officer: Why were you two fighting?
> Rivetti: Well, I said that the Kirby Silver Surfer was the only real Silver Surfer, and that the Moebius Silver Surfer was shit! And Bennefield's a big Moebius fan... Things got out of hand. I pushed him; he pushed me... I'm sorry.
> Officer: This better not happen again. If I see this kind of nonsense I'm going to write you up. [Semi-smiling] You have to set an example even in the face of stupidity. Everybody who reads comic books knows that Kirby's Silver Surfer is the only true Silver Surfer. Now am I right or wrong?
> Rivetti: Right, Sir!
> Officer: Now get out of here...

The scene is interesting because it is all about setting up characters. The officer and Rivetti bond because they agree that the American Jack Kirby was the best artist on the Marvel superhero series Silver Surfer, and that the Frenchman Moebius, who also had a run on the comic, was inferior. So far, so obvious: but it is what happens later in the film that puts things in perspective. It turns out the officer and Rivetti are among a group of crew members who take over control of the sub in order to avert a nuclear catastrophe—thus proving themselves to be the heroes of the piece. Bennefield, meanwhile, sides with the baddies, and consequently gets his nose broken by Rivetti, who in the process refers to him derisively as 'Moebius'. Good triumphs over evil, and patriotism in its 'true'—in this case individualist—sense wins the day. The message of the story seems to be this: how can a (loyal) American of any intelligence be a fan of a French comics artist?

Perhaps it is going too far to see so much in such a small snippet of a movie. Even so, it was one of a number of scenes that were added or modified by a 'script doctor' in order to make it more hard-hitting— specifically, to deliniate the characters more clearly. (The name of the script doctor? Step forward Quentin Tarantino—the then 'bad boy' of Hollywood.[1]) The fact that the scene was designed to speak to the audience in such a shorthand manner, that the 'common senseness' of what it had to say was supposedly so self-evident, was clearly meant to be indicative of an attitude that exists in the US towards foreigners, and by extension towards foreign comics. Could this attitude, this insularity, be one of the underlying causes of the failure of BDs to gain any kind of significant foothold in the US market?[2]

'Failure' is a relative term, of course, but it is interesting to note that the disappointing performance of translated BDs has been across the board. Although the focus of this paper is on 'BDs pour adultes' (which in Europe outnumber kids' titles by a considerable margin—though rarely outsell them), it is worth mentioning that at the children's end of the comics spectrum even the Tintin books have not fared particularly well in the US. In comparison to other parts of the world where Tintin album sales are comparable to that of Disney products, they have only reached a very limited readership among American youngsters (in Europe, Tintin is marketed to a broad age-range, and the sales pitch has always been: 'For readers aged seven to seventy-seven'; in the US, however, the books are seen as almost exclusively juvenile). One of the first American articles to take a detailed critical look at Tintin appeared in *The Comics Journal* in 1983, and concluded that despite the fact that the books had been available in translation since 1959, 'Tintin is still relatively unknown in the US'.[3] Nothing that has happened since 1983 has altered that general conclusion, despite the fact that today publishers

---

[1] Tarantino was unaccredited. Already by this time he was notorious for the debateably racist tone of his scripts (e.g. for *Reservoir Dogs* and *True Romance*)

[2] For the purposes of this essay I am using the term 'BD' as a loose synonym for 'European comics', as opposed to its more strict definition as 'comics deriving from the Franco-Belgian tradition'.

[3] See Mills 1983, p.60.

Little, Brown and Co. do have a Tintin presence in most bookstores.[4] Similarly other characters that are huge draws in Europe (e.g. Astérix, Blake and Mortimer, Lucky Luke, etc.) have never garnered significant American followings.[5]

When it comes to translations of adult-orientated Eurocomics, we might expect the story to be a happier one, because arguably these had a better chance of succeeding in the context of the changing nature of the US comics scene since the 1970s. The growth of the specialist comics store market in the US and its concomitant support for adult-orientated subject matter should theoretically have allowed for a situation in which European material could make a significant impact.[6] Equally, Eurocomics' chances should have increased because of the similarities between the European album format and the American 'graphic novel'.[7] But it was not to be, and Euro-albums soon found themselves relegated to a few out-of-the-way shelves, and sometimes not stocked at all. The situation led one exasperated critic in *The Comics Journal* to declare in 1997 that '[Adult Eurocomics] were the biggest disappointment of the last ten years' (Robert Fiore 1997, 68). More recently, another expert has described their impact as being comparable

---

[4] Steven Spielberg has made public his long-held desire to make a Tintin movie. If this ever happens, it can be predicted that the fame of the comic will soar. However, anti-fascist and Jewish groups have made their opposition to the project clear, based on the perceived role of Hergé as a Nazi collaborator during the Second World War. See Peeters, 2002. For this reason, some commentators believe the movie to be doomed.

[5] Once again, in Europe these characters are commonly marketed to an adult as well as juvenile readership.

[6] On rise of this market, see Pustz 1999.

[7] Indeed, historically speaking, the relative sophistication of the European industry had been an inspiration for certain creators working for American companies, and a spur to the development of the graphic novel. Briefly, the rise of the European album culture in the late 1970s and 1980s helped demonstrate to US/UK creators what could be done creatively in comics of a larger scale—as opposed to the traditional American 28-page comic book. The possibilities for greater characterisation, the generation of atmosphere, and so on, were very appealing, as was the fact that many of the European albums were being produced to a much higher standard than US comics (fully painted art was de rigeur, for example). Also, European creators would retain copyright over their work and commonly receive two royalty payments—one for the pre-serialisation of their story in a magazine and one for the album itself. This was in contrast to the prevailing working conditions in the US industry which were based on a work-for-hire system, commonly involving no creative control and payment on a fee or per-page basis. The European paradigm, in other words, came to be seen by some as a clarion call for change. See, for example, the comments of Bryan Talbot in Hasted 1997, 95-103.

to 'dropping a stone into a bowl of sludge—no splash, no ripples, nothing...'.[8]

It is clear that this lack of interest has taken both publishers and critics by surprise. Today there are small pockets of devoted fans of particular creators (names like Moebius, Enki Bilal, Hugo Pratt and Milo Manara—all of whom have fan websites devoted to them), and there are certain fanzines that make an effort to cover BDs in translation and also, occasionally, in the original (*The Comics Journal* has a regular column entitled 'Euro-comics for Beginners'). There are also publishers like NBM ('Nantier-Bell-Minoustchine'), Heavy Metal/Metal Mammoth Inc and Humanoids Publishing which concentrate on BD translations, and a few adventurous comics stores that stock a small selection of untranslated fare. But compared to the brief period between the end of the 1980s and the mid-1990s, when there was a wave of optimism about the future of the graphic novel, and a hope expressed in the media that the US market might soon transform itself into something akin to the European system, the market for European product can be said to be depressed (indeed, the publisher that led the pack back then—Catalan Communications—no longer exists).[9] Finding a mass market audience is now seen to be out of the question, and even securing a viable cult readership has become increasingly difficult.

But why? It is tempting to look for clues among the kinds of comics that have been published, to sift the more successful ones from the outright failures. What becomes immediately apparent is that the ones that do (relatively) well are those that best conform to existing American tastes—and that those tastes are fairly limited. Take, for example, science fiction. The American market has been dominated since the 1960s by one particular kind of science fiction story—the superhero comic. As the specialist/fan market developed in the 1970s and 1980s, so readers that had grown up with superhero comics continued to read 'adult' versions of the genre (*The Dark Knight Returns, Watchmen, Animal Man*, etc.), but also showed themselves to be sympathetic to other forms of SF yarn. (It is often forgotten that comics fandom itself had historically been an offshoot from SF fandom.)

---

[9] Kim Thompson, co-founder of Fantagraphics Books, interview with the author, 2 April 2001.

[9] The most high profile evangelist for Eurocomics in this period was the tireless Paul Gravett, who as well as featuring European material in his co-edited *Escape* magazine also wrote numerous pro-BD journalistic pieces (in *Print, Jamming, iD* and elsewhere). He was responsible for opening many people's eyes, and would later be hired by Penguin (UK) to oversee their graphic novels list, which included European albums as we shall see below.

This is how *Heavy Metal* made its mark. For the uninitiated: this Americanised version of a French science fiction magazine was an early hit in terms of adult comics (it was first published in 1977—the only previous adult European SF mini-success had been *Barbarella*), and was marketed both to the newsstands and to the growing number of specialist comics stores. Its upbeat anthology format included stories that ranged from 'hard SF' to fantasy and 'sword and sorcery', while its look incorporated intricate full colour art on glossy paper. What was particularly new about the title was its emphasis on sex and violence: the tone was certainly influenced by the underground comix movement, while at the same time drawing on trends in SF cinema. Although the comic did feature artists from America and the UK, it was the contribution from Europeans that made the most impact. Thus, American readers were introduced to BD stars such as Phillippe Druillet, Enki Bilal, and, of course, Moebius, a creator who had been deeply influenced by undergrounders like R. Crumb, and whose 'Arzach' and 'Airtight Garage' strips came to be seen as classics.[10] Later, other names would join the roster, such as Paolo Serpieri, Juan Giminez, and today's favourite cover artist, Luis Royo.

The *Heavy Metal* formula spawned copyists—notably Marvel's *Epic Illustrated* and the UK's *Pssst!*—and also set in train a move towards collecting individual stories as albums, in imitation of the European model. (There were also *Heavy Metal* animated movies and computer games.) The title's influence on the look and formatting of adult comics in the US and UK should thus not be underestimated—though sales were never spectacular.[11] If nothing else, it established that European creators could garner some kind of American following if they stuck to familiar genres and styles—albeit with a bit of extra sex appeal. As a consequence, American companies dabbled with employing European creators, and it did not seem too outrageous in the 1980s that even the mighty Marvel should open its doors to Moebius, and moreover allow him a run on *The Silver Surfer*—the subject of Tarantino's *Crimson Tide* rant.[12]

The second biggest genre in the US has almost always been comedy. But here the fit with European tastes has not been nearly as

---

[10] On Jean Giraud see also Matthew Screech's essay in this volume.

[11] The comics trade press has frequently run stories during *Heavy Metal*'s near quarter-century of existence that it was going to the wall, but today it continues under the ownership of millionaire Kevin Eastman, one of the duo responsible for the *Teenage Mutant Ninja Turtles*.

[12] Several Moebius titles were republished by Marvel, including *The Incal* and *Lieutenant Blueberry*.

snug as that with science fiction. Humorous work has been translated in various forms: some better known creators have been the subject of perfect-bound albums (Claire Bretécher, Mattioli and Max are obvious examples), while more often cheaper comics-sized anthologies have been preferred (for example, *French Ice*, with Lelong and Binet, *French Ticklers*, with Lelong, Binet and Franquin, and *Trombone*, with Edika, Maester and Reiser). Individual strips have also been included among home-originated fare in some humour anthologies, while more 'avant-garde' humourists, such as Max Andersson and Joost Swarte, have appeared in alternative comics such as *RAW* and *Zero Zero*—more about which in a moment. But despite much critical praise in the fanzines, none of the humour translations have taken off, and indeed many have performed disastrously badly. The anthologies tend to last for a few issues only, and albums have commonly ended up in the dumpbins (for example, Sokal's *Shaggy Dog Story* did badly for Fantagraphics, and was such a flop for UK publishers Fleetway that it contributed to the cancellation of its Xpresso Comics line).

Within Europe itself, one can generally say that the comedy comics find an appreciative 'European' audience, with French creators doing reasonably well in Germany, Italy and Spain, and vice versa. But when it comes to the USA (and the UK), there is a brick wall. Clearly, the subtleties of pacing, language and so on do not travel well, and are just too different—too foreign. Thus, it remains a source of astonishment to European comics fans that some of their best-loved characters and creations are all but unknown across the Atlantic—even national institutions like France's Bidochons and Germany's 'Little Asshole'.[13] As one critic said of *French Ticklers*: 'Humour is obviously not as universal as we'd like to think' (Jerome 1997, 224).

There are other genres, of course, but these run into their own problems when it comes to translations. One popular theme in European comics, for example, is historical drama—stories set in a particular period and place, be it the American frontier in the early settler period (*Indian Summer*), medieval Belgium (*Towers of Bois Maury*) or 1930s Budapest (*Hungarian Rhapsody*). Why these albums have not found favour with American readers is—as ever—a matter for debate, but one recurring and somewhat uncharitable theory is that Americans shy away from stories that require some knowledge of past events. As Terry Nantier of NBM comics, the biggest publisher of this kind of material, puts it: 'Americans can't be bothered with history—unless it's in a fantasised form, like Middle Earth history. Even Astérix requires some

---

[13] On the national specificities of the Bidochons, see Libbie McQuillan's essay in this volume.

historical knowledge, and I think that might partly explain that comic's lack of success.'[14]

Another possibility is that the European approach to historical storytelling has an unfamiliar tone (after all, what was *Prince Valiant* if not a period drama). This exhibits itself in two main ways. The first is in the attention to detail—which often goes hand in hand with slow pacing. Nantier explains that, 'European historical dramas are often quite studied and "quiet"—as opposed to the more dynamic science fiction approach.'[15] Kim Thompson of Fantagraphics has experience of how negatively this style can be received: 'The reaction to some of the more detailed, photo-realist historical material among American readers has been visceral. I've shown people—people who've been reading comics their whole lives—books by Hermann [*Towers of Bois Maury*], and they've screamed: "take this away from me!"'.[16] One series that managed to fare slightly better than the rest was Hugo Pratt's classic Corto Maltese—but even then, as publisher Nantier explains, 'it's still on the scale of art house cinema versus Hollywood'.[17]

This question of tone can have other implications, and it has been argued that American readers are turned off by the level of sexual content in some of the historical stories (it is not unusual to be reading a fifteenth-century set yarn and suddenly have the plotting and swordfights interrupted by a fairly explicit double-page sexual encounter). The French publisher Glénat became notorious for this kind of formula in the 1980s, yet their albums still did not sell in translation: this was ironic since in France the company had been severely criticised in the comics press and elsewhere for 'going American'.[18]

'Avant garde' material—so-called—from Europe has made an impact, but again only in a very niche way. Individual strips are commonly included in alternative anthologies: in the 1980s, the trend was set by *RAW* (Meulen, Swarte, Caro, Baru, etc.) and by the British title *Escape* (Baudoin, Mattotti, Varenne, etc.), while in the 1990s the baton was taken up by *Drawn & Quarterly* (Baru, Tardi, Marti, Berberian, etc.), *Graphic Story Monthly* (Tardi, Franquin, etc.), *Zero Zero* (Ott, Andersson, Reiser, etc.) and many others. However, gauging the popularity of such material was difficult because it was mixed in with American strips. Kim Thompson, who admits he was on a 'crusade'

---

[14] Terry Nantier, interview with the author 15 April 2001. Nantier was one of the founders of NBM.
[15] Terry Nantier, interview.
[16] Kim Thompson, interview.
[17] Terry Nantier, interview.
[18] Reported *The Comics Journal*, October 1988, 125, 31.

to introduce fans of alternative comics to European creators while he was involved on the editorial teams of Fantagraphics titles like *Honk!*, *Prime Cuts*, *Graphic Story Monthly* and *Zero Zero*, takes a sceptical view: 'The feedback I was getting was not positive. Although fans of alternative comics are certainly more broadminded than those of mainstream comics, the feeling I had was that the European strips were not welcome. Readers would say they were boring—just pretty pictures. It was an uneasy mix.'[19]

When such unconventional material was republished discretely in album form, Thompson's fears seemed to be borne out, and sales were generally dismal. Fantagraphics had several tries, but despite praise from critics the sales for albums by creators like Max Andersson never materialised. The lesson was not learned by less experienced publishers. When Penguin Books decided to enter the graphic novel market in earnest in the early 1990s (they had had a one-off success with *Maus* in 1986), they reasoned that the best way to cater to a literate, sophisticated audience would be to publish some of the more literate, sophisticated BDs. This was a bad mistake, and the failure of Lorenzo Mattotti's *Fires* and *Murmur* (written by Jerry Kramsky) contributed to the collapse of its graphic novel list within five years. Other mainstream publishers have similarly been burned (e.g. Andre Deutsch with Hendrik Dorgathen's *Space Dog*).

Finally, there is the genre that is either known as 'erotica' or 'porn', depending on who is making the judgement. Here, translated BD sales are relatively good, and although there is no data on the readership it would appear that they find an audience outside the usual fanbase for comics (in other words, people – men—are buying albums who wouldn't otherwise buy comics). '[Erotica] sells to wankers', Kim Thompson explains bluntly but not unreasonably. 'The Europeans draw in a realistic style that the wankers like—the wankers don't care what the national origin is.'[20] Today, NBM's 'Eurotica' line epitomises the trend, with work by old masters such as Guido Crepax (*Story of O*, *Emmanuelle*), and Milo Manara (*Click!*, *Butterscotch*, etc.) joined by newer favourites such as Belore (*Lolita*) and Juan Emilio (*I Can See You Comin'!*). The erotic genre hardly existed in the US until the 1990s, but today it is thriving, and the biggest publisher in the field Fantagraphics (with its 'Eros' line) frequently supplements its stable of American creators with European talent.

So much for the comics genres themselves. In the end, the variations in their performance can only tell us so much. Therefore, we

---

19    Kim Thompson, interview.
20    Kim Thompson, interview.

need to investigate other angles—particularly the context for their reception. In other words, 'message analysis' must necessarily be supplemented by a 'political economy' approach—an exploration of how the economics of the industry can influence comics' content.

The reasons for the rigidity of the US market have already been hinted at, but for readers of this essay who may not be familiar with its industrial dynamics, it is important to underscore the differences in the three basic retail outlets. These are: the newsstands, specialist comics shops, and bookstores. The first of these, the newsstands (under which heading it is also common to include sales via drugstores and supermarkets), have been in decline in terms of comics sales since the 1950s. In the late 1940s, comics reached their peak sales, with the top titles selling in the millions, and a range of genres including westerns, love stories, war adventures and superheroes each doing well. The backlash against 'crime' and horror comics in the mid-1950s, however, brought this era to an end, and led to the introduction of a Comics Code that banned all but the most innocuous of content. Thereafter, comics sales went into decline, with only the superhero and humour genres continuing to thrive. (There have also been a few one-off crazes, such as those surrounding the 'Teenage Mutant Ninja Turtles' in the early 1990s and the dreaded 'Pokemon' nearly a decade later.) Thus, as a venue for translations of European adult-orientated product, this market was always going to be problematic: *Heavy Metal* remains the exceptional success—sold as a magazine rather than a comic *per se*.

The specialist comics shops represent a different kind of distribution network, and since the early 1980s have constituted the 'new mainstream'. By the end of that decade there were something like 4000 such shops in the USA (and a further 400 in the UK): in the 1990s, there was a downturn following the collapse of the 'speculator' market, and today the number of shops is down by something like one third. Nevertheless, it is still true that approximately 85 per cent of all new comics product is sold via this source. The core readership tends to be men in the 15-30 age-range, and therefore the tone of the comics is generally 'adult'. As such, the publishers of comics aimed at this market utilise a 'direct sales' system—i.e. selling directly into the shops using an advance ordering system—and typically ignore the Comics Code. As we have seen, this is where the vast majority of BD translations have been tried.

But how marginalised those BDs have been is explained by a breakdown of the domination of this market by the superhero genre. Estimates vary, but roughly 95 per cent of all comics sold here involve such subject matter. This means that two or three publishers rule (Marvel, DC Comics, and frequently Image) while what is left of the shelf space is fought over by smaller publishers (many of which still deal in superhero fare). A sub-set of these smaller outfits are the publishers of alternative comics (Fantagraphics, Drawn & Quarterly, etc.) which put out comics involving a wider range of storylines and art styles (sometimes—as we have seen—including translations of more left-field European fare). Finally, existing as an even smaller sub-set, there are the companies that deal solely or primarily with foreign material—which usually means either Japanese (manga) or European comics.[21] In the 1980s, the European comics comfortably outnumbered the Japanese, but since the mid-1990s the trend has been reversed, to the frustration of *bédéphiles*, and today a manga publisher, Viz, is the biggest publisher of translated material in the US.[22]

Thus, today's leaders in Eurocomics publishing (the aforementioned NBM, Humanoids and Heavy Metal/Metal Mammoth Inc) are relatively tiny operations, literally forced into a corner by the economics of the direct sales/specialist store system. What this means is that they are vulnerable. For example, whenever there is a crisis in the comics market, or an economic downturn, they are among the first to suffer. Shop managers do not cut back on their superhero titles: these are the ones that make the money, and no sane manager is going to alienate the powerful distributors and publishers. So, for example, when the speculator collapse happened in the mid-late 1990s, although the comics involved were superhero titles, it was the alternative and translated comics that were cancelled first.[23] Moreover, as a consequence of this economic environment, it has not been uncommon for shop managers to use the perceived sexual content of European material as an excuse not to carry it. The occasional busts of sexually explicit comics (and shops that sell them) in certain states has only added ammunition to this argument.

We can go further and say that ownership concentration has other consequences. Conglomerates consisting of different companies can use the profits from one to subsidise the others, and thus comics prices can be kept artificially low, therefore adding pressure on

---

[21] To take an example year: in 1997, Marvel Entertainment Group Inc accounted for 33% of the market; DC Comics 28%; and Image 17%. The other 22% was divided among a total of 496 smaller companies. (For up to date information, see www.comicbookresources.com.)

[22] The manga influence has been widespread in Europe in the late 1990s, which in turn has meant that American publishers are translating BDs that have a Japanese style. See Beaty 1997.

[23] On the collapse of the speculator market, see Evanier 1996, Pustz 1999, and Sabin 2000.

competing publishers who may not share this advantage. Similarly, toys and other merchandising can be used to advertise the comics, not to mention the publicity around movie and game spin-offs. Finally, preferential treatment is given to such companies by distributors for obvious economic reasons (the role of Diamond Distributors has been controversial in this regard). The effects of this kind of synergistic integration have been thoroughly explored in an excellent essay by Matthew McAllister (2001).

Finally, the third market is the bookstores. This ballooned quite suddenly in the late 1980s and early 1990s following the canny marketing of three US-originated graphic novels (*Maus*, *Watchmen* and *The Dark Knight Returns*). The contraction that followed still left a situation in which graphic novel shelves were a feature of every major store, and it is not surprising that a publisher such as Penguin should have thought it was worth taking a risk. The problem, however, is that the kind of comics material that gets ordered by the stores tends to replicate what sells in the direct sales market—i.e. a preponderance of superhero titles. Under these circumstances, the effects of ownership concentration are still significant, though arguably less so than in the specialist stores. Translated BDs are bound to struggle, and the '*objet-livre*' culture that exists in much of Europe, much vaunted by critics when the bookstore market began to take off, still seems a long way off.

Taking into account the intransigent nature of the US system as a whole, therefore, perhaps it is surprising that Eurocomics have made any impact at all. Even the biggest 'hits' are very small beer, and at best can only hope to sell the equivalent of a 'low-end' American comic. With this in mind, it is no wonder that publishers are cautious—especially since putting out a BD translation entails so many more costs. First, there are the rights to the comic: according to the publishers interviewed for this essay, often these will be quite expensive because European publishers and creators have typically seen their comic do well in Europe and other parts of the world, and are therefore loathe to let the rights go cheaply. Then there is the cost of the translation, and of new lettering. Finally, new film is required for the publication process. All in all, the overheads can be extensive. This combined with the aforementioned economic obstacles makes it all the more remarkable—and praiseworthy—that any US publisher would attempt to touch BDs in the first place.[24]

---

[24] Perhaps this assessment should be extended to include European-based publishers who intend to sell translated BDs into the US. The foremost among these is the French L'Association, a small scale outfit with big ambitions: their anthology *Comix*

This political economy analysis is compelling, but there is one nagging post-script that brings us back to our opening film clip— namely, how far has naked xenophobia played a role in this story? Is it true, for example, that American readers have an irrational dislike of European comics? Does Tarantino's movie script reflect an uncomfortable reality? It is impossible to say with any certainty, of course. Terry Nantier is unsure: 'I just think it's a case of two very different cultures'.[25] Kim Thompson has no doubts: 'Americans HATE European comics! There's is a real and tangible resistance there'.[26] Other commentators are angry at how little (some) Americans have bothered to find out about comics history. For example, when in 1996, the US media and sections of academia went into overdrive about '100 Years of Comics', i.e. 100 years since the publication in the US of 'The Yellow Kid', they completely ignored the much longer history of the medium in Europe (not to mention pre-Yellow Kid comics in the US). Thierry Groensteen, former director of the CNBDI (*Centre national de la bande dessinée et de l'image*) concludes: 'American people are convinced that comics are, by definition, an American artform, that it is "their" artform, and therefore they are not very open to anything that comes from outside.'[27]

Such pessimism is not necessarily at odds with the sometimes reverential comments on BDs in comics studies and histories (e.g. 'Continental Europe is where comics have found the most respect in the Western world' (Rothschild 1995, xvii)) and in the media (e.g. 'Europe is where comics have made inroads into high culture' (Hornblower 1993)). Indeed, the sense that BDs are more admired in an abstract sense than actually liked is very reminiscent of the typical attitudes of the American public towards European cinema and literature.[28]

In conclusion, this chapter has been about observations. As such, it is impressionistic: perhaps if other publishers had been interviewed, and other statistics quoted, a different picture would have emerged. But a pattern is clear, and one final quote serves to add emphasis. It comes

---

*2000* was largely wordless and tested the waters, and was followed in 2002 by a full scale translation of David B's remarkable autobiography, entitled *Epileptic*.

[25] Terry Nantier, interview.

[26] Kim Thompson, interview.

[27] Thierry Groensteen, interview with the author (by e-mail), 5 June 1999. Groensteen's thoughts on the Yellow Kid 'centenary' can be gleaned from his withering review of the Bill Blackbeard and Dale Crain (1995). See Groensteen 1997.

[28] This is not to denigrate in any way the serious interest taken in BDs by a minority. (To give just two examples from an academic context; the *International Journal of Comic Art* (IJOCA) has regular in-depth essays, while the library at the University of Michigan boasts the finest BD collection in the country.)

from the aforementioned, and highly recommended, 'Euro-comics for Beginners' column in *The Comics Journal*: 'The most common reaction [to this column] asks why European comics anyway? We can't find them, we can't buy them, we can't read them and ipso facto, we're not interested in what you have to say about them...' (Beaty 1999, 25). One can sympathise with the exasperated writer. Despite all the efforts of committed *bédéphile* critics and publishers, it is hard to escape the verdict that, for the overwhelming majority of American comics readers, BDs are at best an irrelevance.

## Bibliography

Beaty, Bart 1997. 'Euro-Comics for Beginners: L'auoroute du soleil: European manga', *The Comics Journal*, July, 197, 23-27.

Beaty, Bart 1999. 'Euro-comics for Beginners: *la comédie illustrée*', *The Comics Journal*, December, 218, 25-30.

Blackbeard, Bill, and Dale Crain (eds) 1995. *The Comic Strip Century: Celebrating 100 Years of an American Art Form*, Northampton, MA: Kitchen Sink Press.

Evanier, Mark 1996. 'POV', *Comics Buyers' Guide*, January 5.

Fiore, Robert 1997. 'A Nice German Trench', *The Comics Journal*, December, 200, 67-71.

Groensteen, Thierry 1997. 'Retour sur une controverse: la bande dessinée avant (et après) le comic strip', *9e Art*, January, 114-15.

Jerome, Fiona 1997. Review of *French Ticklers*, in *The Slings and Arrows Comic Guide*, UK: Aurum Press.

Hasted, Nick 1997. 'Interview with Bryan Talbot', *The Comics Journal*, March, 194, 87-108.

Hornblower, Margot 1993. 'Beyond Mickey Mouse', *Time*, November 1, 42.

McAllister, M. 2001. 'Ownership Concentration in the US Comic Book Industry', in McAllister, M, E. Sewell and I. Gordon (eds), *Comics and Ideology*, New York: Peter Lang, 15-38.

Mills, T.F. 1983. 'America Discovers Tintin', *The Comics Journal*, November, 86, 60-69.

Peeters, Benoît 2002. 'A Never Ending Trial: Hergé and the Second World War', *Rethinking History*, 6.3, 261-71.

Pustz, Matthew 1999. *Comic Book Culture: Fanboys and True Believers*, Jackson, MS: University Press of Mississippi.

Rothschild, D. Aviva 1995. *Graphic Novels: A Bibliographic Guide to Book-length Comics,* Westport, CT: Libraries Unlimited Inc.

Sabin, Roger 2000. 'How Synergy Killed the Comics', *Speak Magazine* [San Francisco], Spring, 64-69.

'The Dance of the Visible and the Invisible':[1]
AIDS and the Bande Dessinée

Murray Pratt
Institute for International Studies
UTS (University of Technology, Sydney)


Making links between HIV and Comics may not be an obvious thing to do. What connections can there be between, on the one hand, what is arguably the epidemic with the greatest impact this century, affecting an estimated 40 million people worldwide, and calling into question medical, social and political organisation in each country affected—and, on the other, an art form often trivialised as picture books for children or, at best, a humorous diversion? One answer among others is, of course, that comics can be taken a lot more seriously than they have been as a communicative medium, offering what Scott McCloud calls an almost 'limitless potential as an art form' (McCloud 1994, 201). Likewise AIDS, described by Alain-Emmanuel Dreuilhe as 'avant tout une maladie mentale... parce que l'isolement et l'angoisse où il nous plonge fait de nous des aliénés' (1989, cited in Benhaïm and Broda 1994, 110), requires imaginative communicative action on all fronts, especially in educative contexts, and, why not, using humour effectively as one weapon against silence.

Indeed publications such as those developed by the Australian state-funded 'Streetwize Comics', and *Smack in the Eye*, distributed among drug users in the North West of England, have aimed to deploy the comic's resources of humour and familiarity as part of health promotion campaigns, including the dissemination of safer sex messages. Both have received positive evaluations (see Selwood 1993, 48-49, and Gilman 1989, 89), in particular for their ability to bridge the 'credibility gap' (Gilman, 1989, 116) which can have otherwise have the effect of distancing health authorities from the people they intend to

---

[1] The quotation is borrowed from McCloud 1994, 205.

reach in an accessible and non-prescriptive way. Mark Gilman's account of *Smack in the Eye*, for instance, details the project's ability to offer 'a context recognisable to drug users', employing humour 'to attract attention yet leave behind a meaningful harm reduction message' (15). Comics therefore offer immense scope as an effective and assimilable form of HIV prevention. However, this potential has been better exploited in the Anglo-Saxon world than in France, where, as Videlier and Piras point out in *La Santé dans les Bandes Dessinées*, the BD 'ne s'est pas réellement emparée du Sida' (1992, 95). I will shortly outline some of the successes, and failures, of texts produced for this purpose as part of my exploration of representations of AIDS in Francophone BDs. There is, however, a second and perhaps less obvious link between Comics and AIDS, one which I intend to argue, not only hinders the medium's ability to communicate clear safer sex messages, but which also typifies the ambivalence of French responses to the epidemic, specifically national anxieties about the place and legitimacy of visual signs of AIDS, and it is here that I would like to begin.

According to McCloud, the specificity of closure, what happens between images, in the blink of an eye, makes of comics a 'dance of the visible and the invisible'. It is this interplay, he contends, which lends the medium an enhanced power of 'viewer involvement and identification' (204). In addition, the use of simple visual iconography, 'allow[s] readers to MASK themselves in a character and safely enter a sensually stimulating world' (43), the icon functioning as 'a VACUUM into which our identity and awareness are pulled' (36). In *Comics: Ideology, Power and the Critics*, Martin Barker goes beyond McCloud's reading of 'identification' in showing how this is subjected to dialogical elements motivating the text towards the proposal of a specific world view, '*a "contract" between texts and audience*' (261) 'invit[ing] a certain kind of response' (272), in particular through a tendency to offer a thematically coherent 'evaluative accent' (Barker 1989). Barker's analysis of 'Scream Inn' in the 1970's British comic *Shiver and Shake*, for instance, charts the ways in which the strip functions as a space for children to explore and test the bounds of adult authority. Its logic therefore projects a readership of a certain age and range of experience, which, as it grows up, moves on to 'other forms of resistance, of both fantasy and real kinds' (114). The implication subtending his argument is that the medium plays as a kind of hyper-charged ideological site, often characterised by the uniformity and directness of both its environmental texture and the simplicity of its repeated narrative transformations.

Now, from the outset, the AIDS epidemic has been marked by a range of questions about visibility, in terms of both the virus's capacity to pass undetected between bodies, and its initial absence of symptoms, followed by highly visible ones such as lesions, often facial, and the 'wasting' of the body characteristic of the later stages of illness. A few examples from the French context show how similar concerns pass into discourses of AIDS at all levels. In the 1980s, the earliest response to the threat of a plague affecting gay men unseen was effectively to deny its existence. Even prominent thinkers such as Michel Foucault and Guy Hocquenghem reacted in this way, worried about the implications that rumours might hold for the recently acquired, and still fragile, visibility of a gay community in France. In later years, the interventions of the Front National, the scandal of contaminated blood, and the controversial nature of what can legitimately be represented in safer sex campaigns each, in various ways, turn around issues of seen and unseen (see Pratt 1998). There is a sense in which McCloud's blinking eye of 'closure', as well as Barker's site of hypercharged ideology, could apply equally well to competing political, medical and discursive responses to the epidemic in France, as they select and arrange the narrative sequences through which their particular version of AIDS is either given prominence or occluded from discourse.

What is more, HIV itself has come to be figured iconographically—most often as the blown-up spiky molecule appearing behind the presenter's head on news broadcasts. As Mireille Rosello has demonstrated, 'the fetishised virus is an image that packs its narrative very tightly and is therefore able to smuggle metaphorical meaning without taking responsibility for it' (Rosello 1998, 339). The icon, as with its use in the comic, offers a highly controlled visual message which 'safely' projects a coherent world view, in this case one which can connote biotechnological engagement against the 'time-bomb' of AIDS and scopically promoting both fear and dependence on science's solution in hand. But while the virus as icon is certainly a compelling visual image, a code which has become, according to Rosello, 'intertextual, international and culturally compulsory' (338), it is also clear that the narrative which it conveys is only 'safe' in as much as it as universalising, encouraging conformity to dominant scripts. In more specifically French terms, as David Caron has argued with respect to the 1996 Sidaction broadcast (1998), the epidemic is given visual space in the national consciousness solely in its universal, sanitised and consensual forms: the red ribbon connoting solidarity, the 'tale of family tragedy, medical heroism and government compassion' (289) reinforcing the myth that we are all equally at risk from contamination—while the actions and words of gay men in as much as they constitute a distinct interest group are airbrushed out of the picture. In other words, depictions of the virus are permissible in France only to the extent that

AIDS can be used to 'replicate and reinforce the ethical values of the Republic' (291) against the greater risk of the emergence of uncontainable political communities within its boundaries.

It is my contention then, that alongside the comic's ability to use familiarity and clear visual messages in outreach HIV prevention, the medium's consensual and universalising tendencies must also be taken into account in analysing its functions within the context of the epidemic. In the case of 'Smack in the Eye', the publication appealed to, and importantly appeared credible to, a specific reading community who recognised and shared its assumptions. In France, however, the AIDS crisis has been characterised by a Republican refusal to acknowledge collective or community groups of any kind whatsoever. Larys Frogier is correct to point out that, as a result, '"public health" came to signify only the welfare of the dominant population', with '[t]he many specific factors associated with HIV, in particular where homosexuals and drug addicts were concerned [being] ignored' (Frogier 1997, 352). French representations of AIDS in the enhanced ideological field of the comic, then, come up against two interlinked problems. Firstly, to the extent that reader identification, the deployment of humour, and thematic coherence in the BD require a readership which is clearly targeted as well as consensual, its ideology will largely be able to reflect only a national consensus, with all the pitfalls of basing health promotion uniquely on the assumptions of 'le grand public'. And secondly, where images from the margins do enter into discourse, they are likely to gain favour only at the expense of avoiding or derouting any risk of a communitarian political message, or even of figuring the subjects of HIV and AIDS in allegorical or other disguised forms, if not avoiding them altogether. I would like to test out each of these hypotheses in turn, looking first at the ideology of BDs designed specifically for HIV prevention purposes, and then looking at some recent French BDs with gay themes.

One of the most widely available BDs dealing with AIDS in France, entitled simply *Le Sida*, was produced in 1995 in collaboration with the Institut Alfred Fourier as part of the 'Prévention Sourire' series (Moloch 1995).[2] Aimed at a young audience, its intention was to inform its readership about the disease using humour as a form of 'dédramatisation', its introduction setting the tone with the announcement that '[c]hacun d'entre nous doit se sentir concerné par les "messages" qui y sont véhiculés' (4). As the front cover shows, the HIV virus, represented as a little green monster hovering above the heads of

---

[2] See Pratt 1998 for a fuller discussion of this text's engagement in 'a guerrilla war with HIV' (278) characterised by policing the borders of the French straight state.

an otherwise blithe straight couple, is depicted as a threat to heterosexual love rather than health. As the narrative develops, it becomes clear that the main threat that HIV poses is conceptualised in consensually straight terms. At no point are homosexual relations or couples illustrated, and indeed homosexuality only merits one direct mention in the book. However, in tandem with the text's omission of homosexuality as such, is its depiction of the body's immune system as a national army complete with berets and coloured in the red, white and blue of the 'tricolore' (6), draws on the dominant cultural metaphor of AIDS as a threat to French identity. A later 'planche' (12), aiming to allegorise the impact of the HIV virus on the immune system, represents the threat of infection as a dramatic fireworks explosion of the 'tricolore', and its multiplication into a plurality of alien entities, each ready to mount further attacks on France and heterosexual romance.

The immune system army can be understood in terms of 'border guards', operating as shared cultural references deployed in discourse and serving to police the boundaries of what constitutes national identity. '[Border guards] are closely linked', Anthias and Yuval-Davis explain (1992), 'to specific cultural codes of style of dress and behaviour as well as to more elaborate bodies of customs, literary and artistic modes of production, and of course language' (33), a list of codes not dissimilar to those deployed within homophobic social policing. The army of *Le Sida* is effectively engaged in border guard duty against un-French representation as much as in a guerrilla war with HIV. Anthias and Yuval-Davis situate border guards in the deeper context of a national 'mythomoteur', that is 'the constitutive myth of the ethnic polity which describes how and why the collectivity was created, why it is unique, and what its mission is' (34). Any speculation as to what might constitute the French national has more to do with the assertion of reproductive heterosexuality than the promotion of AIDS awareness.

One of the most insidious effects of national heteronormativity in French HIV policy throughout the 1990s can be measured in its tendency to target prevention campaigns at 'la jeunesse'. Despite their good intentions, as both Jean de Savigny (1995, 57) and Franck Arnal (1993, 73) point out, these campaigns have been marked by an assumption of universal heterosexuality, masking a reticence to acknowledge any potential gay-identifying children among the targeted readership. More generally, the universalising discourses of children's BDs severely restrict the medium's ability to offer detailed practical information. The humouristic style of Moloch's *Le Sida* requires that its illustration of condom use figures as a series of escapades effectively problematising and ridiculing safer sex—a sequence of 9 frames illustrates straight or non-defined men struggling to use condoms correctly (26-27), while *Pas de sida pour Miss Poireau*, Mandryka's 1987 album, uses the allegory of the 'le jardin potager' to engage its readers—although it is unclear what message children will take away from the text other than the idea that you get AIDS from vegetables. In each case, a uniform iconographic and ideological field posits a consensual and universalising reading, but in the contolled context of AIDS in France, one which is restricted in how much it can say about its ostensible subject matter.

The 1991 album *Jo*, aimed at an older readership and produced in Switzerland although well distributed in France, is described by Videlier and Piras as 'une *love-story* parfois naïve mais émouvante' (186). Again, there is no possibility of tackling issues such as homosexuality, drug-taking or prostitution, and significantly no space for the inclusion of narrative dissent from the predominantly rosy and coercive message that (heterosexual) love conquers all. This contrasts markedly with the excellent Gabonese album, Fargas's *Yannick Dombi, ou le choix de vivre* (1992), where a range of alternative responses to safer sex messages are followed through the different characters in the comic. Notably, the irresponsible behaviour of Yannick's two schoolmates, Ngania and Régis is shown as having direct social and medical consequences, as with Ngania's refusal to use the condom offered to him by Hermine (visually replacing the Levi's label on her boyfriend's jeans), which leads to her turning down sex with the phrase 'La capote ou rien' (29). This approach is similar to the 'Wise Guys' and 'Daft Bastards' approach used by *Smack in the Eye*, offering a more dialogic and ultimately democratic reading than those proposed by French BDs. Likewise, the album's innovative embedding of the icons used in more formal AIDS education in a sequence of OHP-type frames containing the formal prevention message brought into school (21) is accompanied by voices-off which Fargas uses to to contextualise this message and figure resistant responses, such as 'C'est des histoires tout ça', within the narrative, effectively opening up the comic to its readers' own hesitancies.

By contrast, state-funded prevention material such as the 1995 brochure produced by the French national organisation AIDES, uses a similar sequence to convey the same information, but in a much more directive and abstract way. Here, a sequence of three frames, depicting different levels of 'risk' in male homosexual relations, is accompanied by lists of highly prescriptive advice, particularly around condom use. The effect is that even the moments of closure in the guttering, where readers ought to be given space for their own response and reflection, are taken over by a didactive and monoglossic discourse which over-classifies sexuality into distinct acts, often bearing no relation to the more obscure and nameless forms of intimacy which take place in reality. While the depiction of condom use along the bottom of the leaflet does provide a step-by-step illustration over time, it nonetheless offers a less detailed and annotated account than the similar episode dramatised in Fargas, despite using five 'cases' as opposed to four. For instance the AIDES leaflet is full of florid but practically meaningless phrases such as 'pour un meilleur confort', 'au niveau de l'anus' and 'vérifier le sens de déroulement', while, by contrast, in the Fargas comic, the educator's account is clear and direct ('toujours mettre le préservatif avant le début de chaque rapport sexuel' [21]). Moreover, Fargas also manages to include three different stages of putting a condom on to an erect penis within his four frames, while the airbrush AIDES brochure skips coyly from some crazy notion about squeezing toothpaste into the inside of a condom in the second frame to a successfully covered member in the third. Here, as is endemic in material of this kind, the pictures accompanying AIDS preventions in France, despite the BD's built-in ability to convey sequences of action, fail to take advantage of this, providing instead static images. In the case of the three main frames depicting homosexual relations, there is not even a sense of intended sequence, to the extent that the illustrations of different levels risk in the same brochure could be either unassimilated, or more dangerously, read as advocating unsafe sex. Rather than using the illustrations to address and depict the interpersonal skills needed to accompany the mechanics of sexual relations, the brochure has opted instead for three temporally isolated images. If anything, our tendency to posit a series of similar pictures as a narrative sequence of actions leads us to read these images as a session that passes from the ludicrously safe (heavy petting) through to highly risky behaviour and back again to safer sex practices.

The model of using comic style illustrations in AIDS prevention in France dates as far as back as 1986, when *Libération* (17 December 1986) announced everything you need to know about AIDS in the form of a chart containing highly stylised icons representing safe and unsafe situations. At a stage when little information about the epidemic was being circulated in France, this chart fulfilled a simple but useful purpose, even if the icons are a bit too reminiscent of those used to symbolise different disciplines in the Winter Olympics to convey much information. Recent research into prevention work in France[3] stresses the need for information to be actualised and made relevant to its readers, in a way which a narrative BD could have done in both AIDES brochures and national press depictions, and yet eight years later, the

---

3   See for example Fernandez 1997: 'L'identification a été reconnue comme un des facteurs-clefs pour une meilleure intégration des messages de prévention' (207).

same primitive chart used by *Libération* was still being published, this time in *Télérama*.

AIDS prevention in France, it would seem, has made less successful use of the BD than elsewhere in the world. The reasons for this communicative failure, one replicated across other French media, lie in an anxiety about the place of AIDS in public discourse, visibilised and managed as a symbol of national solidarity and uniformity, yet made to disappear whenever it threatens to signify any form of collective identity. Consequently, BD representations of the epidemic have drawn on certain of the medium's attributes at the expense of others. Rather than its more challenging properties of dialogism, fictional identification, narrative complexity, counter-identification or imaginative engagement, the comic forms taken by AIDS in France tend more towards the consensual and universalising discourses of the icon. Nowhere is this more evident than in the fetishisation of the condom, and its unnuanced marketing style appearance on billboards across the nation as the principal comic character in the national script. From the initial Catholic legacy of a ban on the advertising of contraception, condoms have emerged through France's AIDS crisis as friendly, almost cuddly, little animals popping up all over the place, shiny and playful, and successfully integrated into society as a whole. Perhaps due to their ambivalent function as both contraceptive and prevention aid, condoms have become the acceptable face of HIV, the ostensible solution to the problem of how to control its visual infiltration into French society. In both *Pas de sida pour Miss Poireau* and Moloch's *Le Sida*, the condom functions as 'deus ex machina'. Moloch even goes so far as to attribute some predictable national European stereotypes to his little rubber friends (27). In many ways this trend has served as a useful social dedramatisation and mobilisation of a previously taboo and maligned weapon in the fight against AIDS. However, in its deployment as icon, it has also provided France with the ideal meaningless and decontextualised BD image capable of ousting more problematic representations of the virus.

I would like to conclude by briefly outlining a more hopeful development in the BD, and to preface this with a qualification of my earlier position on the absence of collective groups in French public life. The exception to the Republican model, increasingly prominent, is of course the existence of targetable consumer identities. The global market requires specialisation and diversification, and the tentative emergence of a gay community in France is, if anything, due to the perception of a niche-identified purchasing power. On a worldwide scale, as Mark S'·npson has argued (1996), being gay is becoming less about sexuality than about consumer choices across a range of products, including, of course, the kind of BD you buy.

In some cases, such as Jean-Paul Jennequin's *Les Folles nuits de Jonathan* (1997), it is a case of you-get-what-you-deserve. A gay love story to outmatch *Jo* in its naïvety, it tells of a young gay man's adventures in losing his virginity before settling on a cosy one-to-one with his boss. What is astonishing about this BD clearly set among, aimed at and distributed via the gay consumer community in Paris, is its faithful replication of the national reluctance to figure AIDS. Not once are safer sex or AIDS awareness raised as an issue for this poor bland 'ingénu': he is even provided with a Jiminy Cricket type conscience resembling a worrying cross between a penis and, of course, a condom, which pushes him on to further conquests regardless with the injunction 'Sortir! Draguer...' (4). A second, more interesting BD to sell well among gay men in France is Ralf König's 'polar' series featuring the adventures of the killer condom (1991). Perhaps due their internationalism (the stories are set in New York, the hero is Sicilian, and the text translated from the German) König's stories convey a strong sense of gay community, and offer a complex and fantastical narrative allegory of the sense of dread and threat which AIDS holds within it. In this volume, the condoms are indeed depicted as killers complete with ferocious teeth which offer the ultimate representation of the castration complex (86), but the greatest menace of all comes from a stereotypical hypermasculinised gay male body, the latex replica of porn star Billy Bullcock (34-37). Bullcock's sexual originality lies in its ability to ingest whole his passive anal partners, sucking them in through his flies and spitting them out as fully stripped skeletons through his mouth. König's work, for all its imaginative warpedness, may not be particularly original stylistically, but it does offer a rich and complex allegory which can be seen as transgressing the codes by which gay men and PWA's have been othered in French BD's, particularly through its ascription of agency to them (the detective is a well-adapted and easy-going gay man, and clearly has the upper hand over his 'straight' sidekick), and the subversion of the skeleton 'icon' which had figured in earlier homophobic depictions such as those by Reiser and the *Fluide glaciale* series.

There is, however, one *dessinateur* in France producing BDs with a gay subject, whose work is quite outstanding, both visually and ideologically, and who, although yet to address issues of AIDS explicitly in his work, is operating at the forefront of subsequent necessary debates about the organisation and place of the gay community within national consciousness. Fabrice Neaud is in the process of producing a wide-ranging, thematically complex and stylistically innovative BD autobiography of his life in Angoulême (1996, 1998, 1999), one which confronts issues of isolation and relations, and examines the social structures of cohesion and division behind the concept of a gay community in often engaging and provocative ways. While it is not within the remit of this chapter to explore the many issues raised by Neaud's work at the length they deserve, it is worth pausing briefly to consider it as a response to some of the problems encountered here.

Refusing and recasting the ready-made of the iconographic, Neaud's black and white drawings persist in subverting the visual images of the everyday, subjecting them to the autobiographical gaze of the social outsider, depressive, and 'marginalised' by both straight society and what he sees as the hypocrisy of its commodified gay counterpart. The resulting experimental style—by turn layered, partial, subjective, expressionistic, heteroglossic, symbolic—allows him to develop an acerbic but heartfelt critique of the social structures which impose the visual tyranny of desire for the 'healthy' body of masculinity in contemporary French society. Simultaneously caught up in and repulsed by his obsession to possess on the page that which he is denied (or meted out in doses of 'la tolérance') in reality, the journals achieve what other gay or AIDS-related BDs in France fail to do. Leading their readers on a dance of the visible and the invisible, at once harrowing and joyful, Neaud offers a dynamic and engaged landscape fully capable of tearing apart the structural homophobia behind the 'safer BD' approaches encountered in so much of the work discussed in this chapter.

## Bibliography

Anthias, F. and F. Yuval-Davis (in association with H. Cain) 1992. *Radicalised Boundaries, Race, Nation, Gender, Colour and Class*, London and New York: Routledge.

Arnal, F. 1993. *Résister ou disparaître? Les homosexuels français face au sida: la prévention de 1982 à 1992*, 'Logiques Sociales', Paris: L'Harmattan.

Barker, M. 1989. *Comics: Ideology, Power and the Critics*, Manchester: Manchester University Press.

Benhaïm, M. and J. Broda 1994. *Sida, luttes à vif*, Grenoble: Editions La Pensée sauvage.

Boulé, J-P. and M. Pratt (eds) 1998. *French Cultural Studies*, 9.3, Special Issue 'AIDS in France'.

Caron, D. 1998. 'Liberté, Egalité, Séropositivité: AIDS, the French Republic, and the question of community' in J.-P. Boulé and M. Pratt (eds), 281-94.

Derib 1991. *Jo*, Geneva: Fondation pour la Vie.

Dreuilhe, A-E. 1989. *Corps à corps*, Paris: Gallimard.

Fargas 1992. *Yannick Dombi, ou le choix de vivre*, Libreville: Multipress-Gabon and Société internationale d'Edition et de Diffusion.

Fernandez, Dana 1997. *Jeunes, sida et langage*, 'Communication et civilisation', Paris: L'Harmattan.

Frogier, L. 1997. 'Homosexuals and the AIDS crisis in France: assimilation, denial, activism', in J. Oppenheimer and H. Reckitt (eds), *Acting on AIDS: Sex, Drugs & Politics*, London and New York: Serpent's Tail.

Gilman, M. 1989. *Comics as a Strategy in Reducing Drug Related Harm*, Manchester: Lifeline Project.

Jennequin, J-P. 1997. *Les Folles nuits de Jonathan*, Paris: Bulles Gaies.

König, R. 1991. *Le Retour de la capote qui tue*, Grenoble, Editions Glennat, originally published 1990, Editions Kunst der Comics.

Libération 1986. 'Tout ce que vous avez toujours voulu savoir sur le Sida', 17 December 1986, 24-25.

Mandryka, N. and C. Moliterni 1987. *Pas de SIDA pour Miss Poireau*, Paris: Giphar.

McAllister, M. 1992. 'Comic Books and AIDS', *Journal of Popular Culture*, 26.2, 1-24.

McCloud, S. 1994. *Understanding Comics*, New York: Harper Collins Publishers.

Moloch (Drawings) 1995. *Le Sida*, 'Prévention sourire', Paris: FG Editions.

Neaud, F. 1996. *Journal (I) février 1992 – septembre 1993*, Angoulême: Ego comme X.

Neaud, F. 1998. *Journal (II) septembre 1993 – décembre 1993*, Angoulême: Ego comme X.

Neaud, F. 1999. *Journal (III) décembre 1993 – août 1995*, Angoulême: Ego comme X.

Pratt, M. 1998. 'The defence of the straight state: heteronormativity, AIDS in France and the space of the nation', in J.-P. Boulé and M. Pratt (eds), 263-80.

Rosello, M. 1998. 'Pictures of a virus: ideological choices and the representation of HIV', in J-P. Boulé and M. Pratt (eds), 337-50.

De Savigny, J. 1995. *Le SIDA et les fragilité françaises: nos réactions face à l'épidémie*, Paris: Albin Michel.

Selwood, S. 1993. *Harmful Publications: Comics, Education and Disenfranchised Young People*, London: Art & Society.

Simpson, M. 1996. 'Gay Dream Believer: Inside the Gay Underwear Cult', in M. Simpson (ed.), *Anti-Gay*, London and New York: Freedom Editions, 1-12.

Videlier, P. and P. Piras 1992. *La Santé dans les Bandes Dessinées*, Frison-Roche: CNRS éditions.

# Let's party!
## Astérix and the World Cup (France 1998)

### James Steel
### University of Glasgow

'Drôle de pays que cette France qui s'est trouvé un héros du nom de Mémé' (Belot 1998, 4), and one could add 'funny country' that turns this Mémé (which has an endearing connotation, meaning 'Gran' in familiar French) into a mythical Astérix fit for the twenty-first century. As will be seen, references to comic strips and their heroes abound in the French media throughout the remarkable Summer of 1998. This article will concentrate on the significance of those in the media equating Aimé Jacquet, the coach of the French football team, with Astérix, the comic strip hero. As we shall see, references to characters from the album Astérix are also made about members of the French football team, as well, of course, as to other successful French sporting personalities, of both sexes (despite the notorious absence of main female characters in Astérix). In view of the constraints of a short article, we shall limit ourselves to football, to the French team victory in the World Cup in particular, its impact, its (alleged) political and sociological significance, and the resonance the French implied between the sporting exploits of their football team and the fictitious exploits of such quintessential 'French' heroes as Astérix, Obélix, Panoramix, Abraracourcix and Assurancetourix in a tiny Gaullish village surrounded by Roman soldiers in the year 50 BC.

Let us start by eliminating the odd idea that the victory of the French team in the World Cup changed the country. As Serge July, editor of the daily *Libération*, indicated only too clearly in his editorial: 'Une victoire en coupe du monde ne change pas la réalité sociale mais elle peut changer l'image que les Français se font d'eux-mêmes' (14 July 1998). It is this particular self-image that we find interesting, all the more so since it was and is disseminated by, among others, the comic strip Astérix.

The fact that a journalist can write, 'Merci à Manu, Fabien, Lilian, Titi et David, qui êtes encore là pour longtemps, et malgré tout déjà installés dans nos têtes comme des héros de bande dessinée' (Droussent 1998) and that *Télérama* end its editorial by declaring, 'Aimé Jacquet est notre nouvel Astérix' (22 July 1998) forces us to a salutory reappraisal of what constitutes a comic strip character in general and Astérix in particular. It would be tempting to dismiss this preoccupation as a mere reaction of an intellectual thus endorsing to some extent Goscinny's response when asked whether the success of Astérix was expected: 'Ce que nous n'avions absolument pas prévu en tout cas c'est les sociologues, les psychologues voire même les psychiatres [...] qui se sont emparés d'Astérix et y ont vu toutes les choses que nous n'y avons pas mises et qui n'y sont vraiment pas' (Vidal, Goscinny and Gaumer 1997, 92-93). To this list we can add political scientists, historians, academics, journalists and sports commentators. And, whether 'these things' are there or not, if the readership at large thinks they are there, who is to argue. In short, Astérix shares the fate of works of art or works of fiction, whether in literature, cinema, painting or even music: once completed they become public property and the public's perception supplants the artist's intentions. Therefore, even if Goscinny and Uderzo insist that their aim in creating Astérix was merely to create a kind of *French* strip-cartoon Laurel and Hardy in order to entertain their readership at a time when France was suffering from 'gloomosis', the readership at large is entitled to read more (or less) than what the authors claim to have put in. Furthermore, its international appeal alone would tend to deny Astérix's French exclusiveness.

However, for a foreign observer it seems legitimate to ask for further clarifications concerning the identity and nature of a strip cartoon character such as Astérix who can be referred to in an editorial on a footballing event without any explanation whatsoever by a journalist writing for a non-specialist readership in excess of 750,000. Clearly it suggests that Astérix is well-known, that it can be taken for granted that readers in France will understand immediately the connection between Aimé Jacquet and Astérix, or for that matter between Zorro and Zinédine Zidane or Emmanuel Petit, or between Laurent Blanc and Obélix. We can conclude therefore that this type of reference is self-explanatory.[1] What is however of interest here is to determine why such a reference

---

[1] In July 1994, out of a sample of 1000 people aged 15 or more, 68% had read at least one Astérix album. See 'Le rire d'Astérix. 35 ans d'esprit gaulois', *L'Express*, 10 November 1994, 20.

should be so clear to a French readership as to warrant no explanation and what is its actual meaning.

It will become quickly apparent that both Aimé Jacquet, henceforth 'Mémé', and Astérix are 'embodiments of values' and that they encapsulate ideals widely shared by the French or at least deemed to be so. The French media were peppered with references to comic strips and to Astérix in particular at the time of the World Cup and immediately afterwards. This should come as no real surprise in a country which officially named its first space satellite Astérix (A-1), whose well-known political scientist, Alain Duhamel, spoke of the 'Astérix complexe' (Duhamel 1995) when writing on France's foreign policy, where an editorial in the daily *France-Soir* (Morrot 1996) compared members of the French government, including President Chirac, to characters in Astérix, where some of Obélix's characteristic expressions such as 'Ils sont fous ces Romains' or variants such as 'Ils sont fous ces Anglais' and 'Ils sont fous ces politiciens' have become an integral part of every day language.[2] In short, Astérix belongs to the linguistic, political and cultural repertory of the French since the 1960s.[3]

But why should one compare the members of the French national football team to the characters of a comic strip? Interestingly enough, a similar phenomenon has not taken place in Britain, although we are not short of 'national' cartoon strip heroes. The super strong Desperate Dan, the athletic ace Alph Tupper, who won all his races on 'fish and chips', or the football wizard Roy (Race) of the Rovers who single-handedly could turn around any game come to mind. There is of course Superman, but that was reserved for 'SuperMac', i.e. Harold MacMillan, Prime Minister from 1957 to 1963. But Superman and Astérix are as different as chalk and cheese, physically and above all in the values they embody. No one however would think it appropriate to equate Alex Ferguson (God forbid!) or David Beckham and the England team with comic strip characters. One of the reasons could be that we do not have a universally loved and acceptable strip cartoon character and, more importantly, in matters of sport (or, for that matter, war), the Anglo-Saxons perhaps tend to believe that nothing is impossible and that with grit and determination any competition can be won. The French psyche does not quite work that way, despite the fact that France became

---

[2] On the cover of *L'Express* (10 November 1994), Marianne, holding up on a tray two politicians, exclaims: 'Ils sont fous ces politiciens',

[3] If anything, the Astérix mania has increased. The cover of *L'Événement* (28 January-3 February 1999) refers to 'La folie Astérix' and, in the same issue, an article on the forthcoming European election candidate, Daniel Cohn-Bendit (known as 'Danny le rouge') is entitled: 'Les mésaventures de Danix chez les Gaulois' (8).

a formidable sporting country in the last decade of the twentieth century. But at the time of the World Cup she still had not quite come to terms with her new sporting pedigree and, in any case, history weighed against France's self-confidence whether on a battlefield, tennis court or football pitch, and victory in a major international tournament was usually greeted as a 'divine surprise'.

The World Cup was no exception and a French victory was but a dream, an impossible dream, for 60 million French people until at least the semi-finals, hence the description of the French players as 'des combattants de l'impossible' ('Le Mondial' [cahier central], *Le Monde*, 14 July 1998, iv). To imagine a win for the home team in the World Cup was therefore wishful thinking, comparable to the May 1968 slogan declaring that 'Il faut croire à la réalité de ses désirs'. It is not all that unusual however for the French to make their comic heroes into sporting heroes, such as Les Pieds Nickelés in the 1950s who were either Tour de France winners or world record holders.[4] But in the case of Les Pieds Nickelés, fiction was merely reflecting reality—albeit with unlikely characters—since the French had produced an impressive number of cycling champions in the twentieth century. But to do likewise in football was tantamount to day dreaming.

This might explain why Michel Platini, a brilliant French footballer in his day, and one of the organisers of the 1998 World Cup, was emphatically to declare shortly before the start of the competition that his most cherished wish before the World Cup, *his* World Cup, was for it to be:

---

[4]   It is interesting to note that 'Les Pieds Nickelés', published for the first time on the 4 June 1908 in the weekly *L'Epatant*, created by Louis Forton and continued by other cartoonists after his death (1934) until 1981, never gained the wide acceptance of Astérix, Tintin or for that matter Spirou and Bibi Fricotin. Probably because they were untidy (even the drawings gave the impression of a hurried, unfinished job, admittedly in keeping with the behaviour and 'values' of the characters,) but they epitomised a French 'wheeler-dealer' approach to society which was gradually becoming socially unacceptable; they were also too anarchistic, unscrupulous and definitely on the margin of society to be as popular as Tintin, Spirou or even Bibi Fricotin. However all these characters, whether Belgian of French, have something in common: they are all street-wise, astute and, to a lesser degree, intelligent, qualities which enable them to emerge victorious from tricky situations. But to each generation its own references. Talking about financial skulduggery, Jean-Pierre François, an eminent French banker, refers to his activities in the 1950s in the following terms: 'Nous étions vraiment une bande de Pieds Nickelés. Nous possédions une incroyable témérité et naïveté' (cited in Violet 1998, 84.) It is however doubtful whether a younger generation would understand the allusion nowadays or would wish, in the age of financial scandals, to be associated with such shady characters!

d'abord une fête. Une fête indécente, planétaire, gigantesque, obscène et tout ce que voudront bien lui reprocher ses contempteurs, mais une fête. (*Le Monde*, 10 June, 1)

The word 'Fête' (here in the sense of Party) was on the tip of everybody's pen and was usually associated with the notion of conviviality, joy, laughter, songs, dance and solidarity before, during and after the World Cup. The competition proper and the festive mood it generated were such a resounding success that Fila, the sports equipment manufacturer and sponsor to various football players, decided to cash in on it and coined the slogan in its post-World Cup publicity, 'Que la fête continue' (*L'Equipe*, 18 July 1998).

In fact the notion of partying, the ability to enjoy life, to share enjoyment with others, in short, 'conviviality', is a consumate French artform (even if not necessarily a Gaullish one) which brings us back to the world of Astérix and the Gauls as represented in the Astérix albums. The Romans, in most of the Astérix stories, are killjoys precisely because they lack the partying spirit, they have no sense of humour, and indeed every single Astérix album ends on a banquet held in honour of our Gaullish heroes for their victory over the Romans. The French football team behaved—unwittingly?—in exactly the same fashion when, after their victory in the World Cup final they decided to: 'encore passer une soirée dans l'intimité de Clairefontaine, entre eux' (*Le Monde*, 14 July 1998).

One could be tempted to infer from this that the characters of Astérix truly behave like the French in the second half of the twentieth century, or vice versa, and that consequently this comic strip is a faithful reflection of the nation's mentality. As we shall see later, this is not quite the case. Contrary to what *L'Humanité* wrote in an article entitled 'Nous sommes tous des footballeurs', where it was claimed 'tout un pays match après match, jour après jour, a semblé s'identifier aux Bleus qui reflètent la diversité de la population française' (*Le Monde*, 12-13 July 1998, 1), this French team was far from being a carbon copy of contemporary French society, as had been somewhat hastily declared. We shall come back to this.

It can already be inferred that the numerous references to comic strips betray an inferiority complex on the part of the French who often feel the need to transcend a rather gloomy reality (or perceived as such) and to entrust their (impossible) dreams to imaginary characters. Proof that winning the World Cup was but a wild dream. The world of dreams is never far from the world of childhood and it is significant that journalists and other (sport) commentators should have been quick to establish a connection between the obvious youthfulness (and innocence, in terms of international football experience) of the French football team (not a single member had previously taken part in a World Cup, a previously unknown phenomenon), and the world of childhood. Their articles revealed a mixture of affection, of anxiety—will they be up to it?—and of dreams, emotions central to comic strips. This point is well illustrated by *L'Équipe Magazine* (18 July 1992) and other newspapers: 'Juste des hommes égaux dans un *bonheur d'enfants*'; 'les *gamins* démarrent en trombe ce Mondial'; '*les petits bleus* devenus des géants'; 'au fond ils sont là nombreux, *enfants* de ce France-Bulgarie [France had been eliminated from the previous World Cup in its last qualifying game in Paris against Bulgaria], qui scella leur désir de revanche...'; 'Thierry Henri et David Trézéguet: deux *gamins* heureux'; 'c'est le soir des *minots*'; the Dutch daily *De Telegraaf* would refer to '*des petits coqs* [qui] pour la première fois dans l'histoire sont souverains' (*Libération*, 14 July; my emphasis).

However the importance of team spirit, of the right kind of atmosphere, of the will to win, and of panache will be emphasised time and again and is reminiscent, at least to an older reader, of the spirit of Alexandre Dumas's *Three Musketeers*. But, a sign of the times, nobody thought of comparing our footballing heroes to D'Artagnan, Athos or Aramis, or to the Chanson de Roland, or even to such a historical figure and heroic Knight as Du Guesclin. Who would have understood the allusion anyway? One journalist however went as far as comparing the Muslim Kabyl Zinédine Zidane to Bayard, 'chevalier sans peur et sans reproche', a christian hero par excellence (*Télérama*, 22 July 1998).[5] This, of course, should be ascribed to a political discourse aimed at integration. At the time of the World Cup therefore, most frequent 'literary' references are to comic strip heroes and in some cases even the players refer to themselves as strip cartoon heroes. Emmanuel Petit for instance would have liked to be 'le Zorro qui dénonce les injustices' (*Le Monde*, 28-29 June 1998). Platini's football career is a pretext for a journalist to play on words, in fact to display the extent of his modern culture which may not necessarily be understood by all: 'Comme Tintin, la vie de ce garçon semble avoir été dessinée par un adepte de "la ligne claire" qui préfèrent que les gentils petits l'emportent sur les grands méchants' (*Le Monde*, 'Le Mondial' [supplement], 18 June 1998, vii).[6]

The message is clear: the big villains are Brazil, Germany, England or Italy (in footballing terms, of course) and the 'gentils petits'

---

[5] This is a telling reference since *Télérama* is part of the 'Groupe des publications de la vie catholique'.

[6] 'La ligne claire' is of course a reference to the style of Hergé's school of graphic artists.

can only be the French. Echoes here, of the universal appeal of Astérix who is the 'gentil petit' battling against the big, powerful and wicked Romans,[7] an emblematic image that enjoys world-wide currency and which General de Gaulle himself, although referring to Tintin, applied to the position of France in world politics.[8] There are other 'cultural' references which are revealing of the success and influence of comic strips in France. Marcel Desailly's description as 'un roc, une assurance tous risques' (*L'Équipe Magazine*, 18 July 1998) immediately brings to mind one of the characters in Astérix precisely called 'Assurancetourix'. When a journalist ends his editorial with the expression 'Alors, que la fête commence' (*Le Monde*, 10 June 1998), the reference is clearly—for a French readership—to Abraracourcix, the quick-tempered chief in Astérix. Guy Roux, manager of the French football team Auxerre and a well-known TV sports commentator, who had followed Laurent Blanc's football career since the very outset, also resorted to a reference to Astérix when searching for a striking image to illustrate the multi-talented and exceptional young footballer:

> L'intelligence du football [...] est chez lui hyperdéveloppée, tel un surdoué du foot comme certains le sont en maths. Il comprend tout, par intuition ou réflexion. Franchement s'il existait la potion magique de l'intelligence, on pourrait dire qu'il est tombé dedans étant petit. ('Le mois du Blanc', *L'Equipe*, 6 July 1998, 4)

As is well known, in Astérix, the magic potion is made by the Druide Panoramix. It is this elixir which endows the Gauls with near invincibility and the whole of France, judging by Guy Roux's reference, knows that Obélix never touches the stuff precisely because he fell into a basin full of magic potion when he was a toddler.

In order to make his readers fully appreciate the sense of relief felt all round when Zinédine Zidane (Zizou for those in the know) scored twice in the first half of the final between France and Brazil, a journalist could not think of anything more telling and presumably more universally understood than the expression : 'enfin Zorro est arrivé' (*L'Équipe Magazine*, 18 July 1998), thus referring to both the cinema (Douglas Fairbanks, Tyrone Power, Alain Delon and more recently

---

[7] For Romans, one can read Americans, Brussels technocrats, multinationals, the global economy, the government. In fact it is an up-to-date version of David vs. Goliath, hence its universal appeal. But it also reflects the French siege mentality on the eve of the twenty-first century.

[8] 'Au fond vous savez, mon seul rival international, c'est Tintin! Nous sommes les petits qui ne se laissent pas avoir par les grands. On ne s'en apercevait pas, à cause de ma taille'. Cited in Moliterin, Mellot and Denni 1996, 50.

Antonio Banderas in the eponymous films) and the comic strip character Zorro. 'Zorro est arrivé' is a fairly common and familiar expression in French meaning a timely intervention by a 'saviour' or 'righter of wrongs'.

But let us not forget that in Astérix or in the World Cup, it is not so much physical power that enabled the Gauls or the French footballers to outplay their opponents, but intelligence, shrewdness, cunning and skill. It comes as no surprise therefore to learn that these qualities are to be found in abundance in somebody like Aimé Jacquet and in some of his players—we saw above what Guy Roux had to say about Laurent Blanc's football intelligence. But what is *the* ingredient or attribute which is the decisive factor enabling Astérix and the Gauls to outsmart their opponents? There is no doubt that in Astérix the magic potion—i.e. physical might—plays a considerable role, especially as regards such a colourful but somewhat dim character as Obélix, but on closer examination it soon becomes apparent that references to the Druid's intelligence as well as to Astérix's outnumber references to the physical prowess of the Gauls in general and of Obélix in particular. Everybody is well acquainted with the fact that intelligence is an eminently French attribute (or so the French would like us to think). They are quick to let it be known, openly or through innuendo, that it is largely thanks to their superior intellect that they can compete and hold their own against nations that are more powerful and populous (the 'villains' referred to above), but not as 'clever'. This intellectual arrogance landed France into diplomatic trouble with some Arab countries at the time of the Knom Kippour war (1973) when the French media coined the jingoistic slogan : 'On n'a pas de pétrole, mais on a des idées', thereby echoing Astérix 'Ce qu'il y a de bien, avec nous, c'est qu'on est bourrés d'idées' (Goscinny and Uderzo 1961, 42). This slogan was immediately withdrawn after a number of Arab countries complained that it was insulting towards them. So be it. But on that count, Astérix is insulting towards every other nationality, at least as far as intelligence is concerned. Astérix systematically makes up for his puny physique by using on one hand the magic potion to make him strong and invincible but on the other hand, and more often than not, by using his wits and his sharp intelligence. The latter is innate, therefore a Gallic trait. Let us consider this more closely.

In *Astérix chez les Bretons*, the Gauls from the mainland, who are on their way to help their Breton cousins in England, lose their barrel of magic potion when they come under attack from the Romans whilst navigating on the river Thames (Goscinny and Uderzo 1966, 43-44).[9] This incidentally becomes a pleasant way of explaining the traditional superiority of the English in sport since the content of the barrel, which has suffered a direct hit from the Romans, is spilled into the river (written before the World Cup and the dismal performances of the England cricket team). Faced with the risk of undermining the morale and determination of the Gaullish army should it find out about the loss of the magic potion, Astérix decides to concoct a drink with a few leaves which he took from the Druid's house before setting out for England. This drink, which will have the same effect on their Breton cousins as the magic potion, is none other than tea, as we discover at the very end of the album.

In *Astérix le Gaulois*, the Druid speaks to Astérix in the following manner: 'Non, Astérix. Reste ici pour garder le village. Ta force vient de mon breuvage mais ton intelligence et ta ruse n'appartiennent qu'à toi' (1961, 23). Moreover it is through cunning that Astérix became an Olympic champion (Goscinny and Uderzo, 1968). He indeed managed, through a shrewd stratagem, to induce all his opponents to drink some of the magic potion, whereas he himself did not take a drop of it, thus enabling him after the race, in which, predictably, he finished last but 'clean', to denounce the other competitors to the race officials and have them disqualified. The way in which Astérix lured his opponents into taking the illegal substance and then failing the equivalent of a drugs test is testimony to his intellectual superiority.[10]

In *Astérix le Gaulois*, Astérix again used his wits to persuade a cattle merchant to take him to the Roman town of Petitbonum, which was nowhere near the cattle merchant's destination. Astérix suggested that he should change trade, become a cart merchant and sell his cart here and now and go back home with his cattle. However to do this he has to go to Petitbonum which is the biggest regional cartmarket town. Faced with such a brilliant and simple stratagem, our cattle merchant exclaimed (and his exclamation is printed in bold black letters on an orange background, taking up about a third of the 'frame'): 'Merveilleuse, lumineuse, prodigieuse idée!' (1961, 25). Later on, in the

---

[9] However, the magic potion, before its loss, had enabled the Camulodunum rugby team to 'demolish' the opposition, the Durovernum team (36-42). Rugby being rugby, physical might prevailed and Obélix had a rare time.

[10] It is interesting to note that Goscinny and Uderzo could have ill-afforded an Astérix Olympic victory through cheating at a time when sport and drugs was making the headlines in the media and was beginning to undermine the authority of the Olympic Committee. Furthermore, *Astérix aux Jeux Olympiques* appeared in 1968, the year of the Winter Olympics in Grenoble, where the French skier Jean-Claude Killy, who became a legendary figure, won three gold medals.

same album, Astérix decided to have fun at the expense of the Romans and boasted of having 'quelques idées' on the subject. Later on still, the Druid noted that Astérix's ideas 'ont du bon'. Even his Roman enemy, the military chief of the Roman camp, had to concede that Astérix's suggestion was 'une excellente idée' without realising that he himself was being manipulated by Astérix (1961, 36-7).

The ambiguities of the type of discourse between Astérix and the Roman chief, typical of Goscinny and Uderzo, reveals the mirror effect of the Astérix albums in that the character, here Astérix, addresses both another character in the story and the reader, but with a completely different meaning when addressing the latter. The same technique is at work towards the end of *Astérix le Gaulois*, when the Druide declares that he has 'un plan' and Astérix replies: 'CE QU'IL Y A DE BIEN, AVEC NOUS, C'EST QU'ON EST BOURRES D'IDEES' (1961, 42). This 'nous/on' can refer to both characters, Panoramix and Astérix and/or to the two authors, Goscinny and Uderzo, and/or even, in a total and national identification process, to the readers, especially French readers. As a result, 'Aimé Jacquet est notre nouvel Astérix' takes on an entirely new dimension which is not as innocuous as might have been thought initially.

Mémé is more than a mere new 'star', more than the realisation of a child's dream or the successful completion of 'mission impossible' which was achieved 'envers et contre tous' (echoes here of the three Musketeers). Instead, it represents a somewhat arrogant assertion of the supremacy of French intelligence in a field where it had not yet excelled at the top. It is a fair bet to say that the majority of French people will have recognised themselves in Jacquet-Astérix. Sweet revenge for brains over brawn. Therefore, when it comes to beating the Romans, becoming Olympic champion or helping distant British cousins in fiction, or winning the World Cup in reality, the magic potion or physical fitness are not enough in themselves. Intelligence is required.[11]

In sport, whether rugby or football, when the English media talk about 'French flair', the French prefer to talk about 'intelligence', in expressions such as 'L'intelligence du jeu et du positionnment' (*L'Equipe*, 6 July 1998). In the case of Laurent Blanc, the French daily *L'Équipe* talked about 'une intelligence du football hyperdéveloppée' (*L'Equipe*, 6 July 1998); in the case of the duo Deschamp-Blanc, 'c'est du physique et l'intelligence tactique enviés par toutes les formations du monde' (Françoise Inizan and Dominique Rousseau, *L'Équipe*

---

[11] We should not however neglect the self-parody element in Astérix. It remains to be seen to what extent the general (French) reading public is aware of it.

*magazine*, 18 July 1998, xxix).[12] In Zinédine Zidane's case, the expression 'coup de génie' was used to describe his game in the final against Brazil (Françoise Inizan, *L'Équipe magazine*, 18 July 1996). Another aspect of the French football team which evokes the world of Astérix is the display of a collective effort, a phenomenon admired and commented upon by a majority of journalists. It was noted that it was 'de la force du groupe qu'est née la performance' (*L'Équipe Magazine*, 18 July 1998), and, as the player Laurent Blanc explained, if talent is a necessary prerequisite, 'il faut la force collective. Moi, je crois beaucoup à la force collective' (*L'Equipe*, 6 July 1998). Numerous references will be made to 'la bande à Platini'[13] or 'la bande à Mémé' in order to emphasise the strength of the bonding of the French team. Even the President of the World Football Association, Havelange, will declare: 'Je veux féliciter [...] cette équipe [de France] qui joue avec une force de caractère et une solidarité admirable. C'est impressionnant' (*L'Equipe*, 13 July 1998, 17). On closer examination, these remarks could equally apply to Astérix, to the Gauls, to their village, where they all display a remarkable degree of solidarity when facing the enemy. In their case too, performance is the result of a collective effort. Furthermore there is a remarquable affinity between the Gauls' village and the entranched camp of the French football team, Clairefontaine. The name alone has a medieval, rural French ring about it and its numerous descriptions in the French press were on more than one occasions evocative of Astérix, the Gauls and their tiny besieged village.

What is of interest here, as far as the behaviour of both the Gauls in Astérix and the French footballers on the pitch and at Clairefontaine is concerned, is that we are witnessing a type of behaviour which although far from typically French, or Gaullish, is sold to us as being eminently French. The solidarity displayed by the French team and the Gallic village in Astérix are closer to a figment of French imagination than to reality.

Indeed, what is 'l'esprit gaulois'? Without dwelling on it at length, it can nevertheless be said that there is little evidence of solidarity, tolerance and team effort in the history of the Gauls, a fact which was bemoaned recently by a French parliamentarian who

---

[12] The use of the verb 'envier' is revealing in that it suggests something exclusive to the French, something the others do not have and are unlikely to ever possess, not unlike the magic potion in Asterix, which is the envy of the Romans. Interestingly enough the driving force behind the Romans in Astérix is neither territorial conquest nor lust for Gallic women or food. What they are after is the elusive magic potion, this 'je ne sais quoi' which somehow defines the Gauls, a kind of ancient equivalent of today's 'exception française'

[13] A reference to the French football team coached by Platini in 1992-94.

underlined that 'les Gaulois étaient en permanence soumis à des divisions et à des guerres tribales et l'esprit français est resté à ce niveau-là, très gaulois'.[14] The same MP admitted nevertheless that 'aujourd'hui les mentalités évoluent'.[15] Let us note briefly that, seen from this angle, Astérix is an embellished version of history and does not correspond to reality at the time or worse, suggests that only the Roman occupation brought Gallic intestine quarrels to an end. Some 2000 years later, another Occupation....

Yet the most striking connection between Astérix and Aimé Jacquet is to be found on another level. Aimé Jacquet is the embodiment of values, values which stand in marked contrast to the values of today's frenetic consumer society. Mémé stands out like a denial of the cliché of an ultra-modern, high-tech, materialistic and americanised France. His are sterling values, like those embodied by Astérix, whose values and life style are traditional and on a human scale, represent a kind of humanist hedonism, another cliché if ever there was one. This really is a case for quoting the proverb 'Chassez le naturel, il revient au galop'.

After the French team's victory, Le Monde (14 July 1998) could hardly conceal its surprise: 'vingt-deux anti-héros menés par un monsieur-tout-le-monde aurait donc hissé la France sur le "toit du monde" pour reprendre l'expression de Didier Deschamp'. This ordinary man was then compared to a man who has 'l'archaïsme de ces artisans qui ne sacrifient jamais le savoir-faire au faire savoir'. Expressions such as 'le triomphe d'Aimé-le-modeste'; 'le travail paye' were to be coined by the media. An unfavourable comparison will be drawn between the 1980s 'les années fric, où le spectacle devenait démagogie au service de l'enrichissement frauduleux de quelques uns'—a clear reference to Bernard Tapie[16]—and the 'valeurs dépréciées sinon passées de mode,

---

[14] Goscinny was only too aware of the divisions of the Gauls and found evidence of this in Julius Caesar's La Guerre des Gaules. He seemed to believe that things had not changed much in 1960. See Arte documentary, 'René Goscinny, profession humoriste' (first screened, 16 July 2000).

[15] Patrick Ollier (RPR Deputy) who at the time of the interview was bemoaning the fact that it was nearly impossible to get communes within the one Department to work together. Interview with the author (on another subject), June 1995.

[16] A self-made French businessman, an MP, Mayor of Marseilles, Minister under Mitterrand, who became a millionaire in the 1980s and spent some of his money on purchasing the sports shoe firm Adidas, on setting up a professional cycling team (La Vie claire) which provided two Tour de France winner (Bernard Hinault and Greg Lemon in 1985 and 1986) and who, as Chairman of Marseille Football Club, won the European Cup. Soon after these remarkable successes he was to be accused of various financial frauds at the expense of the Crédit Lyonnais and of bribing a football team during the French championship. As can be seen, he is the antithesis of Aimé Jacquet

comme l'effort, la ténacité, l'abnégation, la simplicité ou le travail' (*Télérama*, 22 July 1998) which Aimé Jacquet upheld, despite being the butt of cruel and unfair jokes by some of his contemporaries, especially in the sporting press.

We are witnessing here a strange phenomenon which reveals a social malaise as some quarters in the media seemed to oppose 'real' France, the one symbolised by Aimé Jacquet, to superficial France, that of the media, of the banks, of the new rich, of unbridled capitalism. It is striking to note that the values defended in Astérix—courage, solidarity, conviviality, modest happiness, a lifestyle close to nature and above all a sense of belonging—are a true reflection of 'real' France's aspirations. And let us not forget that originally football was a working class game which has recently been lost to Big Business and has become, to the despair of its most ardent and erstwhile supporters, a multi-million dollar show business *à la Hollywood*. Therefore one can understand the satisfaction that some lovers of the beautiful game may have derived from Aimé Jacquet's triumph, from this straight, plain speaking and modest son of a provincial worker, a former worker himself and from a football team, not made up of mercenaries as in most top European clubs, but of truly mixed-race players, totally devoted to the national cause. Cocorico.

Aimé Jacquet in the world of football in the 1990s and Astérix in the world of the comic strip in the 1960s struck a pleasantly refreshing note. In a way, the success of the French team and of its manager constitutes a form of revanche for (idealised) 1940s and 1950s petit bourgeois and working class values. There is an interesting parallel to be drawn between Aimé Jacquet and Alex Ferguson, the Manchester United manager, both products of the same era and icons of working class values, both belonging to the pantheon of French and British football. Both started life as sons of workers, became workers themselves, cut their teeth in an industrial environment, one in Saint-Etienne, the other in the Gorbals of Glasgow, both saw their working class pedigree praised by the press and turned into a virtue. The British and French press use a similar lexical range to describe these two men who, according to the media, have come to symbolise the solid and sterling qualities of France and Scotland. In an editorial entitled 'An old-fashioned success', *The Herald* (27 May 1999) paid homage to Alex Ferguson in the following terms:

---

and of Astérix. He was tried, convicted and emprisoned. If he were to be equated with a comic strip character, it would have to be with one of the Pieds Nickelés.

But spending millions on players is no guarantee of success. That depended crucially on the manager, Mr Alex Ferguson, who invested wisely but who, more importantly in the age of the rootless, gilded, mercenary footballer, instilled in his players the age-old virtues of quiet self-belief and honest endeavour to the death. These are Scottish virtues. Mr Ferguson acquired them growing up in Govan. He has never forgotten them or the place in which he learned them, even in his moment of greatest triumph that surely confirms him as the best manager ever in the British game.

These very words could have been equally applied to Aimé Jacquet. But are they not all products of the distorted and selective memories of nostalgic observers? The fact that the French identified with a 'black-blanc-beur' national team and with its coach 'Aimé-le-modeste' (*Le Monde*, 14 July 1998) does not necessarily mean that their team is a true reflection of their society at the end of the twentieth century. In the same way as Astérix, as we have seen, is a positive distortion, but a distortion nevertheless, of the Gaullish/French spirit rather than a faithful reflection of it, 'Aimé Jacquet et sa bande figurent la société *telle qu'elle s'idéalise*, diverse mais tendue vers un but commun' (*Le Monde*, 14 July 1998), 'incarnent la morale républicaine, réconcilient les Français las et défaitistes avec eux-mêmes, en leur offrant *l'image qu'ils ont envie d'avoir d'eux-mêmes*' (*Télérama*, 22 July; my emphasis).

Thus we begin to understand that the identification of an entire nation with Mémé, mentioned and/or hoped for by *Télérama*, *Le Monde* and *L'Equipe*, reveals a nostalgic hankering for an allegedly simpler and more honest era. As a result, the potential affiliation between Mémé and Astérix becomes more evident. To the question: 'what does Astérix represent?', the answer for a majority of French people would be that it is somebody who enables you to dream, who entertains, who is clever, handy, brave, convivial, and who throws back to the French a rather flattering image of themselves. As has been seen, it is a distorted image which owes more to wishful thinking than to reality.

It is however on an ideological plane that the duo Mémé-Astérix acquires a particular significance. Astérix, as a comic strip character, is reassuring (as opposed to disturbing), he is Mr Clean, fairly conformist, predictable, straight, patriotic, non-ideological, a rallying point or a unifier through military exploits and above all somebody who evolves in a non-contentious period of French history. Aimé Jacquet (let us free him from his nickname) is also endowed with these qualities and he too was the author of a non-polemical and unifying feat, winning the World Cup. They are therefore both eminently suitable 'heroes' for our time, replacing the traditional god-sent hero, the great man of History, the individual saviour of France. But as History has taught us, the French tend to get easily carried away by exceptional 'national' events. In the

Summer of 1914, it was the short-lived 'union sacrée', in 1936, the equally short-lived Popular Front, in 1968 they believed in the 'réalité de leurs désirs' and in 1998 in a 'black-blanc-beur' society. As we all know, the road that leads to hell is paved with good intentions. This is however no reason for dismissing the 'good intentions' of enthusiastic journalists, football fans and intellectuals (such as Alain Duhamel, Edgar Morin and Alain Touraine) who have been instrumental in giving Astérix a mythical status nearly on a par with that of Joan of Arc and Charles de Gaulle. Factual history has little to do with all this, what matters and what drives the French is the perception they have of the past, their history, their national heroes and themselves. As Alain Duhamel pointed out, 'En politique', and we can add 'dans la vie quotidienne', 'ce ne sont en effet pas les faits bruts qui comptent mais la perception que l'on en a' (Duhamel 1995, 7). Subjectivity, therefore, reigns supreme.

It is nevertheless a sobering experience to realise that Zinédine Zidane, for instance, asked for the following sentence to be removed from the reedition of his biography, which had been written in the euphoric wake of the World Cup victory: 'c'est un fils de Kabyle qui offrait la victoire, mais c'est la France qui devenait championne du monde. D'un seul coup, d'un seul, deux cultures n'en faisaient plus qu'une' (Etchgoin 1998, 10). Frank Leboeuf, another member of the French World Cup team, answered, in an equally revealing fashion, a question concerning the 'black-blanc-beur' nature of the team and its impact on French society. To the question, 'Quel regard portez-vous sur ces idées black-blanc-beur, cette union sacrée que tout le monde a louée après le titre?', he answered:

> Franchement, c'est de la futilité, des conneries. Comprenez-moi bien: dans l'équipe on vivait ça comme des gens normaux. Sans nous poser les moindres questions sur les différences de celui-ci ou de celui-là. C'était naturel, c'est tout. Après, cette image d'Epinal que certains intellectuels ont voulu avancer... De toute façon la France est restée un pays individualiste. Où chacun regarde devant sa porte s'en essayer de sortir le type d'à côté de la mouise. C'est le monde moderne qui est comme cela. Je ne juge pas. Je constate. (*Tribune de Genève*, 18 April 2000, 44)[17]

This outburst brings to mind the remark made by Goscinny and Uderzo concerning the possible—and tempting—political and ideological

---

[17] As the date of this interview indicates, it was a long time after the World Cup. Edgar Morin, the French sociologist, was ecstatic about the team spirit displayed by the French footballers: 'L'amour communautaire accomplit le dépassement de soi dans le grand Nous' (quoted in *Le Nouvel Observateur*, 24-30 December 1998).

interpretation of Astérix by various intellectuals, merely that their aim in creating the blond little Gaul was essentially to enjoy themselves and entertain their readers. There is no doubt that intellectualising events and issues is a French hobby, be it in the cinema, sport or comic strips. Nevertheless, we cannot dismiss the Astérix-World Cup phenomenon as a mere passing intellectual fad. The fact that Astérix albums are bestsellers, that Astérix himself has become a reference point for politicians, journalists and intellectuals, let alone the general public, points to a strong identification process with our puny but clever comic strip hero and reveals the extent of the cultural impact in France of comic strip heroes.

Jacquet-Astérix, the same fight? Probably. But let us not forget that there are two sides to Astérix, a reactive one with which a fair proportion of French identify, largely motivated by apprehension on the eve of the 21st century, by a spirit of 'resistance' to change and global capitalism, by a survival instinct, by a siege mentality, by an identity crisis, and a proactive one, Astérix as a winner ('La France qui gagne'), an optimist, a clever and ressourceful operator whose wit enables him to win through whatever the circumstances.

Therefore 'le phénomène Astérix' conceals and reconciles two conflicting sets of values, two conflicting 'dramatis personae', and it is not always clear which one the public endorses. Not unlike founding myths in the history of nations, Astérix, like Joan of Arc and Charles de Gaulle, can reconcile the French, can become a unifying force, albeit in a very different fashion. But Astérix has one advantage, which might explain his immediate success, he does not have Joan of Arc's religious connotation or de Gaulle's ideological one. He is a genuinely lay and Republican hero, contextualised in such a distant past that he has become somehow a-historical, a character with whom French people of all walks of life can identify. For let us face it, to equate the French football team and their coach with Astérix le Gaulois, in view of their mixed races (and religions) is as odd as the indigenous population of former French colonies talking about their ancestors 'les Gaulois'. It only makes sense if what people identify with are the values embodied by Astérix. It should not come as a surprise, therefore, to see a magazine such as *Télérama*, which is part of a Catholic publishing group, endorse a man and a comic strip character, both embodiments of traditional and reassuring values. It is tempting to draw a parallel with the Tintin of before the present polemic, with the proviso that Tintin's ideology is far more apparent than Astérix's, and very different. Tintin is a hero, he belongs in a way to the breed of individuals who make History, who, like 'Great Men', can change the destiny of a nation single-handedly, whereas Astérix is an anti-hero, like Aimé Jacquet, and like him he belongs to a community, he is a member of a team, not a lone individual like Superman or de Gaulle. Jacquet-Astérix corresponds to the post World War II democratisation of national heroes, very much in keeping with the interest shown by contemporary historians and writers in the 'petit peuple' and its role in shaping twentieth-century France.[18]

It is therefore significant that at the end of the twentieth century, the coach of a winning football team—'un Monsieur tout-le-monde', to quote *Le Monde*—, should be equated with a non-controversial, quaint, slightly old-fashioned and in many ways anti-materialist character such as Astérix. Even more telling, is the fact that this journalistic comparison should have been widely endorsed by the French themselves. This cultural phenomenon alone tells us a lot about the state of mind of the French, their fears and aspirations on the verge of a new century.

But equally revealing is the fact that for others, admittedly a minority, Astérix is a bold, adventurous and positive character who 'avec son baluchon, part à la conquête du monde' (Bernamon 1999). Precisely what the French football team, under the aegis of Jacquet-Astérix, achieved by becoming 'champions du monde'. Of course, some 'esprits chagrins' will point out that this victory was achieved on home soil and that the French team, like the Gauls in Astérix, only perform well in or near their 'village', thus confirming Astérix's 'esprit pantouflard' and entranching the position of those who think that the French way is the best way. For some, Astérix is the epitome of 'l'exception française' and Aimé Jacquet its legitimation. Others, on the other hand, will derive comfort and confidence in the fact that the French football team took on the world and won.[19] Thus, the World Cup victory and its aftermath prove, yet again and more than ever, that Astérix is a hero for all seasons.

## Bibliography

Belot, Jean 1998. 'L'effet Mémé' [editorial], *Télérama*, 22 July, 4.

Bernamon, Georges-Marc 1999. 'Le symptôme Astérix' [editorial], *L'Evénement*, 28 January-3 February.

Droussent, Claude 1998. Editorial. *L'Équipe magazine*, 18 July.

---

[18] For example novels by Jean Rouaud and Didier Daeninckx, and Bertrand Tavernier's film, *La Vie et rien d'autre*.
[19] This attitude was of course vindicated by the French football team's victory in Euro 2000 on foreign soil.

Duhamel, Alain 1985. *Le Complexe d'Astérix*, Paris: Gallimard.

Duhamel, Alain 1995. *Politique imaginaire*, Paris: Flammarion.

Etchgoin, Marie-France 1998. 'Zidane, homme de l'année', *Le Nouvel Observateur*, 24-30 December, 10.

Goscinny and Uderzo 1961. *Astérix le Gaulois*, Paris: Dargaud.

Goscinny and Uderzo 1966. *Astérix chez les Bretons*, Paris: Dargaud.

Goscinny and Uderzo 1968. *Astérix aux Jeux Olympiques*, Paris: Dargaud.

Moliterin, Claude, Philippe Mellot and Michel Denni 1996. *Les Aventures de la BD*, Paris: Gallimard.

Morrot, Bernard 1996. 'Où est passée la potion magique', *France-Soir*, 10 October, 1.

Vidal, Guy, Anne Goscinny and Patrick Gaumer 1997. *René Goscinny. Profession: humoriste*, Paris: Dargaud.

Violet, Bernard 1998. *L'Ami banquier: le mystérieux conseillé de François Mitterrand*, Paris: Albin Michel.

# List of Illustrations

Every effort has been made to contact copyright holders, to whom the contributors wish to record their gratitude for the permission granted to reproduce illustrative material.

**BD Theory Before the Term 'BD' Existed**
**Laurence Grove**

**Figure 1** 'Préface des Editeurs' of an early edition of Töpffer, *Voyages en zigzag* (1846)

**Figure 2** An example of 1930s bandes dessinées

**Figure 3** Extract from Parker and Renaudy, *La Démoralisation de la jeunesse par les publications périodiques* (1944), which includes 'les Petits Journaux illustrés' as 'littérature pornographique'

**Figure 4** The inside cover of Parker and Renaudy

**Figure 5** Gerin, *Tout sur la presse enfantine* (1958) – the first self-conscious analysis of the workings of the bande dessinée in terms of its text/image interaction

**Figure 6** *Pilote*. First episode of the series, 'Le Roman vrai des bandes dessinées' – © *Dargaud*

**Figure 7** Example of *Le Rire*

## *De nouvelles formes naissent*: Le Corbusier and the bande dessinée
## Judi Loach

**Figure 8** Le Corbusier, 'Lettre de Le Corbusier à Mme. Meyer, avec croquis' in *Oeuvre Complète* (1929, I, 89) – © *Fondation Le Corbusier*

**Figure 9** Le Corbusier, 'Détail du Pavillon', Pavillon de l'Esprit Nouveau, as presented in Le Corbusier, *Oeuvre Complète* (1929, I, 101) – © *Fondation Le Corbusier*

**Figure 10** Le Corbusier, *Almanach d'architecture moderne* – © *Fondation Le Corbusier*

**Figure 11** – Le Corbusier, 'Immeubles-Villas' (collage) in *Oeuvre Complète* (1929, I, 98) – © *Fondation Le Corbusier*

**Figure 12** Le Corbusier, 'La Maison Standardisée' in *Oeuvre Complète* (1929, I, 69) – © *Fondation Le Corbusier*

**Figures 13-14** Le Corbusier, 'Un fragment de façade', 'Immeubles-Villas' in *Oeuvre Complète* (1929, I, 43) – © *Fondation Le Corbusier*

## *Le Grêlé 7/13*: A (Communist) Children's Guide to the Resistance
## Laurent Marie

**Figure 15** A strip vividly depicted a scene of torture, and another calls one of the *résistants* 'an enemy of Franco-German collaboration' – © *Lécureux Production*

**Figure 16** *Vaillant* no. 1101 – © *Lécureux Production*

**Figure 17** L'Ermite, his local double, who will accompany him throughout his adventures – © *Lécureux Production*

**Figure 18** In *Le Grêlé 7/13*, every social category supports the Resistance including workers, peasants, small shop-keepers, and the bourgeoisie – © *Lécureux Production*

**Figures 19a-19b** 'Mauvaise année Colonel Hartz' (*Pif-Gadget* n° 1285) – © *Lécureux Production*

**Figure 20** 'La Belle et la Belle' (*Pif-Gadget* n° 1250) – © *Lécureux Production*

**Figures 21a-21b** 'La Caverne d'Ali-Baba' (*Vaillant*, n° 1157 to n° 1163) – © *Lécureux Production*

## *Pilote*: Pedagogy, Puberty and Parents
### Wendy Michallat

**Figure 22** Michel Vaillant, 'Le Circuit de la Peur', *Tintin* (5 November 1959) – © *Dargaud*

**Figures 23 and 24** Buck Danny 'Prototype FX-13', *Spirou* (22 October 1959) – © *Dargaud*

**Figure 25** Laverdure faints – © *Dargaud*

**Figure 26** Laverdure: 'jus de fruits bien entendu' – © *Dargaud*

**Figure 27** 'L'école des aigles' – © *Dargaud*

**Figure 28** 'C'est moi, ça vous ennuie peut-être?' – © *Dargaud*

**Figure 29** 'Les Japs attaquent' – © *Dargaud*

**Figure 30** The rejection by Darnier of the past as St Helier's means to earn credit in the present – © *Dargaud*

## Jean Giraud / Moebius: *Nouveau Réalisme* and Science Fiction
### Matthew Screech

**Figure 31** Moebius, The racist has awoken, *Cauchemar blanc* (1980-85, I, 107) – © *Les Humanoïdes Associés, SAS, Paris*

**Figure 32** Moebius, Arzach and the pterodactyl revived in *Arzach* (1980-85, II, 44) – © *Les Humanoïdes Associés, SAS, Paris*

**Figure 33** Moebius, A dislocated sequence of images, with Grubert and the 'aéroplane de la destinée' in *Le Garage hermétique* (1980-85, III, 105) – © *Les Humanoïdes Associés, SAS, Paris*

**Figure 34** Moebius, Stel and Atan in *Les Jardins d'Edena* (1987, 24) – © *Casterman*

**Figuration and configuration: mapping imaginary worlds in BD**
**Teresa Bridgeman**

**Figure 35** Werth, *Text worlds: Representing Conceptual Space in Discourse* (1999, 109)

**Figure 36** Crepax, 'Les Souterrains' in *Valentina* (1983, 28) – © *Editions Albin Michel*

**Figure 37** Juillard, *Le Cahier bleu* (1994, 28-29) – © *Casterman*

**Figure 38** Juillard, *Le Cahier bleu* (1994, 6-7) – © *Casterman*

**Figure 39** Juillard, *Le Cahier bleu* (1994, 8) – © *Casterman*

**Figure 40** Tardi, *Brouillard au Pont de Tolbiac* (1992, 74-76) – © *Casterman*

**Figure 41** Juillard, *Le Cahier bleu* (1994, 48-49) – © *Casterman*

**Figure 42** Mathieu, *La Qu...* (1991, 6-7) – © *Delcourt*

**Figure 43** Franc, 'Le Roi du monde' in *Le Marchand d'opium* (1984, 26) – © *Dargaud*

**Figure 44** Mathieu, *Le Processus* (1993, 8) – © *Delcourt*

**Figure 45** Mathieu, *Le Processus* (1993, 28) – © *Delcourt*

**Figure 46** Juillard, *Le Cahier bleu* (1994, 32) – © *Casterman*

**Figure 47** Juillard, *Le Cahier bleu* (1994, 67-69) – © *Casterman*

**Narratives of Adolescence, Ethnicity and Masculinity in the Work of Baru**
**Ann Miller**

**Figure 48** Baru, Front cover, *La Piscine de Micheville*: under the sign of the paternal signifier (1985b) – © *Editions Albin Michel*

Illustrations

**Figure 49** Baru, *La Communion de Mino* (1985, 7): a visual equivalent of the style indirect libre

**Figure 50** Baru, *L'Autoroute du Soleil* (1995, 14-15): the destruction of the blast furnace signals the demise of traditional types of working class masculinity – © *Kodansha*

### Femmes en Images et Images de Femmes: L'Héroïne de *La Femme Piège* d'Enki Bilal
### Dominique Le Duc

**Figure 51** Bilal, *La Femme Piège* (1990, 41) – © *Les Humanoïdes Associés, SAS, Paris*

**Figure 52** Bilal, *La Femme Piège* (1990, 14) – © *Les Humanoïdes Associés, SAS, Paris*

**Figure 53** Bilal, *La Femme Piège* (1990, 8) – © *Les Humanoïdes Associés, SAS, Paris*

**Figure 54** Bilal, *La Femme Piège* (1990, 13) – © *Les Humanoïdes Associés, SAS, Paris*

**Figure 55** Bilal, *La Femme Piège* (1990, 49) – © *Les Humanoïdes Associés, SAS, Paris*

**Figure 56** Bilal, *La Femme Piège* (1990, 20) – © *Les Humanoïdes Associés, SAS, Paris*

PRÉFACE DES ÉDITEURS. VII

blicité de famille. Ce sont ces Albums très-recherchés, mais extrêmement rares, dont nous publions ici la reproduction fidèle, bien convaincus que nous sommes que le public est aujourd'hui d'autant mieux préparé à goûter ces pages sur la Suisse et sur les Alpes, qu'elles n'ont pas été primitivement écrites pour lui.

M. Calame, qui a fait des contrées parcourues par M. Topffer et ses jeunes compagnons le sujet préféré de ses études d'artiste, a bien voulu apporter aux *Voyages en Zigzag* le concours de son admirable talent. Parmi les plus importants dessins qui accompagnent ce livre, on trouvera plusieurs dessins de paysage signés du nom de ce peintre célèbre. Le mérite de ces compositions sévères, grandes malgré l'exiguité du cadre, et dans lesquelles l'étude sérieuse et approfondie de la nature se montre toujours unie au sentiment poétique, sera apprécié, nous en sommes certains, comme le sont en France toutes les œuvres du même artiste.

Enfin, nous acquittons, au nom de M. Topffer et à notre propre nom, une dette de reconnaissance envers M. Karl Girardet, qui a traduit et dessiné sur bois, pour les graveurs, la plus grande partie des sujets de cette collection, avec une perfection qui témoigne en lui d'une habileté au-dessus de cet emploi modeste, habileté déjà prouvée ailleurs par des compositions originales qui annoncent l'artiste consommé, et à laquelle les preuves les plus éclatantes ne manqueront pas dans l'avenir.

En deux ou trois rencontres, M. Topffer fait allusion à des personnages qui figurent dans les histoires comiques qu'il a publiées, et dont les plus connues sont celles de *M. Jabot*, de *M. Vieux-Bois* et de *M. Crépin*. Afin que ceux d'entre nos lecteurs à qui ces *histoires* sont demeurées étrangères puissent comprendre ces allusions, il nous suffira de dire que M. Jabot est le type du sot vaniteux, ou, si l'on veut, de la marionnette que font agir, se mouvoir, bouger, les cent mille ficelles du *paraître*; que M. Vieux-Bois est le type de l'amoureux poétiquement constant et risiblement pastoral; que M. Crépin, enfin, est celui de l'honnête bourgeois qui, aux prises avec les méthodes d'éducation, relancé par la phrénologie et contrarié par sa femme, ne parvient pas sans beaucoup de peine à élever ses onze enfants.

A côté de ces rares allusions, l'on rencontrera quelques termes improvisés, quelques dénominations locales, et aussi des traces d'un argot de voyage, issu tout naturellement du retour annuel des mêmes impressions, des mêmes besoins, des mêmes habitudes. Ainsi *spéculer, spéculation,* l'action chanceuse d'abréger la route en coupant par ce qu'on croit être le plus court; *ruban,* route rectiligne; *burette,* petit repas d'extra; *halter,* faire des haltes; *nono,* un touriste anglais qui tient à rester digne, ou qui répond tout au plus *nu* (non): *uī uī* (oui), l'inverse, c'est-à-dire affable et amicalement causeur; *blousé,* qui porte blouse; *ambresailles,* petit fruit sauvage, en français myrtille; *séchot,* pour chabot, espèce de poisson du lac Léman; c'est à peu près tout. Il nous eût été facile, sans doute, de remplacer ces termes, d'ailleurs heureux ou commodes, par des circonlocutions explicatives; mais nous nous sommes bien gardés de le faire, dans la crainte d'altérer la physionomie du texte original, et d'entraver la libre allure d'un style toujours vif, piquant et naturel.

Encore un mot pour appeler l'attention des lecteurs sur la belle exécution typogra-

**Figure 1**

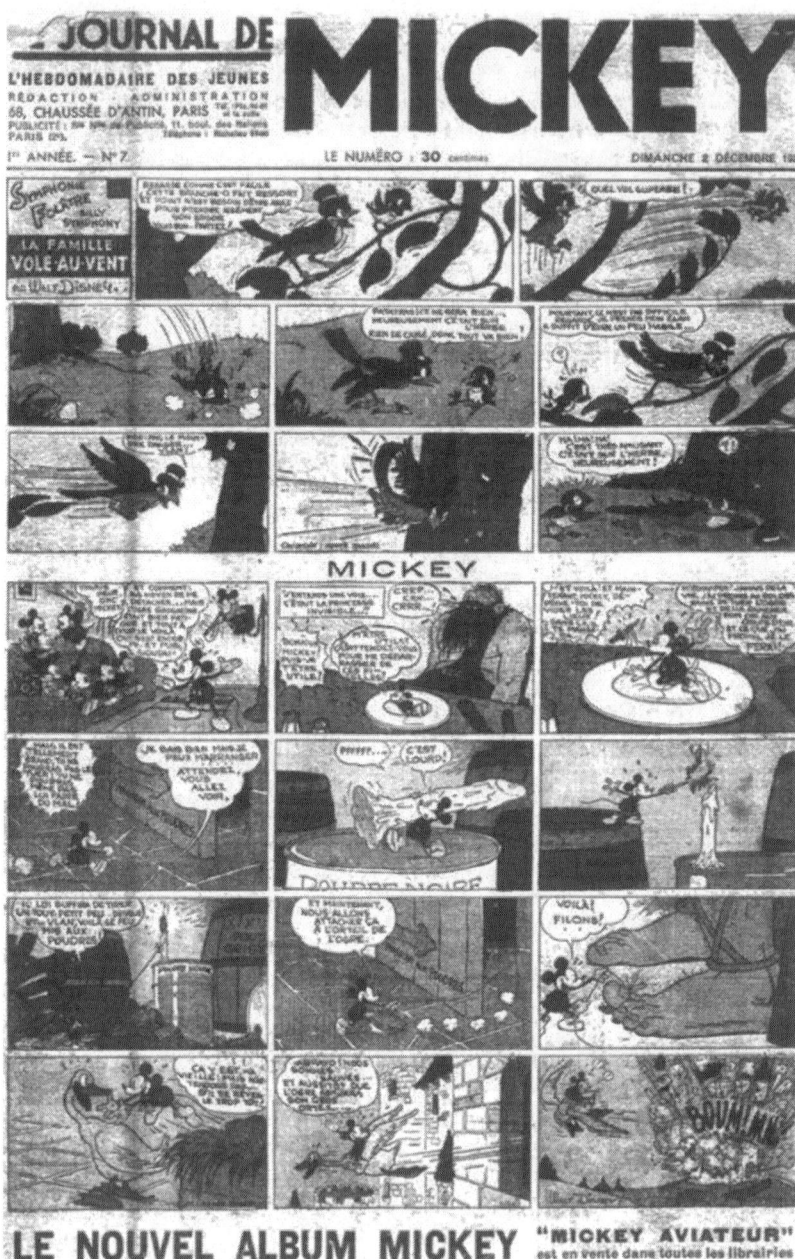

Figure 2

Figure 3

## CARTEL D'ACTION MORALE

Fédération Française des Sociétés contre l'Immoralité Publique

23, place Saint-Georges, PARIS (IX<sup>e</sup>)
Chèques Postaux : PARIS 2313-73

Les adhésions individuelles doivent être adressées à la
**LIGUE FRANÇAISE POUR LE RELÈVEMENT
DE LA MORALITÉ PUBLIQUE**
23, place Saint-Georges, PARIS (IX<sup>e</sup>) — Tél. TRU. 12.20
Chèques Postaux : PARIS 2119 97.

## PRINCIPAUX POINTS du PLAN d'ACTION de la LIGUE

**CINEMA.** — Campagne en vue de la formation de l'opinion publique. Organisation de séances de critique cinématographique. Mesures législatives et administratives réclamées. — Campagne en vue de la promulgation d'une loi réglementant l'accès des mineurs dans les salles de cinéma. Modification de la composition de la Commission de censure cinématographique. Introduction de représentants des Associations familiales et éducatives au sein de cette Commission.

**PUBLICATIONS PÉRIODIQUES.** — Surveillance des publications périodiques. Interventions auprès des pouvoirs publics en vue de faire appliquer les mesures permettant la répression des outrages aux bonnes mœurs (et en particulier, des articles 119 à 122 du Code de la Famille).

Mesures législatives réclamées. — Promulgation de la loi concernant le contrôle des publications destinées principalement à la jeunesse (voir texte dans la présente brochure).

**LUTTE CONTRE LE PROXÉNÉTISME ET LA PROSTITUTION.** — Interventions auprès des pouvoirs publics pour obtenir la mise en application de la loi du 2 mars 1943 contre les souteneurs. Campagnes en vue d'obtenir la fermeture des maisons de tolérance et l'abolition du système de la réglementation de la prostitution. Campagne en faveur de l'établissement, dans chaque région, de « Centres de reclassement professionnel » pour le relèvement des jeunes prostituées. Création de services d'inspectrices de police dans toutes les agglomérations importantes.

**CAMPAGNE CONCERNANT L'IMMORALITÉ DANS LES LIEUX DE TRAVAIL.** — Mesures réclamées. — Promulgation du projet de loi concernant la défense de la dignité et de la moralité des jeunes travailleurs. (Projet adopté par le Conseil supérieur de la Famille le 7 décembre 1943.)

**LIAISON AVEC LES AUTRES ORGANISMES S'OCCUPANT DE LUTTE CONTRE LES FLÉAUX SOCIAUX.** — La Ligue prend également une part active à la lutte contre le Taudis, en liaison avec la Ligue Nationale contre le Taudis et l'Association « D'Amélioration de Logement Ouvrier », à la lutte contre l'Alcoolisme, en liaison avec la Ligue Nationale contre l'Alcoolisme, et à la lutte contre l'Avortement, en collaboration avec l'Alliance Nationale contre la Dépopulation.

« La Ligue réalise l'union des honnêtes gens et la coopération des Associations en vue du redressement moral du pays. »

(1) Consulter pour plus de détails la brochure : Un Plan d'Action d'Ensemble » contre les fléaux sociaux : immoralité publique, alcoolisme, taudis, avortement. Ligue Française pour le Relèvement de la Moralité publique, 23, place Saint-Georges, PARIS (IX<sup>e</sup>). Prix franco : 12 francs. Ch. Postaux 2119 97.

Figure 4

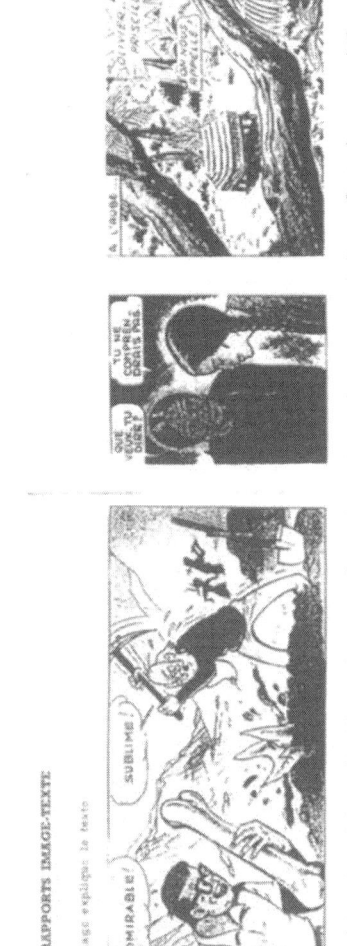
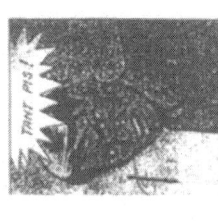
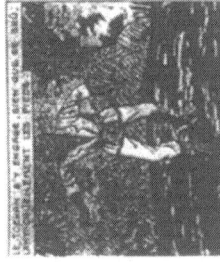

**Figure 5**

**Figure 6**

**Figure 7**

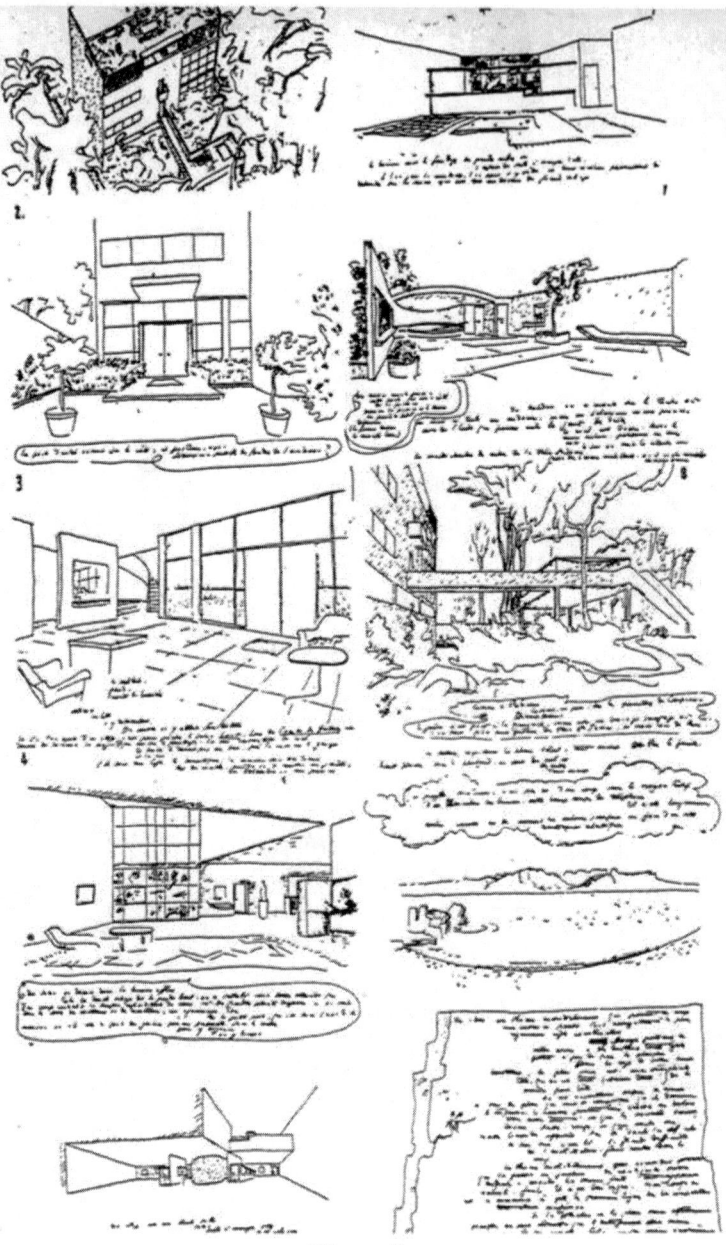

**Figure 8**

**Figure 9**

**Figure 10**

Illustrations

Nous donnons une photographie des échafaudages des magasins du « Bon Marché » qui nous fournissent l'échelle des immeubles-villas dessinés en prolongement

**Figure 11**

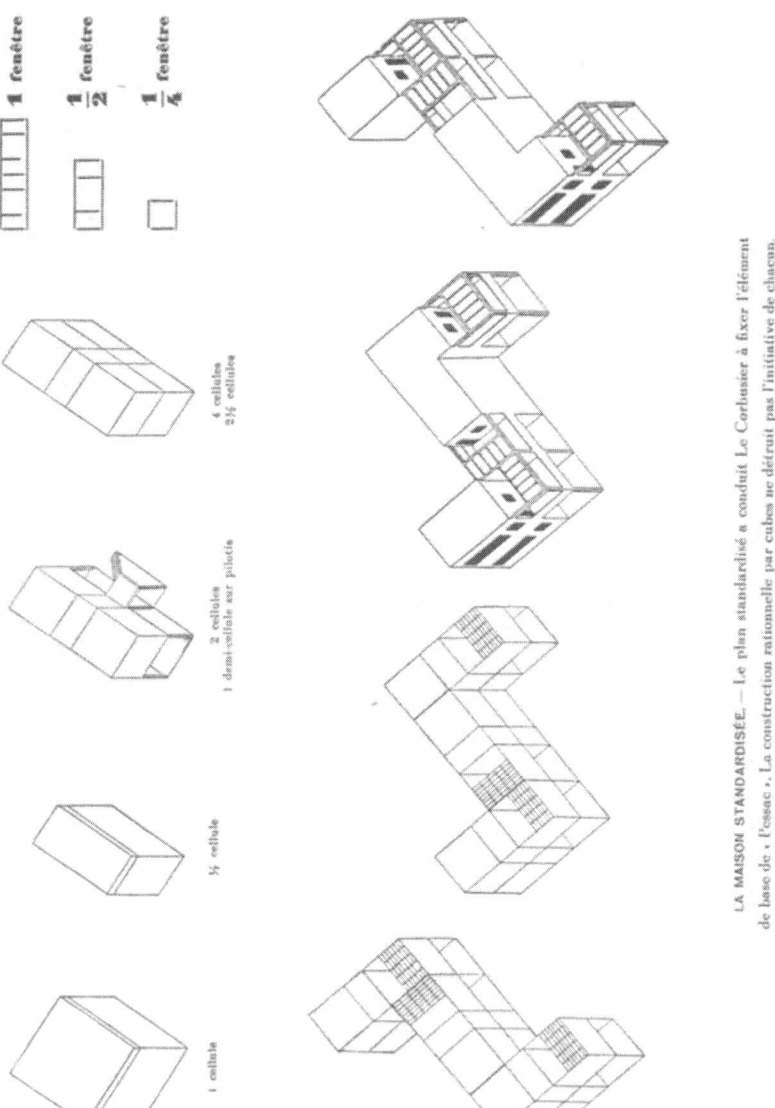

**Figure 12**

Un fragment de façade (première étude)

**Figures 13-14**

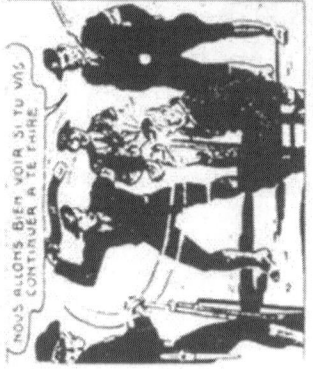

Scène de torture dans Fifi, extraite d'une planche qui ne parut qu'en album.

**Figure 15**

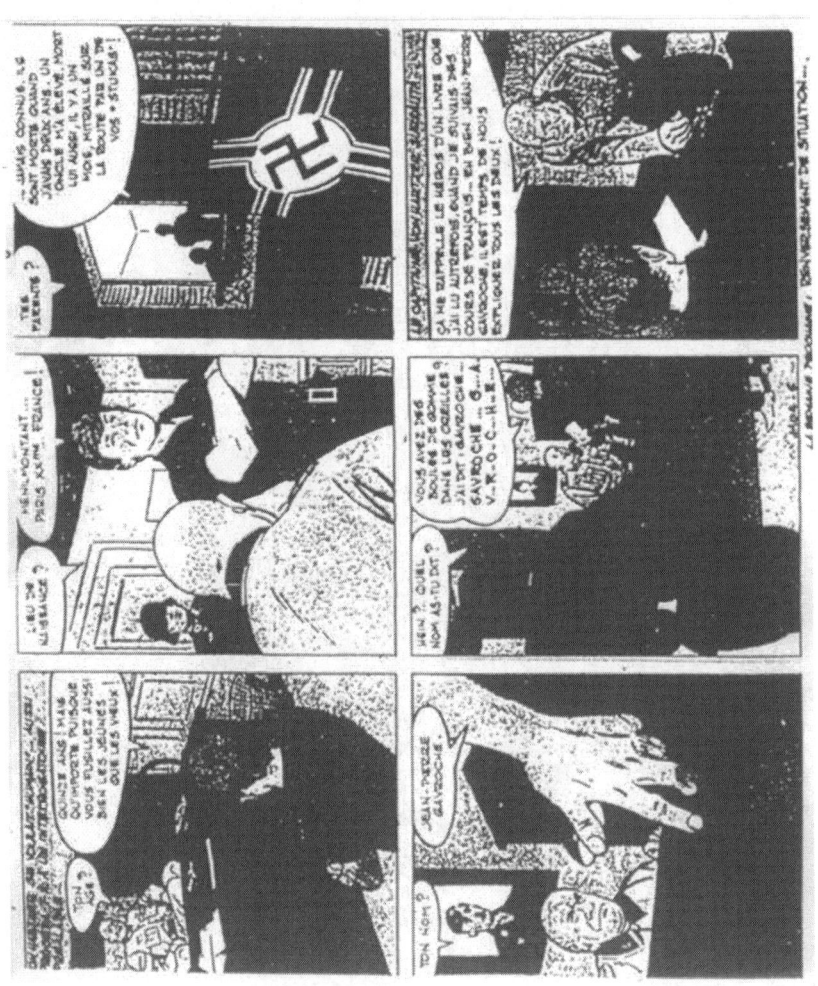

**Figure 16**

**Figure 17**

**Figure 18**

**Figures 19a-19b**

**Figure 20**

**Figures 21a-21b**

**Figures 22-24**

**Figures 25-27**

**Figures 28-30**

**Figure 31**

**Figure 32**

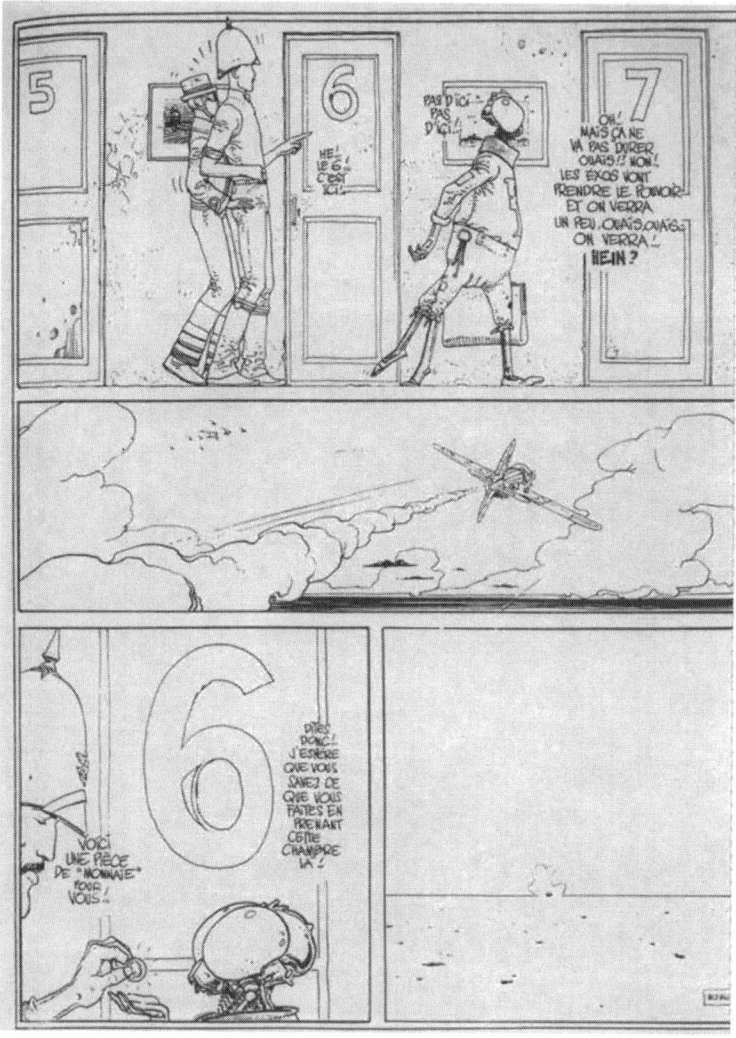

**Figure 33**

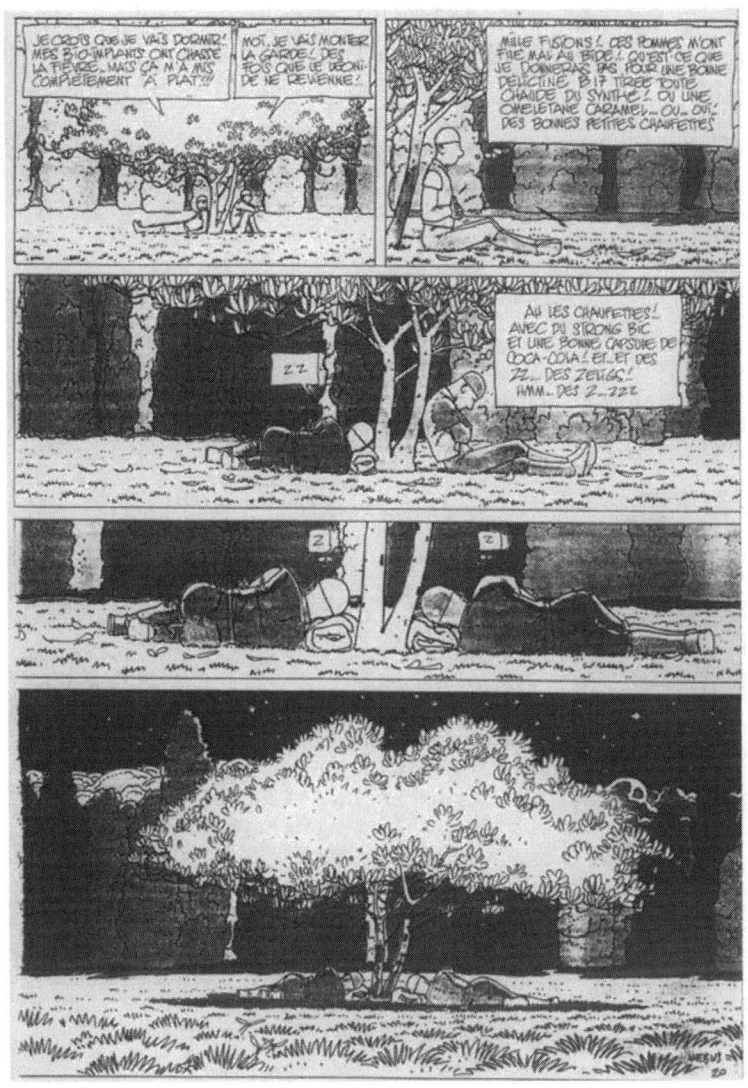

**Figure 34**

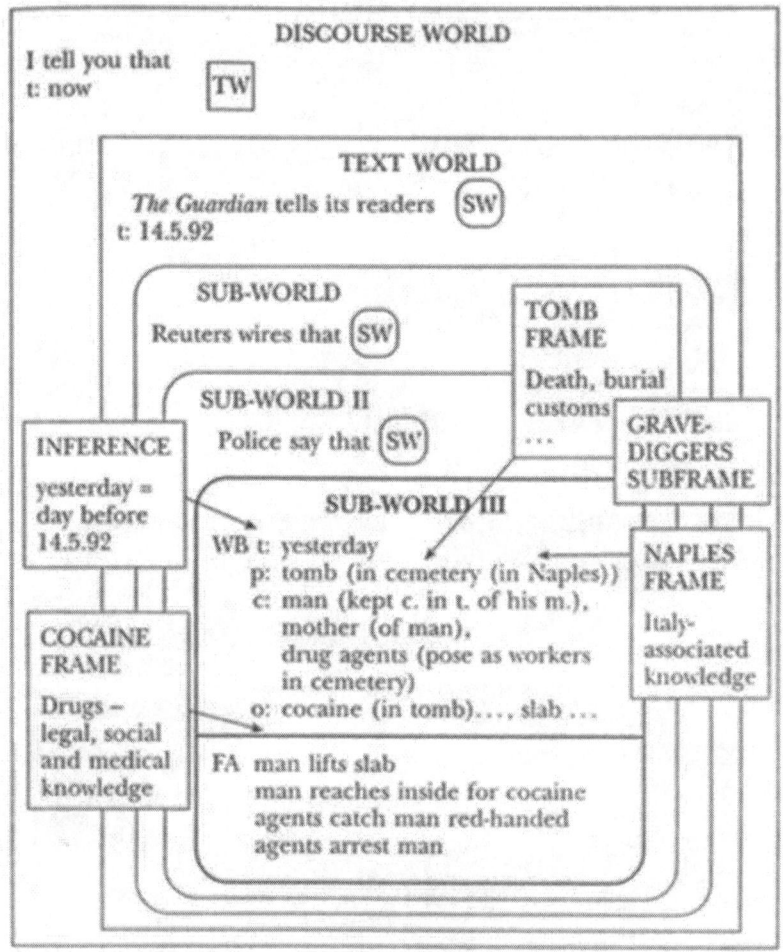

**Figure 35**

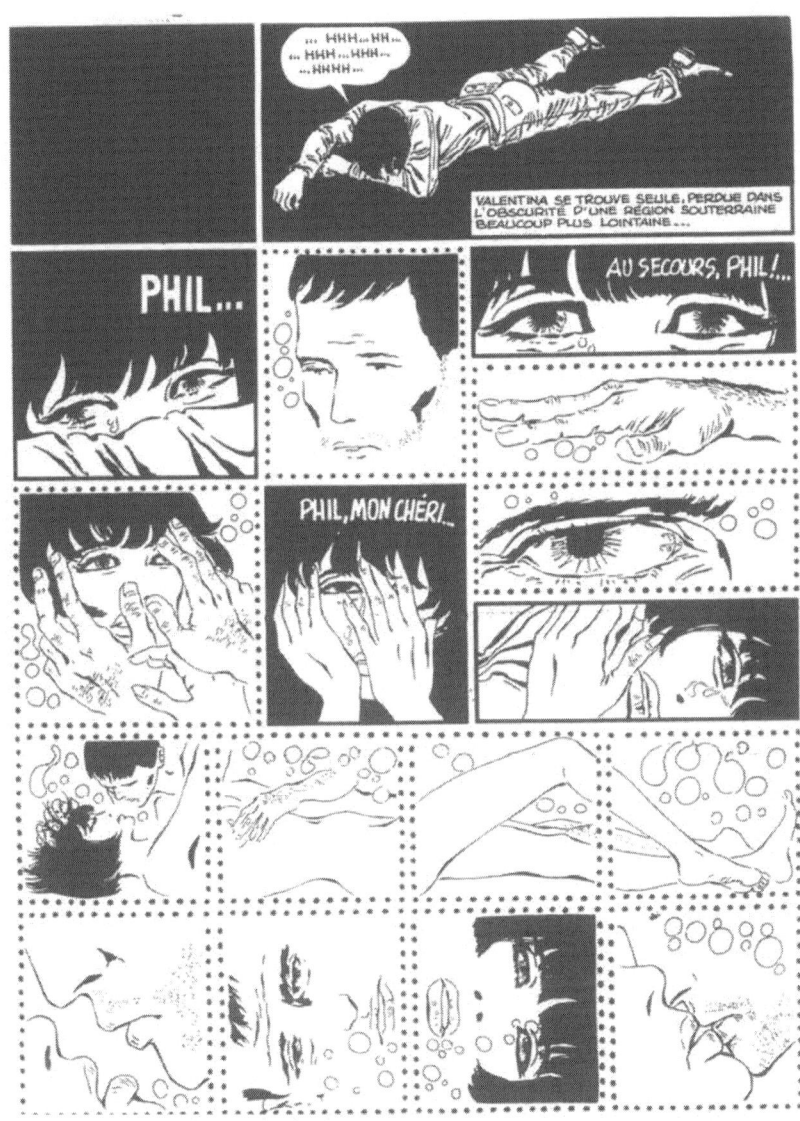

**Figure 36**

**Figure 37**

Illustrations

**Figure 38**

**Figure 39**

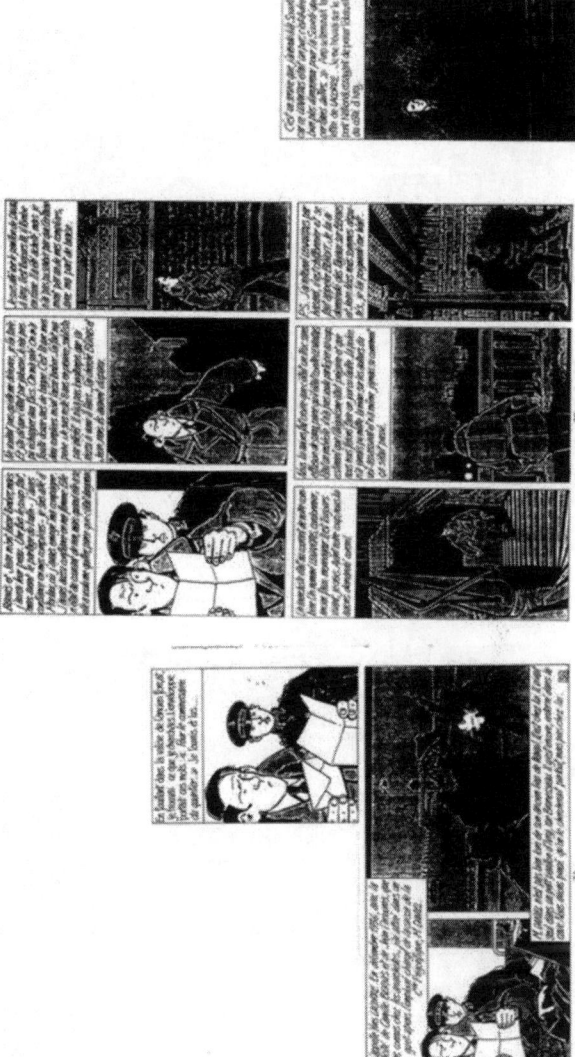

**Figure 40**

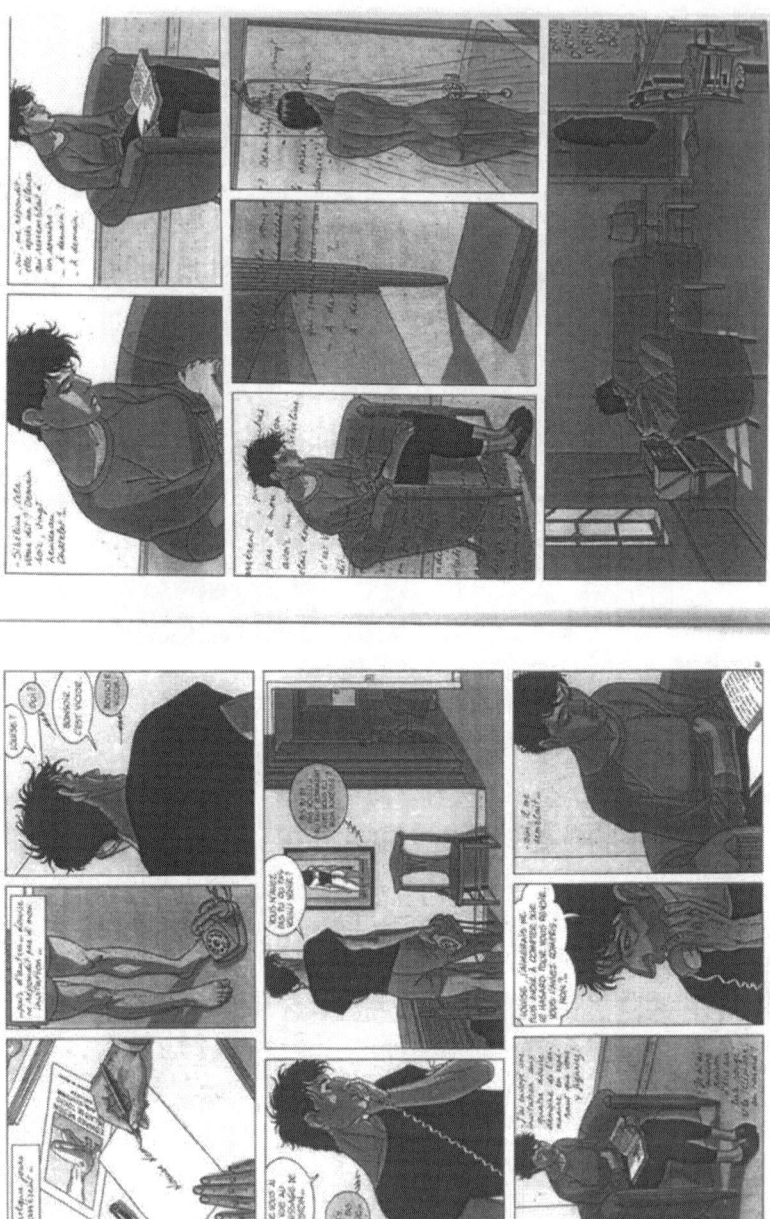

Figure 41

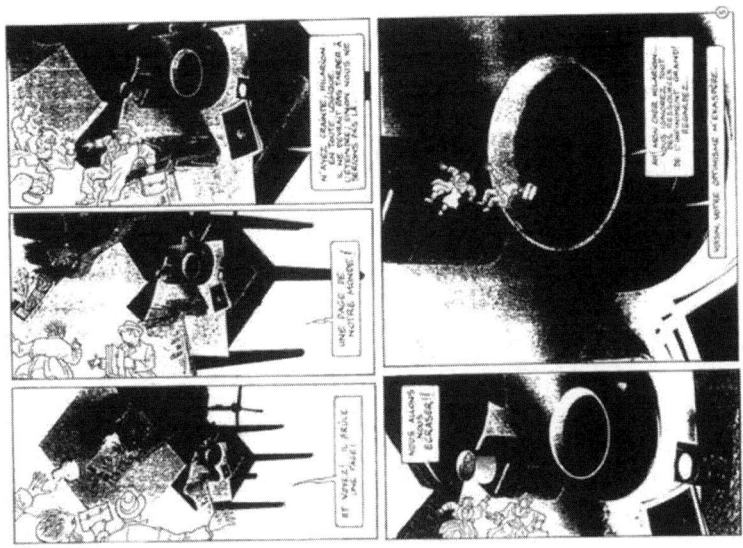

Figure 42

Figure 43

**Figure 44**

**Figure 45**

Illustrations

**Figure 46**

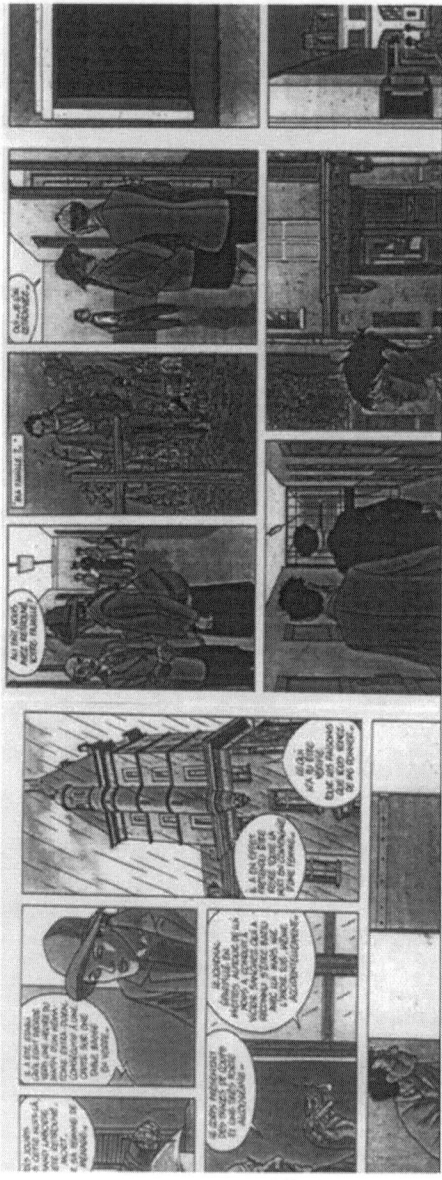

Figure 47

Figure 48

**Figure 49**

**Figure 50**

**Figure 51**

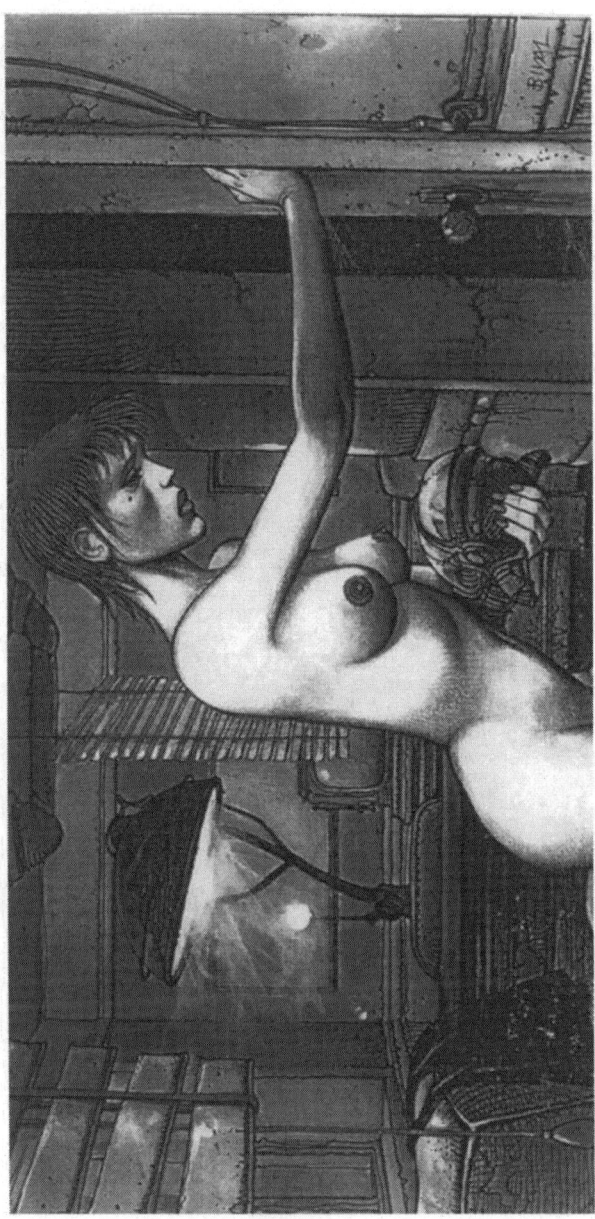

**Figure 52**

**Figure 53**

**Figure 54**

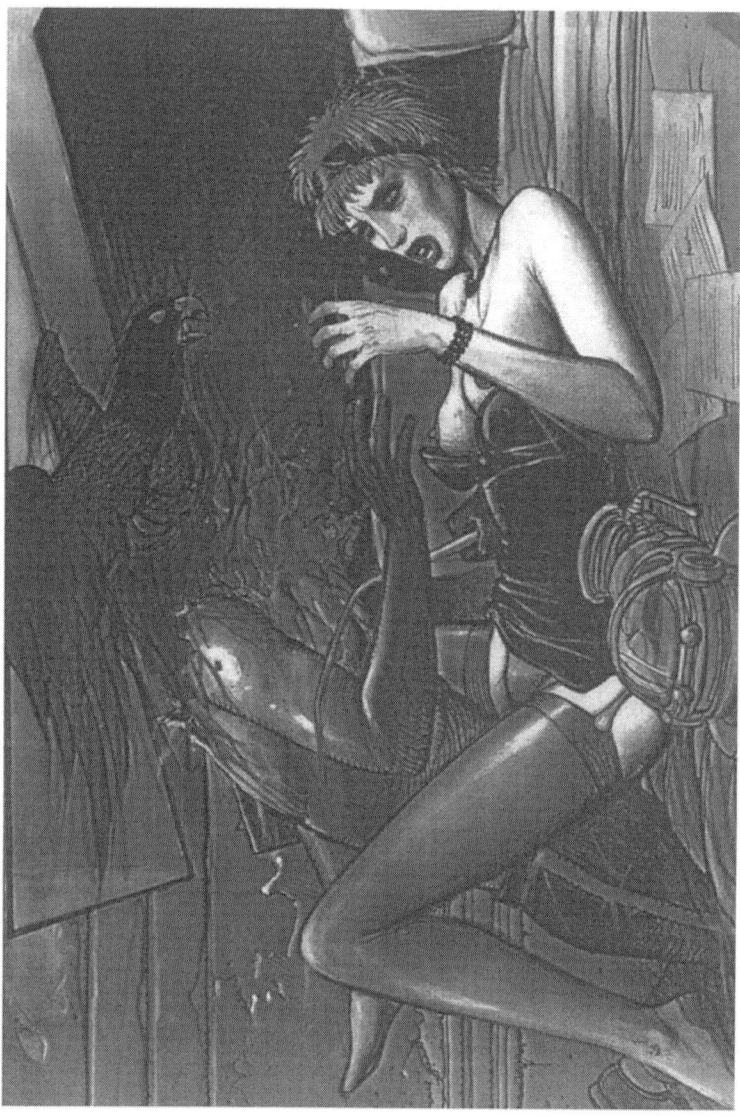

**Figure 55**

Illustrations

**Figure 56**